# Havana

## Autobiography of a City

# Havana

## Autobiography of a City

Alfredo José Estrada

HAVANA: AUTOBIOGRAPHY OF A CITY
Copyright © Alfredo José Estrada, 2007

First published in 2007 by
PALGRAVE MACMILLAN™
175 Fifth Avenue, New York, N.Y. 10010 and
Houndmills, Basingstoke, Hampshire, England RG21 6XS.
Companies and representatives throughout the world.

PALGRAVE MACMILLAN is the global academic imprint of the
Palgrave Macmillan division of St. Martin's Press, LLC and of Palgrave
Macmillan Ltd. Macmillan® is a registered trademark in the United States,
United Kingdom and other countries. Palgrave is a registered trademark in
the European Union and other countries.

ISBN-13: 978-1-4039-7509-6
ISBN-10: 1-4039-7509-4

Library of Congress Cataloging-in-Publication Data
[cip tk]

A catalogue record of the book is available from the British Library.

Design by Letra Libre

First edition: April 2007
10  9  8  7  6  5  4  3  2  1
Printed in the United States of America.

*For my parents*

# Contents

# Illustrations

# Chronology of Havana, 1492 to 2006

1492   Christopher Columbus makes landfall near present-day Gibara in eastern Cuba and returns to Spain with tobacco.

1508   Sebastian Ocampo circumnavigates Cuba and enters Havana Bay, naming it Puerto de Carenas.

1511   Diego Velásquez invades Cuba.

1512   Hatuey is burned at the stake at Yara.

1513   Ponce de León discovers the Gulf Stream.

1514   Havana is founded by Panfilo de Narváez near present-day Batabanó on Cuba's southern shore.

1519   Havana is relocated to its present location.

1538   Havana is attacked by French corsairs. Hernando de Soto is appointed governor and sets out to conquer Florida. His wife, Isabel de Bobadilla, remains in charge.

1553   Havana replaces Santiago de Cuba as the capital of the island.

1555   Havana is destroyed by Jacques de Sores, known as the Exterminating Angel.

1558   The castle of the Fuerza Real replaces the Fuerza Vieja.

1586   Sir Francis Drake threatens Havana and later sacks Santo Domingo.

1589   Construction begins on the castle of El Morro.

1592   Havana has a population of four thousand and is granted its own coat of arms, with three castles and a golden key.

1674   Havana's city walls are erected.

1748   Coffee is introduced to Cuba.

1762   British forces under Lord Albemarle storm and

briefly occupy Havana. Cuba is later returned to Spain in exchange for Florida.

1791 Revolution in Santo Domingo leads to the growth of the sugarcane industry and the rise of slavery. French planters emigrate to Cuba.

1800 Alexander von Humboldt visits Havana.

1812 José Antonio Aponte leads a slave revolt.

1823 *Sol y Rayos de Bolivar* conspiracy is betrayed. Father Felix Varela is exiled to New York and later joined by José María Heredia.

1851 Filibuster Narciso López invades Cuba and is executed.

1868 Carlos Manuel de Céspedes begins the Ten Year War.

1869 At the age of sixteen, José Martí is imprisoned and later exiled to Spain.

1880 Martí arrives in New York.

1895 Martí and Máximo Gómez reach Cuba, beginning the War of Independence. Martí is killed at Dos Rios.

1898 The American battleship *Maine* explodes in Havana Harbor. Led by Theodore Roosevelt's Rough Riders, America defeats Spain. The American occupation of Cuba begins.

1902 Establishment of the Cuban Republic. Tomás Estrada Palma becomes the first president.

1932 Ernest Hemingway visits Havana for marlin fishing.

1933 The fall of Gerardo Machado. Fulgencio Batista seizes control of the army in the Sergeants' Revolt.

1952 Just before the upcoming election, Batista seizes power, ending the Cuban Republic.

1956 Castro lands in Cuba aboard the *Granma* and finds refuge in the Sierra Maestra.

1959 Batista flees and Castro triumphantly enters Havana.

1960 Relations between Cuba and the United States sour and the trade embargo is imposed.

1961 CIA-backed invasion of Cuban exiles at Bay of Pigs fails.

1967 Che Guevara is executed in Bolivia.

1991 Fall of the Soviet Union brings about the "Special Period." Far-reaching changes include the legalization of the U.S. dollar and the growth of tourism.

1998    Pope John Paul II meets with Castro in Havana.

2002    Oswaldo Payá organizes the Varela Project.

2006    Cuba is defeated by Japan in the first World Baseball Classic.

# PREFACE

# Return to Havana

## Bearings

*If I ever get lost, look for me in Havana.*

—*Federico García Lorca*

*Y*ou can easily find Havana on the map of the imagination.

Few other cities offer such infinite possibility. Arriving by sea in 1895, Winston Churchill wrote: "Here was a place where anything might happen." There has always been an air of intrigue about Havana. It is Casablanca in the Caribbean, where shady characters converge from the dark corners of the planet. Here, conspiracy theories are born and secret agents follow each other about.

But Havana is about pleasure as well as politics, full of lovely *señoritas* and handsome *caballeros*. Its name alone is an incantation. As if on a magic carpet, you are transported to a tropical paradise of sparkling beaches and swaying palm trees, an island described by Christopher Columbus as "the most beautiful yet seen by human eyes."

Yet the mind's eye is easily deceived. Though most Americans have been proscribed from going for nearly half a century, Havana remains oddly familiar. It is the setting for spy novels like *Our Man in Havana*, gangster movies like *Godfather II*, and politically correct documentaries like the *Buena Vista Social Club*. Even if you've never gone, you know what clichés to expect, and you think of conga lines and communism, Ricky Ricardo as well as Che Guevara. You imagine yourself sipping daiquiris at the Tropicana while bearded revolutionaries storm the barricades.

I remember that in grade school my teacher showed the class a disk with all the colors of the rainbow. When spun around, it became a muddy blur, and so it is with Havana. The colors fade, and it begins to resemble those places that medieval cartographers left blank because no one had ever been, or returned.

Havana can also be found on real maps, ninety miles south of Key West. One of the largest cities in Latin America, it is a metropolis with a population over 2 million. From a room at the Hotel Riviera, built by mobster Meyer Lansky in 1957, you can see the Malecón, the splendid boulevard skirting the shoreline. Tom Miller called it "no-man's land between the devilish city and the bluest deep sea."[1] It ends at the fortress of La Punta, which once defended the city from Sir Francis Drake. To your right is Havana itself: a sprawl of crumbling colonial palaces, nondescript apartment buildings, and neoclassical monuments like the Capitolio. And if you look across the harbor you see the lighthouse of El Morro, perhaps the city's most recognizable landmark.

Beyond the Malecón is an endless carpet of ocean, stretching to the horizon. Depending on the weather, its color ranges from gunmetal gray to pale turquoise. On a clear day, the dazzling light glints on the waves and the spray comes over the seawall like a handful of glittering coins. The sky is a peculiar shade of blue not found anywhere else, a brilliant, almost translucent cobalt that the early settlers tried to emulate in pottery. It is impossible not to squint in Havana, or else survey it through dark glasses.

It is a city that assaults the senses. Habaneros douse themselves with cologne, and the city itself has an unmistakable scent. In the morning, the brine of the sea air is mixed with diesel fumes, roasting coffee, cigar smoke, and the sweetish stink of last night's rum. It is a noisy city. Many of the storefronts are protected by corrugated steel shutters that make a fierce racket as they are cranked open. There is no peace to be had from the uncertain engines of vintage DeSotos, Soviet-era Ladas, and paleolithic buses known as *camellos*, or camels. Exiles recall that myriad church bells once resounded over Havana, together with the cries of street vendors. This has been replaced by omnipresent music, often from American radio stations, whether hip-hop, salsa, or the Cuban pop known as *filin*. And from the docks comes the dour foghorn of a freighter and the shrill keening of seagulls.

Havana is a kaleidoscope of cities. There is Habana Vieja, which includes the seamy waterfront and the colonial palaces on the Plaza de Armas. From there, Havana expanded west. After Monserrate Street, the site of the old city walls, comes Centro Habana, the commercial district. If Habana Vieja was built with coral rock, Centro Habana is marble, with the ornate Presidential Palace and the bombastic Centro Gallego. Farther west is El Vedado, originally a suburb of row houses with delicately columned porticoes, but now the geographical heart of the city, with the monolithic Plaza de la Revolución. Across the Almendares River is Miramar, once a swank neighborhood of art deco mansions. Many of these have become embassies, and it is now the diplomatic quarter. Opposite the bay is the fishing village of Regla, with a famous shrine to Havana's patron saint, the black *Virgen de Regla*.

These Havanas from different centuries jostle each other like the old *comparsas* at Carnaval, the Cuban Mardi Gras. They were elaborate bands playing musical instruments such as long *tumbadora* drums, *timbales*, and a flute known as a *corneta china*. Today the closest equivalent would be the samba schools of Rio de Janeiro. Each Havana had its own *comparsa*, with distinctive costumes and dance steps. Many were African in origin, from poor neighborhoods such as Mantilla, though the elegant Havana Yacht Club had one as well. Perhaps the most famous was the *Marquéses de Atarés*, whose members wore white top hats and tails. On Saturday nights in February, all the comparsas paraded riotously down the Malecón and turned left on the Prado led by a *farolero*, a man carrying a lantern on a five-foot pole.

In 1961, Fidel Castro put an end to the *comparsas*, but their rhythm still echoes in Havana. This ghostly rumba gives the city a surreal, hallucinatory quality. The poet Hart Crane found it "hypersensual and mad."[2] If anything can happen, something strange undoubtedly will. The city is a stage set, and what appears real is often an elaborate fantasy, as in a movie by Luis Buñuel. Visitors to Havana themselves become fictional characters. Upon arriving, the novelist Pico Iyer felt himself to be "inside some romantic thriller."[3]

Little wonder that Havana literally drives people insane. Before the Revolution, there was a rich tradition of pixilated beggars wandering the streets, particularly in Habana Vieja. My grandmother spoke of the

*Comparsas* such as the *Marquéses de Atarés* danced up the Prado at Havana's Carnaval. (Historical Museum of Southern Florida)

*Andarin Carvajal*, a young man dressed in white who ran up and down Obispo Street all day. Sometimes he blew a whistle and snagged the coins tossed at him without stopping. Another was the *Marquesa*, a decrepit, heavily rouged mulatta in a tattered hooped skirt who haughtily sneered at passers-by.

But the most famous of all was the *Caballero de Paris*, a white-haired, bearded old vagabond who wore an opera cloak and a shabby linen shirt. It was said that in his youth he had loved a rich man's daughter who spurned him. Like Don Quixote pining for Dulcinea, this unhinged his mind, and he too believed himself to be a knight-errant. The *Caballero de Paris* was as harmless as his colleagues, and became something of a celebrity, signing autographs—often a cryptic mark on a scrap of paper and giving candy to children. His real name was José María Lipez Lledin and he died in a psychiatric ward in 1985, but he is commemorated in a lifesize statue outside the church of San Francisco de Asís, where he is buried. His outstretched hand has a patina from being stroked by Habaneros, who believe he brings good luck.

## SCULPTING CLOUDS

I left Havana in 1961 and returned thirty years later. But I could remember nothing of it.

A child of the Revolution, I was born shortly after Castro triumphantly entered Havana in 1959. A volatile mix of Basque and Catalan blood, my mother's people came to Cuba from Spain. Exile was a family tradition. They fled to Jacksonville during the struggle for independence in 1895, and it was there that my great-grandparents met. My mother's grandfather was a railroad signalman from Stockton, Georgia, named Thomas Crews. Perhaps hoping to impress his bride-to-be, he enlisted in the Rough Riders. After the war, the young couple settled in Havana. As for my father, his family hailed from Germany and emigrated to Matanzas, east of Havana. His grandfather, Alfred Heydrich, is still remembered there as *El Aleman* (the German). He was an entrepreneur who built the first ice factory in Matanzas and was briefly interned during World War I, when U-boats prowled the Caribbean.

This provenance is by no means unusual, since Cuba is a nation of immigrants. Thomas Crews (who lived to be ninety-four, one of the oldest surviving veterans of the Spanish American War) was a leading member of the American colony in Havana, and my mother grew up speaking English. This may have endeared her to my father, who like many bright young Cubans of his generation, studied in the United States He earned an engineering degree at Georgia Tech and went on to work for Shell Oil, managing its refinery in Havana. Its gas flare still lights up the sky at the end of the harbor.

Like much of Cuba's middle class, my parents avidly supported the Revolution. My father even worked for Che Guevara, who served briefly as minister of industry before setting out to start more revolutions. But before long, they joined the diaspora of over 1 million Cubans leaving the island. I was not quite two years old.

We did not go to Miami, like the vast majority, but instead to Spain, where my father found a job with Marathon Oil. A few years later we came to the United States and I grew up in Texas and Connecticut. Neither Cuban nor American, I was trapped in the hyphen between them, more impassable than the Straits of Florida. If the city where I was born was a *tabula rasa*, it nonetheless haunted me. Having nothing to draw upon save what my parents told me and what I could find in books, I fashioned a Havana of my own, complete with an imaginary Malecón and a toy lighthouse of El Morro.

I was in good company, since Havana has often been viewed through the prism of loss. Many of Cuba's greatest poets, such as José María Heredia, have been exiles. Refracted by nostalgia, Havana has often been described as a long lost love, an unforgettable glimpse of paradise. But nostalgia feeds on memory, and Havana was like a dream I could no longer recall once awake. Exiles often sugar-coat their homelands, and this has created a whole genre of Cuban humor. A mutt wandering through the streets of Miami turns down a bone, scoffing that in Cuba he was a German shepherd. Exiles have their mental scrapbooks to draw on, however distorted. But you can lie only if you remember the truth.

Another famous exile, José Martí, likened living in *exilio* (exile) to "sculpting clouds."[4] It is a sublime metaphor for the power of the imagination, and many Havanas have been built in the skies over Miami. But the less used, more traditional Spanish word for exile is *destierro*. The latter suggests that one's *tierra* (land) is somehow shorn away, like an amputated limb, while *exilio* implies escape. *Exilio* is active while *destierro* is passive. The exile takes with him a suitcase of memories, as well as hopes for a fresh start. *Destierro* leaves only a gaping hole, as bleak as a howl in the night.

My love for Havana, then, remained unrequited, as chaste as Dante's vision of Beatrice. At least until I finally screwed up the courage to go.

A lifetime passed, or rather, my life up to that point. In 1991, I was the editor of a magazine in Washington, D.C. This made the usually byzantine process of visiting Cuba easier, since the travel ban does not cover journalists. Though I am an American citizen, I had to apply to the Cuban Interests Section* for a passport since I was born in Cuba. This was accomplished over several lunches at expensive restaurants where I convinced the skeptical but hungry Cuban press attaché that I wanted to interview Fidel Castro.

---

* Since Cuba and the United States do not have formal diplomatic relations and do not exchange ambassadors, each country has "Interest Sections." They are embassies in all but name.

I often wondered what the FBI agents who trailed Cuban diplomats made of me, and perhaps my name can be found in a yellowed surveillance report in the bowels of the Justice Department.

Miraculously, my passport appeared in the mail within a few weeks, looking just like the American version but with the Cuban seal. After a forty-five minute flight from Miami, I arrived in Havana early in the morning, late in April. While other American visitors could wander freely about, as a journalist my visit was carefully chaperoned. I was met at the airport by someone I'll call Carlos. He was from MININT, Cuba's all-powerful ministry of internal security, and he was to be my minder. Carlos was hardly a goon, but rather a courteous, bespectacled young man about my age. He had a car and driver, and for the next week he dutifully showed me around Havana.

It was the darkest phase of the so-called Special Period following the collapse of the Soviet Union, Cuba's sugar daddy for three decades. The streets were full of Chinese bicycles, with long lines even for staples such as bread, and there was a peculiar stench in the air, since soap was in short supply and laundry was done with toothpaste. Prostitution had returned with a vengeance, and young girls known as *jineteras*\* paraded along the Malecón and all but waited in line outside the hotels. Despite this, we visited tourist attractions such as Hemingway's house and even attended a show at the Tropicana. The interview with Castro was dangled in front of me like a distant piñata. I was told at the press office that such things were decided only at the last minute and that interviewers were often summoned in the middle of the night, without warning. I don't recall what on earth I would have asked him, but as I waited for Castro's call I got to know Carlos.

Presumably, only the most loyal cadres were allowed to meet journalists, and Carlos was a smooth customer. Like me, he was a product of the Revolution, but from a family of cane cutters. Though he had never been to the United States, he spoke English well and had studied for a year in Moscow. At first he played tour guide, describing Havana's early history. But before long, our conversations moved from conquistadors to commissars. Carlos had some experience at this game and carefully probed to ascertain where I stood. We circled each other warily, two lion cubs in the bush, until we unsheathed our claws. I struck first, asking why he sup-

---

\* Literally, jockeys. The term applies to male hustlers as well.

ported a revolution that was such a dismal failure. Castro appeared increasingly out of touch with the modern world, his jails were full of political prisoners, and you could smell despair in the street like the dirty clothes. Carlos had heard it all before, and parried with a question of his own: Why did America, winner of the Cold War, pick on a tiny island like Cuba?

I'm afraid I didn't have a very good answer. Carlos knew his stuff and reminded me of the Bay of Pigs invasion and Operation Mongoose, the CIA's attempts to kill Castro with exploding cigars. Pressing his advantage, he brought up the *bloquéo*.* I shot back that Cuba's economic woes were caused by communism, not the United States. My argument had a hollow ring to it, since I believed that the best way to bring capitalism (and with it, democracy) to Cuba was to drop the antediluvian embargo altogether. It had failed to dislodge Castro, but McDonald's, Coca-Cola, and a battalion of tourists with American greenbacks might just do the trick.

"Let them come," replied Carlos when I admitted this. "We'll welcome them with open arms."

He lost his cool only once, at a sarcastic remark I made about the *Maximo Lider*, as Castro is often referred to. In 1948, Castro married the daughter of a *Batistiano* (a follower of the dictator Batista) and spent his honeymoon in Miami, which I found ironic. This was going too far, and Carlos berated me for my arrogance and naiveté. I feared things would end badly and I would be hastily deported, but the next day he was as unruffled as ever and we continued our Cook's tour of Havana.

One day he left me to my own devices, perhaps having reached the same conclusion as the FBI, that I was harmless. But I had a mission of my own, to see my parents' house. My mother had shown me pictures of it, a snazzy, cream-colored bungalow designed by my uncle, a budding architect much influenced by Gropius. Its most elegant feature was a series of brick jalousies that let in the breeze as well as scorpions, according to my mother. Bits of cobalt-colored glass between the openings created an effect like that of the *mediopuntos* of colonial houses, stained glass windows that cast a rainbow of shadows. However, my mother didn't remember the address. It was near the old Havana Country Club, in the area

---

* *Bloquéo* (literally, blockade) is how Cubans refer to the trade embargo imposed by President Eisenhower in 1960 and still in place today.

now known as Siboney, and I repeated her imprecise directions to the cab driver.

After a roundabout drive I found it, though it didn't look much like the pictures. A second story had been added, destroying its sleek lines, and it appeared the jalousies had been boarded up. A window was broken and repaired with cardboard. Though badly in need of paint, it was clearly inhabited, perhaps by several families. Should I go inside? Perhaps someone would remember me. It was here that I had taken my first steps, and something of me remained. Could this be my own madeleine, which would retrieve the memories I had so envied? I didn't dare find out, but took nearly a whole roll of pictures, from every angle.

When I returned home, I showed them to my mother. "That's not it," she said.

"Are you sure?" I said. "It must have changed quite a bit."

"*Claro que sí,*" she said definitively. "I know my own house."

I would have to go back.

And so I did, the following year. This time I found the house, surprisingly in mint condition. The yard was neatly tended, and I suspect that a diplomat or party official lived there. The jalousies were untouched, and the bits of tinted glass my uncle was so proud of sparkled like sapphires. I still didn't knock on the door, leaving the madeleine uneaten by the teacup.

Later I found other reasons to return to Havana. I no longer tried to interview Castro, but there were film festivals, conferences, and even a doomed joint venture between my magazine and *Granma*, Cuba's official newspaper. I traveled throughout the island, visiting Santiago de Cuba, the old capital; my father's birthplace, Matanzas; and Trinidad, a colonial gem in the foothills of the Escambray Mountains. There was much to write: magazine articles, a novel about Hemingway, and finally this book. I married, had children, moved from Washington, D.C., to Austin, to Paris, to Miami, and back to Austin. Throughout these peregrinations, Havana provided a constant. If not at the center of the compass, it was a direction nonetheless. Though it could never be home, it was a place I could always return to.

After the first trip, I was no longer assigned a minder, and happily fended for myself. Sadly, few friendships survived from one trip to another. The cast of characters kept changing: some left for Miami or

Madrid, while others stopped returning my phone calls, perhaps afraid to be questioned by the likes of Carlos. Habaneros are as protean as their city. They can be warm, good-natured, gregarious, and sensual, but also suspicious, morose, stubborn, and bitter. Almost any adjective will do. They are nothing if not contradictory: carefree yet easily offended, open-hearted yet selfish, gentle yet prone to violence. Their constant smiles often hide black melancholy, and their easy familiarity can be shrewdly manipulative. They are sometimes described as "happy-go-lucky," but this apparent simplicity is a mélange of Spanish fatalism, African cruelty, and Chinese guile. If they are quick to laugh at themselves, this self-deprecation often hides the haughty, unyielding pride of the *hidalgos* who arrived with Columbus.

There are conversations in Havana like nowhere else. Habaneros have a true gift of gab that combines endless wordplay, surprising erudition, and a scathing sense of humor. Talk is an art form that glides effortlessly from a song by Carlos Varela, to the latest joke about Raul Castro, to a film by Enrique Pineda Barnet. For a few hours, I could share the intensity of their lives, which made my own seem bland and coddled. But if I envied their passion, they resented the dollars in my wallet (a fortune to most of them) and the fact that I would soon return to *La Yuma*, as the United States is referred to.* They found my endless questions patronizing, and wanted to talk of anything but Havana. My life was elsewhere, as was theirs.

My conversations continued with Havana itself, for I wanted to hear its side of the story. Yet for every answer I found, there was another question.

## LA ENGAÑADORA

Is Havana male or female?

Here I will employ a noncommittal *it*, but many other cities have a well-defined gender, based on their history, architecture, or less tangible factors. London is a burly beefeater, while Paris is an alluring courtesan. New York is decidedly masculine, while New Orleans is feminine. Often the balance is tipped by the name of the city itself: martial Madrid and sexy Sevilla, luscious Lima and craggy Cuzco.

---

* *Yumas* are Americans. Some claim that this all-purpose phrase came from the movie *3:10 to Yuma*, but I suspect it comes from the common greeting "You man!"

At first blush, Goethe's eternal feminine appears to predominate in Havana. In Spanish, the name *La Habana* rolls sweetly off the palate. The *h* is silent and the tongue skips from the article directly to the soft welcome of the *b*. Havana's geography strengthens this conclusion. The curve of the Malecón is like a woman's waist, and from above the city appears to recline gracefully on the blue divan of the Gulf Stream. It has been wryly observed that Havana has one of the few harbors where ships can penetrate directly into the city, almost to the doorsteps of the houses.

Havana has always been celebrated for the beauty of its women. In the nineteenth century, poets such as Heredia swooned over the dark-eyed Creole charmers. Women of good families led closely guarded lives, as in a Moorish harem, but assignations were made with a flick of a fan, often from balconies or a passing carriage. Misunderstandings were common, leading to many a duel.

The beauty of Habaneras was confirmed during Prohibition, when American tourists first visited in great numbers. They came not just for the rum but for the señoritas, somewhat more liberated than their cloistered great-grandmothers. In 1927 Basil Woon gushed "At least two out of three girls on the street . . . are pretty, and half of them, if you like the lissome, languorous, warm-eyed, dark skinned, vividly colored type, are beautiful."[5] If they inspired poetry a century earlier, now it was show tunes. For Irving Berlin, Havana was "Where dark-eyed Stellas light their fellas' panatellas. . . ."[6]

The metaphor of Havana as a lady is much-loved by writers. It has been described as "a woman in love," yet with a dubious reputation, a tart rather than a virtuous wife. Andrei Codrescu compared the city to "a cheap and bountiful mistress."[7] But there is an element of danger as well. Bob Schacochis imagined Havana "beautiful but exhausted, dancing through the perfumed night with a gun in her hand."[8]

Many of the city's landmarks are female. Perched on the castle of the Real Fuerza is La Giraldilla, supposedly a likeness of Isabel de Bobadilla, the wife of the conquistador Hernando de Soto. Just south of the Parque Central is La Fuente India, with a marble statue of a woman in a feathered headdress. On the road from the airport is another, less elegant fountain built by President Grau. It's popularly known as "Paulina's bidet," after Grau's sister-in-law and alleged mistress.

And yet something is wrong with this picture. Despite its lacy trappings, there is a harsh and masculine side to Havana, and its history is marked by conquest, rapine, and slaughter. In its early days, the city was a far-flung outpost of the Spanish empire, a rendezvous for gold-laden galleons returning home from Mexico. In the 1500s, it was repeatedly attacked by pirates and burned to the ground several times. As a result, Havana became one of the best-defended cities in the world, ringed by massive fortifications.

What fueled its growth was commerce in tobacco, coffee, sugar, and slaves. Most of the luxurious palaces from which fetching beauties looked out were built in the 1800s. Until then, Havana was a rough-and-ready emporium where deals were struck, money changed hands, and fortunes were made or lost. To gain independence from Spain, Cuba endured a massacre in which a fifth of its population perished. In the twentieth century, Havana suffered not one but several violent political upheavals, and every manner of repression yet devised, whether by American capitalists, Russian communists, or Cubans themselves.

When you wipe off the lipstick and rouge, you begin to revise your judgment. If Havana is a woman, she may well be *La Engañadora*, the subject of the famous cha-cha-cha by Enrique Jorrín. This was a girl who walked down Prado and Neptuno streets, eliciting wolf whistles until it was discovered that her charms were not what they appeared to be.

## TIME TRAVEL

Havana is a time machine that propels you into the past.

It has been the stage for most of the political drama that shaped Cuba. Despite its small size, this troublesome island has at times decided the fate of the world, as in October 1962, when the United States and the Soviet Union nearly went to war over it. Hugh Thomas titled his magisterial portrait of the island *The Pursuit of Freedom*, and much of Cuban history unfolds as an epic struggle for self-determination. But it also meanders in strange and unexpected ways, down tortuous paths and occasional dead ends.

As in few cities, this history reveals itself in the sun-baked streets of Havana, as if the city were eager to give its own account. Begin in the present, at the Plaza de la Revolución. This is the vast square where Castro still harangues crowds for several hours at a time. If you follow Reina (now Salvador Allende) you reach the Capitolio where legislators met during the Cuban Republic, which ended ignominiously in 1952. It is a stone's throw from the Parque Central with its statue of José Martí, known as the Apostle of Freedom, who led the fight for independence until his tragic death in 1895. He faces Monserrate Street, the entrance to the city in the 1700s, when it was larger than New York or Boston. On the other side is Habana Vieja, the colonial core. If you follow Obispo Street toward the waterfront, you reach the Plaza de Armas, where Havana was founded in 1519.

One of the inherent difficulties of writing about Havana is finding a middle ground between political extremes. There have been a number of books about Cuba in recent years, and it is easy to see where they fall in the political spectrum, either pro or contra. Accounts by Cuban exiles can be nostalgic and bitter, viewing life before 1959 with rose-tinted glasses and condemning the Revolution. Conversely, books by fellow travelers exaggerate the poverty of pre-Castro Cuba and overlook such minor details as the savage treatment of political prisoners. Avoiding either of these traps is like walking a tightrope.

Readers in both camps tend to politicize even the most mundane descriptions of Havana. To mention the outstanding renovations of certain colonial buildings is to support Castro, while to admit that many others are crumbling is to condemn him. To note that Cuban doctors are among the best trained in Latin America is to applaud the Revolution, while to point out that many Cubans cannot obtain medicines such as aspirin is to denounce it. Cuba today is inevitably compared to what it was fifty years ago, or what it might have been with without Castro. What would the United States do without its longest-lived bogeyman? Just before this book went to press, Castro was hospitalized and the question gained urgency. But within a few weeks, he appeared to be recovering. As Voltaire might have said, if Castro hadn't existed, Americans would have had to invent him.

These arguments only muddy the waters further. Even in Havana, a rose can be a rose, sometimes.

This is the story of Havana: an autobiography, if you will, told from the city's point of view. Occasionally it ventures beyond the city limits, since Havana is a supremely cosmopolitan city. You'll find what intrigued me, rather than what others have found intriguing. There is a Cuban expression often used by my grandmother, *"Cada loco con su tema."* Like much else heard on the streets of Havana, it is difficult to translate, but means roughly "To each his own." This applies not just to mad beggars like the *Caballero de Paris* but to those who search the Plaza de San Francisco for the bar where Hemingway set the opening scene of *To Have and Have Not*; who wander in Habana Vieja, trailed by suspicious policemen, looking for the remnants of the old city walls; who comb the Vedado, notebook in hand, for the Doric columns that inspired Alejo Carpentier.

Far too much has already been written about the Revolution, and I have little to add here. More interesting to me is what led up to it. Certain periods of Cuban history—such as the Spanish conquest or the vibrant, violent 1930s—have been ignored or distorted by historians, both in Miami and Havana. For obvious reasons, I was fascinated by the shared destiny of Cuba and the United States going back centuries, and by no means over in 1959. The relationship between my two countries resembles a passionate love affair which ended so bitterly that neither side can forget the other. "Who jilted whom?" they still wonder. As in a romantic comedy, there may yet be a happy ending . . .

Certain parts of Havana remain unchanged after five hundred years, while others will be soon unrecognizable. Like any city, it is a living, breathing organism, one that I could hardly contain within these pages. I once found a snow globe of Havana, perhaps a knock-off from the 1950s, a glass ball containing a miniature lighthouse of El Morro. When I turned it over, it filled with incongruous flurries. That was when I realized an impossible ambition: to hold Havana in the palm of my hand.

# CHAPTER I

# *Hatuey's Revenge*

## *Plaza de Armas*

*T*o find a book in Havana, you go to the Plaza de Armas.

It is a postcard-perfect square on the seaward side of Obispo Street, shaded by banyan trees and royal palms. From the belltower of the nearby Church of San Francisco de Asís, which affords you a seagull's view of Habana Vieja,* it resembles a lush, verdant pool, as though foliage had flooded the cobblestoned streets. But this is deceptive, since beneath the canopy of leaves are marble benches, Moorish-style fountains, and carefully tended flower beds. At the center is a statue of Carlos Manuel de Céspedes, a hero of Cuban independence. Even on the hottest day there is a cool, salty breeze from across the bay, and the gnarled trunks of the banyans are garlanded with bougainvillea blossoms.

Books are a scarce commodity in Havana. What few bookstores there are, such as the art deco Moderna Poesia near the Parque Central, are usually empty save for Soviet-era technical manuals and hagiographies of Che Guevara and other revolutionary icons. Those in the know head for the Plaza de Armas, where each morning the booksellers line the porticoes of the colonial palaces that frame the square. Unlike their counterparts on the Seine, who have permanent stalls, the *bouquinistes* of Havana must display their wares on makeshift shelves or folding metal tables. There are books of every description, from worn paperbacks to tomes of calfskin leather, as well as old newspapers like the *Havana Post* and vintage

---

*Literally and figuratively, "old Havana." In Spanish, the *b* is pronounced the same as *v*, followed by *vee-ay-ha*. Habana Vieja describes the area from the old city walls, which ran along Monserrate Street, east to the waterfront.

magazines like *Bohemia*. Rain is a constant danger, and they have plastic sheets to cover their precious inventory in case of an *aguacero*, as the abrupt midmorning showers are called.

In the 1990s, the Cuban government flirted with free enterprise to attract tourists. This was the time of *paladares*, restaurants in private homes that served the best food in Havana, and *jineteras*, who offered their own fare on the Malecón. Vendors were allowed to troll the streets of Habana Vieja, and a flea market called a *candonga* was set up on the Avenida del Puerto, where you could buy kitschy souvenirs such as bongo drums or carved coconuts. It was then that the *Mercado de Libros* (book market) was established in the Plaza de Armas. It is often described as an old tradition, but there was no need for it before the Revolution, since Obispo Street was cheek-to-jowl with bookstores. Many of the *paladares* were later closed and the *jineteras* were banished to seedier neighborhoods, but Castro left the booksellers alone.

This might seem surprising, given the regime's predilection to control information. For example, access to the Internet is severely restricted and an e-mail address is awarded only to the elite. But a thousand flowers bloom in the Plaza de Armas, and many of the novels on sale are hardly required reading for the New Man. Some are the detritus of the nearly defunct Cuban publishing industry, recycled versions of what can be found at the Moderna Poesía, as well as the usual canon of *The Old Man and the Sea* and *One Hundred Years of Solitude*. But there are other books of doubtful provenance, perhaps left behind by tourists. One morning I found a John Grisham paperback in English, an Inspector Maigret mystery in French, and a translation of Danielle Steel in German. Despite the embargo, there were U.S. periodicals as well, such a recent issue of *Newsweek* and a Land's End catalog. There was even a well-thumbed phone book from Houston, Texas.

The Plaza de Armas appears in countless novels about Havana, drawing literary characters like a magnet. Nearby was Mr. Wormold's vacuum cleaner store in *Our Man in Havana*, and only a few blocks away, Harry Morgan docked his boat in *To Have and Have Not*. But there is no danger that the fictional world will supplant the real one. History keeps intruding, for the Plaza de Armas was bombarded by British frigates when they attacked Havana in 1762. It was here that the head of José Luis Aponte, who led an unsuccessful slave revolt in 1812, was exhibited on a pike, and in 1933 the American ambassador, Sumner Welles, announced the fall of the dictator Machado to a cheering crowd from the balcony of the old

American embassy at the southwest corner of the square. And Castro himself passed through here after Batista fled in 1959.

The scene is much the same as in a print from the *Illustrated London News* in 1869. Then the statue was of Ferdinand VII, the Spanish king. The streets were unpaved, but the royal palms had already been planted and the Plaza de Armas maintained an air of serenity amid the bustle of the harbor. Today it is kept in pristine condition for tourists, and mulattas dressed in ruffled skirts and red kerchiefs pose for pictures. Strolling musicians take requests, and horse-drawn carriages pass by the Palacio de los Capitanes Generales on the western side of the square. Here the street is paved with cobblewood, wooden bricks intended to mute the passage of just such carriages. Once the residence of the Spanish governors, the Palacio is now a museum containing a throne intended for the King of Spain but never used and the bronze eagle that once perched atop the monument to the battleship *Maine*.

Between the Plaza de Armas and the waterfront is another tourist magnet, the Templete. Sheltered by a majestic ceiba tree, it's a mock temple replete with Doric columns, built in the nineteenth century to commemorate the founding of Havana on November 19, 1519. Inside is a vast canvas by the French painter Jean Baptiste Vermay. Entitled *First Mass*, it depicts the Spanish conquistadors celebrating the sacrament while the Indians kneel respectfully. Looking on from above, perched in the spreading branches of the ceiba, is a brilliantly plumed parrot.

This is the sanitized version taught to Cuban schoolchildren, just as Americans learn about the Pilgrims who landed at Plymouth Rock a century later. None of it is true, though there may well have been a parrot.

## DISCOVERING COLUMBUS

*All night long they heard birds passing.*

—Christopher Columbus's log book

In the sumptuous courtyard of the Palacio de los Capitanes Generales is a larger-than-life statue of Christopher Columbus on a pedestal. Sculpted in 1862, it is an indifferent representation at best, though we don't know what he looked like since there are no contemporary portraits. The most famous statue of Columbus is in Santo Domingo, where he fearlessly points to the horizon. Here he meekly stands with his hand upon a globe, dwarfed by two royal palms. The palace is often used for weddings.

The Plaza de Armas, from the *Illustrated London News*, 1869. (Author's collection)

Bridesmaids dressed in crinoline pose on the marble staircase, and pea-cocks strut between the colonnades. The Admiral of the Ocean Sea seems uncomfortable in his marble skin, out of place among the orchids.

I shall refer to the man who "discovered" Cuba by the anglicized ver-sion of his name, but in Spain he was Cristóbal Colón. As a brand, Columbus ranks with Coca-Cola. In the United States he has a day of his own, October 12, complete with a parade; in Latin America it is observed as *Dia de la Raza*. The Quincentennial of his arrival in the Americas was celebrated with much hoopla and auctioned off to corporate sponsors—Budweiser was the "official beer." A movie was even made starring French actor Gerard Depardieu called *1492: The Conquest of Paradise*. Yet his statue in Havana has a somewhat guarded expression. What is he hid-ing from us?

Quite a bit, actually. There are nearly as many conspiracy theories about Columbus as about his contemporary, Leonardo da Vinci. Despite conflicting claims from as far afield as Poland, it is generally accepted that Columbus was born in Genoa, although he mentioned it only once (in a will he drew up in 1498) and there is no record of him ever speaking Ital-ian. Columbus wrote in Castilian, Portuguese, and Latin. His life before 1480 is a blank page, and from then on, much of the traditional Colum-bus narrative is patently false. For example, no sailor of the time worth his salt feared that a ship would fall off the earth when it disappeared over the horizon, and there is no proof that Columbus's crew was about to mutiny when land was sighted. It is equally ludicrous to think that Queen Isabella pawned her jewels to pay for the expedition. Even the date is wrong, since Columbus used the Julian calendar. Under the Gregorian calendar, adopted in 1582, the date of his landfall is not October 12 but October 23.

One problem is that the biographical sources are themselves dubious. The famous log book of the first voyage was transcribed after his death (from a copy, not the original) by the Spanish cleric Bartolomé de las Casas, who condemned Columbus's treatment of the natives. What little else we know of Columbus's life comes from the book by his son Fernando, who hoped to burnish his father's tattered image. Even that was lost—the existing version comes from an Italian translation. Another problem is that Columbus himself was very secretive, and often twisted the facts to serve his purposes. We know only what he chose to tell us, and even that is suspect.

Most scholars agree that Columbus landed on what is now Watling Island, in the Bahamas.[1] Not finding much except for a sandy beach, he sailed on to Cuba and then Jamaica and Hispaniola. But the greatest mystery of all is where he thought he was going. Accepted wisdom has it that Columbus was trying to reach India (hence the name *indios*, which has stuck) or China (familiar to him from the writings of Marco Polo). But if so, why did he formally take possession of Cuba on behalf of the King of Spain? The Chinese had discovered the compass in the twelfth century and possessed the world's greatest navy. Their ships were as long as 440 feet with crews of 500 and ranged as far as Africa. Imagine the scorn of the Ming emperor at the thought of Columbus and his three ragtag ships making a territorial claim!

Columbus christened the island Juana in honor of Prince Juan, heir to the Castilian throne. This, too, is inconsistent with the supposed landfall in China. Why would he rename it? Also puzzling is the feverish quest for gold. Did Columbus really intend to barter bullion from Chinese merchants with the meager glass beads and trinkets that he carried aboard his caravels? In fact, he stole what little gold he found in Cuba and blithely kidnapped several Taino natives to exhibit them at the Spanish court—overt acts of piracy. Did he plan to start a war between Spain and the vast Middle Kingdom? It seems likely that Columbus knew more than he let on. Perhaps the possibility of a lucrative trade route to the Indies was an easier sell to the Spanish throne than rumors of a New World.

Historians have debated this prickly point for generations, and will doubtless continue to do so.

Of course, Columbus no more "discovered" Cuba than he did China. That honor belongs to the precursors of the Tainos, who migrated from the Yucatán to Cuba as early as 4000 B.C.[2] Archaeologists know little of the first Cubans for the simple reason that their departure from the world stage was so abrupt—within a generation after the arrival of Columbus, they would be extinct. *Taino* was their word for "noble," and not necessarily how they referred to themselves. They comprised a flourishing civilization that stretched from Cuba to the Lesser Antilles. The Tainos lived in villages of palm-thatched houses called *bohios* and played the same ceremonial game as the Aztecs, in which a rubber ball was propelled with hips and elbows through a stone ring. They employed a sophisticated system of agriculture, growing yucca, corn, sweet potatoes, and plantains in knee-high mounds called *conucos*, and had trading relations with the Yucatán peninsula and southern Florida. What few artifacts they left behind include bone carvings of ethereal beauty and wooden chairs in the shape of animals called *duhos*.

Columbus came ashore near a Taino fishing village. His description of the natives is contradictory: He noted in his log book that "in all the world there can be no better people," yet he thinks nothing of putting them in chains and comments that they would make very good servants. Columbus dispatched two of his men to explore the interior, and they returned with tales of a "perfumed weed" called *tabaco*, and a remarkably comfortable net for sleeping called a *hamaca*. They might also have returned with syphilis, though this is far from certain, according to historians including Irving Rouse. There was an epidemic of venereal disease in the Mediterranean a few years later, although Columbus's sailors might not have been the source.

Columbus soon departed and would not see Cuba again until his second voyage, a year later. He returned with an armada of seventeen ships carrying fifteen hundred colonists, to establish a permanent settlement. After making landfall in Hispaniola, he left with three ships to explore the southern coast of Cuba, but soon turned back. Had he gone just fifty miles more, he would have rounded the southwestern promontory of Cuba and proved that it was not the Chinese mainland, as he still claimed. He might also have reached the site of present-day Havana.

This would not occur until 1508, when Spanish explorer Sebastián Ocampo circumnavigated the crocodile-shaped island in eight months and entered Havana Bay to careen his two ships. Careening was an essential and potentially dangerous repair for any oceangoing vessel of the time. It involved emptying a ship of ballast and hauling it on land in order to caulk the hull. The serene, natural harbor was perfect for this, and Ocampo found pitch on the rocks along the shore. He named the site Puerto de Carenas.

By then, the Admiral of the Ocean Sea was dead. Columbus was an archetype of the contemporary entrepreneur who has the vision to launch a start-up yet lacks the people skills to manage it. True to form, he was greedy and mistreated his subordinates, and the stock tumbled shortly after the IPO. The colony on Hispaniola fared so badly that Columbus was hauled back to Spain in chains, though he pleaded his case to Queen Isabella and was reinstated as governor. His final voyage ended in shipwreck as Columbus struggled with the mysterious, still-undiagnosed illness that would kill him. His last days are as mysterious as his childhood. Ignored by the Spanish court and embroiled in lawsuits, Columbus died on May 20, 1506, but it is a myth that he was poor. To the contrary, he had amassed a large fortune, like many a disgraced CEO.

His final resting place is one last conundrum. Columbus's remains were taken to Santo Domingo, but then supposedly transferred to Havana and later Sevilla. Then in 1877, a lead casket bearing his name was found hidden in the cathedral of Santo Domingo. This was enshrined in the Las Vegas-style Faro, a huge lighthouse-shaped mausoleum with 157 spotlights that shine a cross on the night sky. In 2003, a team of Spanish forensic experts tested a DNA sample from the remains in Sevilla, but the results were inconclusive. Like much else about Columbus, we'll probably never know for sure.

In recent years, his reputation has been so tarred by revisionist historians that Columbus is likened more to Machiavelli than Copernicus (two other contemporaries.) But during the Quincentennial in 1992, replicas of the *Niña*, *Pinta*, and *Santa María* were built in Spain and sailed across the Atlantic. Sponsored by Texaco, they can be seen today in Corpus Christi, Texas. One has only to stand on the rickety bridge of the *Santa María*, which measured about seventy-five feet from bow to stern, to realize the enormity of Columbus's achievement, and the awe he must have felt when he first saw the Cuban shore. In his last novel, *The Harp and the Shadow*, Alejo Carpentier has Columbus's ghost recite his own epitaph:

*One day, on the coast of Cuba . . . I said that one world ended and another begin. . . . I had rent the veil of the unknown and entered a new reality that surpassed my understanding, for there are discoveries so momentous—though possible—that by their very immensity they annihilate any mortal who dares to enter them.*[3]

His son Diego became the new Admiral of the Ocean Sea. By then, the meager gold mines of Hispaniola were exhausted and the Taínos had been all but eliminated by murder, disease, and forced labor. It was in Hispaniola that the Spaniards perfected the techniques of genocide that they would use so effectively throughout the New World, and there were soon as few as two thousand natives left on that island.[4] In 1511, an expedition of three hundred men embarked to conquer Cuba. But when they landed near the present-day town of Baracoa, the conquistadors were met with a shower of arrows.

This time, the Taínos were ready for them, led by a man named Hatuey.

## AN INDIAN WITH TWO CANOES

*I saw there so great cruelties that never a man will see their like again.*

—Bartolomé de las Casas

Today, Hatuey is best known for the beer named after him. His hawk-nosed profile is on the amber bottle, superimposed on a map of the island. Ernest Hemingway drank Hatuey, the beverage of choice aboard his fishing boat the *Pilar*. It is the quintessential lager of Havana, known popularly as *un indio con dos canoas*,* and has washed down countless plates of *arroz con pollo* since 1926, when it was first brewed by Bacardi. Now the beer can only be found outside of Cuba.

We know considerably less about Hatuey than Columbus, and it is even harder to extract the man from the myth. But from accounts of his heroic resistance against the Spaniards, we can take the true measure of the Taínos. Hatuey was the *cacique*, or tribal chief, of the island of Guahaba (today Gonave in Haiti) off the coast of Hispaniola. Running afoul of the conquistadors, he escaped to Cuba with about four hundred fol-

---

*Translated as "an Indian with two canoes." The word *canoa* is Taíno. Native canoes were hollowed-out tree trunks, and two of them facing each other approximate a bottle. Another theory is that this referred to two glasses, to share with a friend.

lowers. There he rallied the local tribes by warning of what would soon befall them:

> You know that the Christians are coming to this island, and what they have done to the people there. What they did on Hispaniola they will do here. Do any of you know why they behave this way? It is not simply because they are evil. They have a god that they worship and adore, and it is in order to get that god from us that they conquer and kill us.

Hatuey showed them a basket of gold jewelry and continued: "If we keep this god, they will kill us in order to get their hands upon him. Let us cast him into the river!"[5]

To lead the invasion, Columbus's son had appointed Diego Velázquez, a *hidalgo** from an ancient family in Castilla. Nearly fifty, he had arrived on the second voyage and prospered. His wealth figured in the selection, for he had to pay for the ships out of his own pocket. Conquering new lands was very much a financial venture, and investors received most of the loot. Velázquez's secretary was the future conqueror of Mexico, Hernando Cortés.

As in the conquest of Hispaniola, the natives vastly outnumbered the Spaniards but were no match for their superior weaponry. The Taínos fought with bows and arrows, bamboo-tipped spears, and rocks thrown from slings, none of which could penetrate Spanish armor. Mounted on horses, the conquistadors had steel swords that could cleave a man in half, crossbows that killed with deadly accuracy, and the early rifles known as arquebuses, which, though often ineffective in the tropical humidity, created deafening explosions. Among their most frightening weapons were the *mastines*, Irish wolfhounds trained to rip their victims apart.

Despite the gap in military technology, Hatuey waged a tenacious guerrilla war against Velázquez and held him at bay for nearly a year. The Taínos abandoned their villages and hid in the rugged mountains of eastern Cuba (much as Castro would do nearly five centuries later), where Spanish horses were useless and there were no clear lines of fire for the crossbows. Hatuey's strategy was to isolate the armored columns and attack stragglers before dispersing and regrouping for another attack. At

---

*A Spanish nobleman. The word comes from *hijo de algo*, or "son of something."

one point, the Spaniards were forced to barricade themselves in the fort they built at Baracoa.

It is at this point that the mythmaking begins and Hatuey enters the pantheon of doomed Cuban heroes. According to most versions, one of his own betrayed him and led the Spaniards to his hideout. Velázquez was able to capture him alive only by promising to spare his followers. On February 12, 1512, Hatuey was burned alive at the stake near a village called Yara, a few miles from Manzanillo. According to legend, a Franciscan monk told him just before the fire was lit that if he were baptized, he would go to heaven. Hatuey asked if Christians went to heaven. When assured that they did, Hatuey replied that he preferred to go to hell so he would never again have "to meet such cruel and wicked people. . . ."[6] True or not, this story is taught to every Cuban schoolchild and is commemorated not just in history books but on beer bottles.

Once Cuba was pacified, the extermination of the Taínos commenced in earnest. One eyewitness wrote of a horrific encounter near Camaguey:

> . . .we were welcomed with a bounteous quantity of fish and bread and . . . the Indians generously gave us all they could. Then suddenly, without cause and without warning . . . the devil inhabited the Christians and spurred them to attack the men, women, and children who were sitting there before us. In the massacre that followed, the Spaniards put to the sword more than three thousand. . . . [7]

Those who survived such slaughter were parceled out to landowners in grants known as *encomiendas*, presumably for the Taínos' protection. In practice, this entitled the Spaniards to literally work them to death clearing fields or digging trenches in the never-ending search for gold. Those who escaped were hunted down with dogs, branded like cattle, and sold into slavery.

Even today, it is implied that the Taínos somehow lacked the will to fight back. Columbus himself noted in the log book of the first voyage that the Taínos "do not carry arms or know them" and "are very gentle and without knowledge of what is evil." In fact, however, the Taínos were themselves conquerors, having subjugated a tribe called the Guahatabeys, whom they kept as slaves. They waged war on the Arawaks, tough customers who inhabited the Lesser Antilles and practiced ethnic cleansing by raping women and castrating men before eating them. On his second voyage, Columbus found that the sailors he had left behind in Hispaniola had been slaughtered to a man. The original barbecue (from the Taino word *barbacoa)* was a rack used for torturing prisoners as well as roasting meat.

Yet another misconception is that the Taino women were wantonly promiscuous. Actually, rape was cited as one of the greatest Spanish abuses. Most sexual encounters were probably like that recounted by the brutish Michele Cuneo, an Italian nobleman who sailed on the second voyage:

> *I wanted to put my desire into execution but she did not want it and treated me with her fingernails in such a manner that I wished I had never begun. But seeing that (to tell you the end of it all) I took a rope and thrashed her well, for which she raised such unheard of screams that you would not have believed your ears. Finally, we came to such an agreement in such manner that I can tell you that she seemed to have been brought up in a school of harlots.*[8]

Violation of Taino women was probably the reason for the massacre of the Spanish sailors.

But it is certain that the Tainos had never encountered such savagery. Many committed suicide by hanging themselves, eating dirt, or drinking unprocessed cassava juice, which was poisonous. Incredibly, there were soon not enough Tainos to work in the mines, and Velázquez ordered slave raids in Honduras to replace them. Perhaps the great majority were killed by diseases such as measles, influenza, and typhus. It has been estimated that there were about 600,000 Tainos in Cuba in 1492.[9] Within a generation, they would all but disappear.

The extermination of the Tainos was so complete that within a few scant years they were outnumbered by African slaves. Apart from words such as *tabaco*, *canoa*, and *barbacoa*, they left us a meager legacy—except the durable legend of Hatuey. Its source is probably Father Bartolomé de las Casas, who transcribed Columbus's log book. Born in 1474 to a *converso*[*] family, he arrived in Hispaniola in 1502 and was the first priest ordained in the New World. He participated in the conquest of Cuba, but in 1514 had a change of heart and denounced the slaughter of the Tainos. Bitterly opposed by his fellow Spaniards, he pleaded his cause to Charles V, who did little. Ironically, Father de las Casas recommended that slaves be brought from Africa, though he later regretted this. Disillusioned, he joined the Dominican order, and wrote *The Devastation of the Indies,* a searing indictment of the conquistadors.

Did Hatuey truly prefer to go to hell? The account bears Father de las Casas's self-righteous, slightly hypocritical stamp. It was intended as propaganda to sway Charles V, yet it has a bitter ring of truth. In a much-reproduced sixteenth century woodcut, a monk holds up a crucifix to Hatuey as the flames engulf him. In the distance, mounted soldiers cut down other Tainos. Under those circumstances, would Hatuey have engaged his captors in a theological debate? Father de las Casas's objective was to shame the Spanish conscience, but if we take Hatuey's response at face value, then perhaps the unbowed Taino rebel has something to tell us.

It was during Cuba's struggle for independence from Spain that the legend of Hatuey took on a political dimension. Carlos Manuel de Céspedes, whose statue is in the Plaza de Armas, launched the Ten Years War in 1868 when he emancipated his slaves. His estate was only a few miles from where Hatuey was burned at the stake, and his revolt was called the *Grito de Yara* (literally, the shout from Yara). Hatuey became a symbol of heroic resistance against oppression and this continues today, substituting Americans for Spaniards and capitalism for colonialism.

Apart from the label of his eponymous beer, Hatuey appears in other odd places. His profile is also on the seal of the University of Havana, which was founded in 1728. The Tainos were mascots for the athletic teams, much as our own Washington Redskins. Gustavo Godoy, a magazine editor in Miami who often went to basketball games, told me the cheer was:

*¿Quien vive? ¡Caribe!*
*¿Quien va? ¡Universidad!*

Hatuey's consort was named Guarina. Havana's most popular ice cream was named after her, and a middleweight boxer in the 1950s was named Kid Guarina because he once drove an ice cream truck.

Yet Hatuey had the last laugh. His answer to the monk offering him salvation was laced with fatal irony. It was a typically Cuban response, a wisecrack in the face of death. Father de las Casas's version makes Hatuey

---

*Spanish Jews who converted to Catholicism escape persecution.

sound resigned to his fate, yet he was spitting in the eyes of his captors, defiant to the end.

Hatuey might also have taken his revenge in another way. Recent studies have shown that isolated communities of Tainos may have survived in northeastern Cuba, in the rugged mountains where Hatuey sought refuge.[10] Fulgencio Batista, the dictator whose name is synonymous with brutality and corruption, hailed from that region. Batista dealt Cuban democracy a death blow when he staged a coup in 1952, which ushered in the Revolution. Even at the height of his power, he was not admitted to the exclusive Havana Yacht Club because he was of "mixed blood." It was something he never denied, as it was evident in his features. Batista was a Taino.

## THREE HAVANAS

Many cities ascribe mythic origins to their foundation, as if destiny had willed them into being, but with Havana it was trial and error. No sooner had Velázquez put down the Taino rebellion than he set about extending

A sixteenth century view of the death of Hatuey. (Courtesy of Emilio Cueto)

Spanish rule throughout the island. Baracoa was his base of operations and the first capital of Cuba. From there he established six other outposts called *villas*. One of them, San Cristóbal, would grow into Havana.

Velázquez dispatched an expedition from Baracoa led by Pánfilo de Narváez to establish the settlement on July 25, 1514. It was St. Christopher's Day so it was named San Cristóbal, for the patron saint of travelers. Narváez, whom Father de las Casas knew personally and described as "cruel and stupid," committed many of the atrocities detailed in *The Devastation of the Indies* and was brutal even by conquistadorish standards. He was a red-haired giant from the governor's hometown of Cuellar. Arriving in the New World in 1498, he participated in the conquest of Jamaica and from there followed Velázquez to Cuba. He later succeeded Velázquez as governor of Cuba and commanded a disastrous expedition to Florida that ended in shipwreck. Abandoning most of his men, Narváez attempted to sail across the Gulf of Mexico on a makeshift raft and disappeared without a trace.

San Cristóbal was first located on Cuba's southern coast, on the Broa Inlet near present-day Batabanó, from which a ferry departs to the Isle of Pines. There is nothing in this sleepy fishing village to betray its lofty pedigree, though Columbus had landed there on the second voyage. In this, too, Narváez's judgment was suspect; the location of the new *villa* was a mosquito-ridden swamp. It was here that Cortés outfitted his ships for the conquest of Mexico. His chronicler, Bernal Díaz, complained that the provisions consisted of cassava bread* and salt pork, "for at that time there were neither sheep nor cattle in the island of Cuba, it having only recently been settled."[11]

After a few years, the bedraggled colonists moved their settlement thirty miles due north and reestablished the *villa* at the mouth of the Casiguagua River, as it was called by the Tainos. Today it is a sewer-choked stream known as the Almendares. It is guarded by a small fort built in 1674, grandiosely called Santa Dorotea de la Luna de la Chorrera. The Almendares divides the Havana neighborhoods of Vedado and Miramar, and a tunnel passes below the river connecting the Malecón with Fifth Avenue. Why they selected this second location (within present-day Havana) is un-

---

*Also known as *casaba*. A Taino staple made from Yucca, it became standard fare on Spanish galleons. Today it is still eaten in Cuba, though it is more popular in the Dominican Republic.

certain. The river provided fresh water, which was in short supply at Bata-banó, and there may have been a Taino village nearby.

But it proved equally inhospitable. There was no protection from the elements, and the hapless Spaniards were plagued by a host of tropical ail-ments. In 1519, they relocated one last time, a few miles east to the site explored by Ocampo a decade before and known as Puerto de Carenas. They chose the high ground now occupied by the Plaza de Armas, which commanded the superb natural harbor where ships could be easily ca-reened. Curiously, St. Christopher's Day is celebrated in Cuba on No-vember 16 by papal dispensation, since July 25 is also the feast day of St. James (Santiago), the patron saint of the island. November 16, 1519, is therefore celebrated as the date Havana was founded, as portrayed in the Templete with rose-tinted lenses.

The third try was a charm, since few places are blessed with such nat-ural beauty. Now the harbor is clogged with fishing boats and rusting freighters by midmorning, but just after sunrise the water is smooth as glass. From the Plaza de Armas, one can still look across the turquoise bay to the hills of Casablanca, now crowded with ramshackle houses, and imagine those pristine dawns. They must have seemed a blessing after murky Batabanó and pestilential Casiguagua. The *brisa* (sea breeze) swept away the mosquitoes, the surrounding land was easily tilled, and the nar-row entrance to the bay could be easily defended. It was apparently a gradual move, and the previous site was for a time referred to as *Pueblo Viejo* (literally, old town). It is at this point that the *villa* is first known as San Cristóbal *de la Habana*.

The name itself is the subject of obscure debate among the scholarly and not-so-scholarly. One school has it that Havana was named after a local chieftain named Habaguanex. This seems unlikely since the Spaniards quickly eliminated most of the Taino leaders. Another theory is that "Havana" comes from the Taino word *sabana* (the origin of "savan-nah"), though this fits neither Batabanó nor Puerto de Carenas. Havana could also derive from the Anglo-Saxon word *haven*, since the harbor provided refuge from storms.[12] But once again, Columbus holds the key to the puzzle. In a letter that he wrote returning home after the first voy-age, he describes Cuba and writes: "One of the provinces is called Avan, and there the people are born with tails. . . ." Columbus was at least half right, and so christened the city he never set eyes upon.

Each *villa* was established with the Spanish colonial bureaucracy al-ready in place, as was done throughout the Americas. The Cabildo, or town council, was selected from among the property-owning citizens known as *vecinos*. In 1515, Velázquez had moved his capital from the fort at Baracoa to Santiago de Cuba on the south coast, where he built a house that still stands today. The first governor of Cuba* proved to be an able administrator and encouraged the planting of Taino crops such as malangas and maize, as well as sugarcane, which was brought from the Canary Islands. He also introduced a herd of long-legged swine that multiplied rapidly. By 1519, there were probably about three thousand Spaniards in Cuba.[13]

Then Havana was no more than a few huts spread out along the water between what is now the Plaza de Armas and the Plaza de San Francisco. The conquistadors probably imitated the construction techniques of the Tainos, who built their *bohios* with thatched roofs of palm leaves. One of the earliest existing edicts of the Cabildo ordered settlers to build houses of stone. Nonetheless, the indigenous *bohio* was remarkably sturdy and cool even in summer, and can still be found in rural Cuba. The floors were of beaten earth and the walls covered with sun-hardened mud. The only furniture might have been a wooden table and chairs, and the sole luxury a lamp lit by olive oil from Sevilla rather than a smoky candle made from lard.[14]

Following Father de las Casas's recommendation, African slaves were brought to Cuba as early as 1513, though in small numbers. Since there were few women from Spain, the first Habaneros took Taino girls as wives. Many of the settlers worked in the shipbuilding trade, either as carpenters or caulkers, since the Spanish galleons stopped in the harbor for repairs. Others were prospectors, for a vein of gold had been discovered near Havana at La Mina, for which a café in the Plaza de Armas is named.

At night, Havana was overrun with tortoises, which were caught and killed to make *tasajo*, dried strips of meat boiled by sailors on the long journey back to Spain. During the summer, the stench of dead tortoises grew overpowering, and the Cabildo decreed they could only be killed a safe distance away. Needless to say, the Spaniards were slow to adopt the Taino custom of frequent bathing.

But two discoveries rivaling those of Columbus were soon to transform this rough-hewn outpost into the gateway to the New World.

---

*After the death of Prince Juan, the name was changed from Juana to Fernandina, which also wouldn't stick. The natives had called the island Colba, but it was not until the mid-1500s that the Taino name gained acceptance, pronounced as *coo-ba*.

# CHAPTER 2

# The Exterminating Angel

## Hurricanes

*What a troublesome thing it is to go and discover new lands.*

—Bernal Díaz

*I*t was the sea that brought the first settlers to Havana, and you are never far from it there.

Habana Vieja is a cork of land jammed into the bottleneck of the harbor, surrounded by water on three sides. But even if you turn your back on the ocean and from the Plaza de Armas head up Obispo Street, its presence is implacable. The foghorns of ships entering the port are heard throughout the city, as is the rush of the waves against the seawall. The salty air is responsible for the peeling paint on the walls, though it washes away gasoline fumes from the vintage Lincolns and Packards that clog the cobblestoned alleys. Seagulls perch on the balustrades of the old colonial palaces, and terns circle high overhead. And if you look to your right, an occasional glimpse of blue reveals itself through the gray maze of narrow streets.

But while the presence of the sea is comforting to visitors and natives alike, it has always placed Havana at the mercy of the elements. The word *harakan* comes from the Tainos, who viewed these storms as malevolent deities. It first entered the English language as *furacane* in 1555, and John Winthrop coined the current usage in his 1635 account of the "Great Colonial Hurricane."[1] Winds in the Mediterranean could be fierce, but Caribbean hurricanes, which pack almost unlimited destructive potential and reach speeds of 150 miles per hour, were a different matter altogether. Indeed, the Spanish colonists soon viewed hurricanes in much the same way as the Taínos, and Father de las Casas described them as the work of demons.

Columbus encountered one during his first voyage and safely rode it out behind Saona Island. The newly minted Admiral of the Ocean Sea was not so lucky the following year, when a storm sank three of his ships. So when Columbus made landfall at Santo Domingo on his final voyage in 1502, he was understandably wary. There were the same ominous signs he remembered: gusty winds beneath cirrus clouds, an "oily swell" rolling in, and a brick-red sunset. In the harbor was a homeward-bound armada of thirty sail, and Columbus notified the governor, Nicolás de Ovando, of the impending storm. Scoffing, the arrogant Ovando nonetheless sent his ships out to sea. While the fleet rounded the Mona Passage between Hispaniola and Puerto Rico, a fierce wind struck from northeast. Over five hundred lives were lost, and among the ships that went down was the flagship carrying the *cacique* Guarionex and a cargo of 200,000 *castellanos* of gold, including the largest nugget yet found. Only one ship, the *Aguja*, survived and limped back to Spain.[2]

Meanwhile, Columbus brought his four caravels to safe haven a few miles west of Santo Domingo. Anchoring in a sheltered lee at the mouth of a river, he escaped unscathed despite a harrowing night at the mercy of the winds.

This was the first hurricane prediction in recorded history. In his fascinating study *Winds of Change*, historian Louis A. Pérez Jr. describes how the destruction wrought by hurricanes during the colonial years had a decisive impact on Cuba. The island extends lengthwise along the trajectory where hurricanes enter the Gulf of Mexico, particularly during the month of October. Not only were coastal settlements destroyed, but the interior was ravaged by floods as well. From the beginning, fierce storms buffeted Havana and devastated shipping, providing booty for generations of treasure hunters such as Mel Fisher.[3]

Not until the nineteenth century could hurricanes be predicted with any accuracy, when Father Benito Vines began to keep detailed weather logs. In 1870, the canny Jesuit was named the director of the Meteorological Institute of the Colegio Belén in Havana, and became a worldwide celebrity for accurately predicting a hurricane that hit Cuba's southern coast. His predictions were often ascribed to supernatural powers, but Father Vines empirically studied the same signs that had alerted Columbus, such as cloud formations and reddish sunsets.

Not even Father Vines could have foretold the damage to Havana caused by Hurricane Wilma, which sideswiped the island on October 25, 2005. A massive swell breached the seawall, ripping off huge chunks of the Malecón and submerging much of central Havana. According to the blog of former CNN correspondent Lucia Newman, there was waist-high flooding up to a kilometer inland, sweeping away the doors and wooden shutters of houses, with only the blue tops of phone booths visible above the churning brown water. Miraculously, no one was killed, although nearly 2,500 dwellings were damaged and 130,000 people had to be evacuated from the city. Unlike the dire situation in New Orleans a few weeks earlier, there was no looting, and the Cuban army rescued many of the flood victims with an amphibious troop carrier used in Angola. *Granma* reported that 9.5 square kilometers of downtown Havana had been flooded, as well as all three tunnels under the city, and 300 meters of the seawall had to be rebuilt. The one good thing to come of Hurricane Wilma is that American authorities extended humanitarian assistance. Castro uncharacteristically accepted, though the offer soon became a political football and nothing came of it. It was yet another lost opportunity to better U.S.-Cuba relations.

Visiting Havana a month after the hurricane, I saw little sign of it, although the damaged seawall was still under repair. Habana Vieja was spared the flooding, and there was no damage to the Plaza de Armas. The first Habaneros would not have been as fortunate, since the *bohios* and mud huts that were the first dwellings provided little shelter, and the gale-force winds would have devastated what few crops they were able to grow. What kept them in this violent, unpredictable environment?

## THE GREAT BLUE RIVER

Ernest Hemingway called it the "great blue river." When he arrived in Havana to fish marlin in 1932, he began a lifelong love affair with the Gulf Stream. In Marlin off the Morro, an article that appeared in the inaugural issue of Esquire magazine the following year, he wrote: "The heavier the current runs to the eastward the more marlin there are; traveling along the edge of the dark, swirling current from a quarter mile to four miles offshore; all going in the same direction like cars along a highway." Hemingway noted that when he crossed it, in sight of El Morro, the water became dark blue, almost purple, dotted with whirlpools of yellow gulfweed.

It is easy to sense the wonder he felt in the presence of the Gulf Stream, which is the most powerful ocean current in the world, and certainly the most celebrated. Strictly speaking, Hemingway fished in the Florida Current, which originates in the Gulf of Mexico and sweeps past Havana before flowing around Florida and joining the Gulf Stream proper around Cape Hatteras. It then runs north until the Grand Banks of Newfoundland, at which point it veers east toward the Azores and joins the North Equatorial Current, a belt of warm water that flows back toward the Caribbean, to complete the circle. Off the coast of Cuba, it flows at nearly five knots, and by the time it reaches Canada, the Gulf Stream has transported more than 200 million cubic meters of warm water per second, more than all the rivers of the world.[4]

Columbus came within a hairsbreath of finding the great blue river on his second voyage, but this was left to Juan Ponce de León, a nobleman from Castilla. Known for seeking the Fountain of Youth, Ponce de León was appointed governor of Puerto Rico. He was dismissed due to a feud with Diego Columbus, though King Fernando permitted him to mount an *entrada* (expedition) to explore Florida, which the Spaniards called Bimini.

The pilot of the expedition was Antonio Alaminos, who had sailed on Columbus's final voyage. On Spanish ships of the time, pilots had nearly absolute authority over navigation and jealously guarded their lore. Directions were top secret, and contained in elaborately coded pilot books known as rutters. In case of capture by enemy ships, pilots were expected to throw the rutters overboard. Alaminos was reputed to be one of the best navigators in the Caribbean.

They set out with three ships in March 1513 and made landfall on Easter Day near present-day Palm Beach. Easter was commonly known as *Pascua de Flores* (Passover of Flowers) and hence the name Florida. Then Ponce de León headed south along the Florida coast, and in his log on April 21 he noted that they encountered a current so strong they could make no headway against it, despite a strong wind.[5] Indeed, one of the ships was swept out to sea. This observation marks the discovery of the Gulf Stream, the oceanic superhighway for Spanish ships returning home from the New World, but at the time it went unnoticed. Ponce de León later returned to Florida and tried to start a permanent settlement, perhaps in the vicinity of Sarasota, but was killed in a skirmish with natives in 1521 and died of his wounds in Havana. King Fernando himself had died five years before, and it was rumored that his heart failed because of a medicine made from bull testicles given him by his wife to stimulate his virility.

It was in 1521 that Hernando Cortés completed his conquest of the Aztec empire in Mexico, and Ponce de León's death attracted little attention in Spain. We first encountered Cortés during the conquest of Cuba, when he served as Velázquez's lieutenant. He was trained as a notary, and probably handled the paperwork to found the seven original *villas*. Though Cortés was poor, he wore "a plume of feathers, with a medallion and a gold chain, and a velvet cloak trimmed with loops of gold."[6] But he soon grew restless. A slaving raid under Francisco Hernández de Córdoba reached Yucatán in 1517, and another under Juan de Grijalva set out the following year, bringing back some valuable gold objects, which whetted the voracious appetite of the conquistadors. In both these expeditions, the pilot had been Alaminos, and so it was logical that he accompany Cortés when he set out the following year.

Havana was still located on the southern coast, near present-day Batabanó. As the westernmost of the settlements, it became the logical staging point for the conquest of Mexico. In addition to cassava and salt pork, the conquistadors took on cotton, used for padding in armor. The most valuable items, however, were negroes and horses, "worth their weight in gold."[7]

Díaz's firsthand account of the conquest of Mexico remains the most thrilling, five hundred years later. Cortés was an even better politician than a soldier. Realizing the importance of communicating his discoveries to Charles V, he dispatched a ship from Veracruz containing some of the presents the emperor Montezuma had given him. It was essential that it reach Spain as soon as possible, avoiding enemies such as Velázquez, with whom Cortés had fallen out. The pilot was the redoubtable Alaminos, who recalled how Ponce de León's ships had been swept out to sea by a mysterious current. Taking a gamble, he hugged Cuba's northern coast, passing by Puerto de Carenas, the superb natural harbor discovered by Sebastián Ocampo, and entered the narrow Lucuyan Channel through the Bahamas. There he hooked the Florida Current and rode it north until it joined the Gulf Stream. North of Bermuda, at a latitude of forty degrees, he veered east and made landfall in the Azores. In his haste to reach Spain, Alaminos changed history. The Gulf Stream provided a safe, predictable passage across the Atlantic for all the ships that were to follow year after year, like clockwork.

Even today, it is difficult to comprehend the torrent of wealth that flooded Europe after the fall of the Aztec empire and the subsequent conquest of Peru a decade later by Francisco Pizarro. It is estimated that during the first two decades of the sixteenth century, the Spaniards sent back fourteen tons of gold.[8] Within a few scant years, this multiplied exponentially. The threat of pirates required that the ships return to Spain in convoys, and these treasure fleets filled Spanish coffers to bursting. Charles V acknowledged in 1536 that the latest shipment amounted to 800,000 ducados. Ducados (or ducats) were originally Venetian coins and the trading currency of the Mediterranean. More familiar are the "pieces of eight," which derived from pesos. One silver ducado roughly equaled two pesos, though this varied tremendously. They were roughly struck, often square coins bearing the twin pillars of Hercules which stood for the Straits of Gibraltar. This symbol would, in turn, become the American dollar sign, as ubiquitous today as the peso was then. In 1545, a vast silver mine was discovered in Potosi, and the fleet of 1551 carried over a million and a half ducados. After 1565, when the Spaniards conquered Manila, the fleet also included pearls, silks, and spices from Asia. Just between 1596 and 1600, it is estimated that the value of the treasure reached $774 million in today's terms.[9]

The impact on Havana was immediate and irreversible. Just as Alaminos had sailed toward Havana, so would the treasure fleets. The struggling outpost at Puerto de Carenas soon became the entrepôt for the gold-laden galleons hoping to hitch a ride on the Gulf Stream and the key link in the vast commercial chain joining Spain to its colonies. In addition to its proximity to the Florida Current, Havana boasted the superb natural harbor where Ocampo had careened his ships, an essential operation for the voyage home. And the depth of the bay made it possible for the galleons to unload almost at the water's edge.

The route was known as the *Carrera de Indias*, and it began at Sevilla.[10] The Royal Ordinances of 1564 specified that two convoys should leave each year, containing as many as thirty ships each, with military escorts. The first, known as the New Spain Fleet, left in April or May. The second, the Tierra Firme Fleet, departed in July or August. Both fleets followed Columbus's route toward the Canary Islands to catch the trade winds. But when they reached the Antilles, their paths diverged. The New Spain Fleet proceeded north to San Juan de Ulloa, an island off Veracruz that served as the port of entry. The Tierra Firme Fleet continued south to Cartagena de Indias. From there, both convoys rendezvoused in Havana, only two weeks' sail away. Thus there were often as many as sixty galleons at once in the harbor, loading or unloading precious cargo. In 1583, the treasure fleet had to leave a million pesos in Havana because there was simply not enough room in the ships' holds. The galleons were not just careened but outfitted with fresh water, food, and supplies such as sails and rigging. The journey back needed to be undertaken before the hurricane season of late summer. The *Carrera de Indias* followed Alaminos's route home. The treasure fleet reached the Azores in over a month, and from there it reached Sevilla in twenty or thirty days more.

The *Carrera de Indias* not only established Havana as a thriving commercial center, it also changed the balance of power in the Caribbean. Soon after the conquest of Cuba, many of the settlers—like Cortés himself—left in pursuit of new worlds to conquer. Combined with the wholesale slaughter of the Tainos, this left the island largely depopulated. But the *Carrera de Indias* created an intense demand for labor, not just for shipbuilders but also crew, many of whom deserted searching for riches of their own.* According to a census taken in 1544, Cuba had fewer than 7,000 inhabitants: 5,000 Tainos, 800 black slaves, and 660 Spaniards. By 1553, the governor resided in Havana, making it the unofficial capital. The Spanish crown also took notice. Cuba was no longer merely a springboard for the conquest of the mainland but an important possession in its own right, and one that would have to be defended.

## LA GIRALDILLA

The stark castle of the Real Fuerza seems out of place beside the flowers and marble fountains of the Plaza de Armas. Surrounded by a moat filled with brackish water, the ravelined walls are six meters thick and ten meters high. They form a perfect square of thirty meters to a side with an interior courtyard. At each corner are massive triangular bulwarks whose edges cast razor-sharp shadows. The effect is softened somewhat by the red-tiled roof above the sloping, crenellated battlements built to deflect cannonballs, but the windows are barred and narrow, designed as gun

---

*Seafaring is the source of an all-purpose imprecation in Havana, "*¡Véte al carájo!*" This roughly translates as "Go to hell!" but the *carájo* was the crow's nest of the galleon, and a trip up the mast was a common punishment for sailors.

emplacements. The Real Fuerza once housed a garrison of fifty men-at-arms and served as the residence of the governor of Cuba from 1590 to 1762. Subsequently, the governor moved next door to the Palacio de los Capitanes Generales. Complete with a portcullis, it was the first bastioned fortress of the New World. Its cutting-edge military technology was intended not just to protect the harbor from pirates but to safeguard the gold bullion bound for Spain.

During the Cuban Republic, it was the National Library. In 1963, it underwent a massive renovation and now houses the Museo Nacional de la Ceramica Cubana. Tourists enter via a wooden drawbridge, passing through a gate bearing the Spanish coat of arms dating from 1579 and carved in Sevilla. It is a pleasant museum, containing ceramics from contemporary artists as well as exquisite Taino pottery, but the artwork can't conceal that the Real Fuerza remains a fortress of the Middle Ages.

At its founding, Havana was a medieval city. Columbus's log books contain deadpan accounts of sea monsters, two-headed natives, and other marvels. The New World was believed to contain not just the Fountain of Youth but the mystical cities of El Dorado, home of an immortal king who covered himself in gold dust. These legends belong to the fanciful world of knight-errantry lampooned by Cervantes a generation later, and one of the most popular books among the conquistadors was *Amadis de Gaula*, the same romance that scrambled the brains of Don Quixote. A best seller of the 1500s, it recounts the adventures of a heroic knight who rescues beautiful princesses, kills evil wizards, and discovers enchanted islands. Did the founders of Havana imagine themselves to be knights-errant? No doubt they were eminently practical men, but the accounts they heard from Cortés in Mexico and, later, Pizarro in Peru, rivaled anything in *Amadis de Gaula*.

Rising from the northwest bulwark of the Real Fuerza is a cylindrical bell tower built around 1631. It is in keeping with the fortress, a massive structure from which soldiers could scald attackers with boiling oil, and contains a verdigris bell that warned Habaneros of pirates in the harbor. But it is topped by a graceful weathervane called La Giraldilla, named after the Giralda tower in Sevilla. This is a bronze statue of a woman, seemingly floating above the turret, and it is one of the best-loved symbols of Havana. Like Hatuey, she has become an advertising icon, and serves as the logo for Havana Club rum. But the source of her fame is a legend that Amadis would have appreciated.

The statue overlooking Havana is a copy, since the original was knocked down in a hurricane in 1926 and is now in the museum in the Palacio de los Capitanes Generales. It is here that La Giraldilla is best observed, and I found her on an unadorned pedestal by the stairway off the courtyard. She is petite, barely four feet tall, and in her left hand is a flagpole with the distinctive Cross of Calatrava, symbol of the prestigious military order to which the governor belonged. In the crook of her other arm is a palm branch, the leaves of which were broken off in the fall. The artist's name is displayed prominently in a medallion around her neck. His true intent will never be known, but it is generally accepted that La Giraldilla is a young woman named Isabel de Bobadilla.

Isabel was the wife of Hernando de Soto, who in 1538 was appointed the seventh governor of Cuba. He left the following year to conquer the territories to the north explored by Ponce de León. According to the legend, Isabel anxiously scanned the horizon each day just as La Giraldilla looks out over the water, waiting for his return. The news of his death on the banks of the Mississippi River did not reach her for four long years. Heartbroken, she expired a few days later, her fallen husband's name on her lips.

This paean to the fortitude and fidelity of Cuban women has inspired generations of Habaneros since La Giraldilla took her place above the Real Fuerza. But as in the case of Hatuey, something is not quite right here. La Giraldilla is anything but mournful. Her pose is defiant, almost jaunty. Her finely chiseled head is thrown back, with the barest trace of a smile on her lips, and her left arm (which catches the wind on the Cross of Calatrava) is flung back nonchalantly. Though hardly voluptuous, she sports a trim waist and her right leg is thrust outward, exposing a bronze thigh.

Even if Isabel de Bobadilla was not the source of this legend, she was an interesting woman in her own right. Her husband is among the most likable of the conquistadors. Soto was a poor *hidalgo* born around 1500 in Jerez de los Caballeros, a frontier town northwest of Sevilla. He left home as a young boy and, like many of his class, went to find fame and fortune in the New World. This he certainly did. The dashing young conquistador proved his mettle in expeditions to Panama and Nicaragua, and in 1531 served under Pizarro in the conquest of Peru. The Incan empire was significantly more advanced than that of the Aztecs, six times the size of Spain with 6 million inhabitants. Soto participated in the capture of the emperor Atahualpa and was named lieutenant general of Cuzco, the Incan capital. By all accounts, Soto was an outstanding leader—loyal, brave, and extraordinarily handsome. In 1536, he returned to Sevilla a hero, and a wealthy one at that, with his share of the Incan gold.

It is here that Isabel enters our story. She belonged to the powerful Bobadilla clan, and was therefore a good catch. She was in her late twenties, virtually an old maid then, or perhaps a widow. We know nothing of her physical appearance. La Giraldilla is certainly fetching, but she was cast a century after Isabel's death. There is no reason to suppose that the marriage was a love match. Isabel's family connections helped Soto get an audience with Charles V, who was impressed and granted him the right to conquer Florida, with the governorship of Cuba thrown in almost as an afterthought.

Soto spent less than a year in Havana, outfitting his armada. It is significant that he left Isabel to represent him as governor; no woman had ever assumed such authority in the New World. This implies that he had grown fond of her, or at least respected her business sense. He set sail in May 1539 with an army of 600 soldiers, 240 horses, and a small herd of pigs.[11] Soto dreamed of conquering another empire such as that of the Incas, and no doubt he carried *Amadis of Gaula* for bedtime reading. But from the start, it was a disaster. The Spaniards landed near present-day Tampa and spent the next few weeks in skirmishes with the warlike Timucan Indians, who fought with deadly longbows that could pierce chain mail armor. Over the next three years, Soto was to travel four thousand miles through unexplored, hostile territory—twice the distance covered by Lewis and Clark. His route took him through what is now Georgia, North Carolina, Tennessee, Arkansas, and Texas, cutting a swath of disease and destruction among the tribes that had the misfortune to encounter him. He found neither gold nor glory, and in 1542, while wintering near the Mississippi River, he caught a mysterious fever. The exact cause of Soto's death is unknown, and it has even been suggested that his men poisoned him so as to end the disastrous *entrada*. When he died, they were afraid the Indians, who regarded him as a malignant deity, would mount an attack. Perhaps inspired by another knight-errant, El Cid, they mounted Soto's corpse in a dugout canoe and began the journey home. The survivors reached Mexico in 1543.

From there the news would soon have reached Havana, but, contrary to legend, the historical Isabel did not die of heartache. Instead, she promptly auctioned off their joint property and returned to Spain. We know about Soto's holdings because they were the subject of a long, protracted lawsuit brought by a former associate of Soto's against his wife.[12] They included several plantations, a cattle ranch, eighteen household slaves, and numerous personal effects such as a rosary of solid gold beads, totaling 4,000 pesos. Whatever the outcome of the lawsuit, we can assume that Isabel, still in her prime, lived happily ever after.

If her destiny was not as poetic as the legend, it nonetheless casts a new light on La Giraldilla and explains her provocative pose. Perhaps it accounts for her smile as well.

## ATTACK OF THE CORSAIRS

It is difficult to mention the word "pirate" without evoking Long John Silver.

Robert Louis Stevenson's classic adventure story, *Treasure Island*, has been reprinted countless times and introduced the popular vocabulary of eye patches, treasure maps, and talking parrots. At least four film versions have been made, the most recent starring Charlton Heston. But the pirates that ravaged Havana in the sixteenth century were of a different stamp altogether.

To begin with, they were French, and referred to as corsairs.* They were not pirates so much as privateers, vessels operating under a letter of marque. This was a sort of license to plunder on the high seas, making privateering an honorable profession. Columbus himself was no stranger to privateering. He encountered corsairs while sailing in Genoese convoy in 1476, and a few years earlier may even have participated in an attack against an Aragonese merchant vessel. Many privateers, such as Sir Francis Drake, were regarded as heroes in their own countries, although the Spaniards had an altogether different view of them.

The French had their own reasons to attack. In 1494, under papal authority, the Treaty of Tordesillas cozily authorized the kings of Spain and Portugal to partition the hemisphere between them. The French monarch, Francis I, took issue with this, and struck the first blow shortly after the conquest of Mexico. Giovanni da Verrazano was a Florentine

---

*The word was popularized by Byron's romantic poem *The Corsair* and comes from the Latin *cursus*, "to run"—their preferred course of action following an attack.

explorer who reached New York in 1523 and left his name to a bridge over the Hudson River. But he also went by the name of Jean de Fleury, an accomplished corsair in the pay of the French. At the beginning of the voyage that would take him to Manhattan and win him a place in the history books, Verrazano encountered three Spanish caravels near Cape St. Vincent, on the southern tip of Portugal.[13] Capturing two of them after a brief and bloody skirmish, he was astounded to find they contained the Aztec treasure plundered by Cortés. There were three chests of gold ingots, 500 pounds of gold dust, 680 pounds of pearls, emerald-encrusted ceremonial knives, jade masks, and feathered cloaks. All told, the treasure trove was calculated at 150,000 ducados.[14]

Verrazano/Fleury was captured by the Spanish off Cadiz in 1527 and hanged with 150 of his men. A peace treaty two years later ended hostilities, but by 1536, France and Spain were at war once again. Francis I lost no time in sending out more corsairs. It was no easy thing to intercept an oceangoing vessel, depending on the vagaries of winds and currents, and so the primary target was Havana, where the gold was kept until the departure of the convoys. It seems unlikely that the city would have been so vulnerable to attack, but as writer Juliet Barclay noted: "Havana was a treasure chest, and no one had thought to lock the lid."

Accounts of the first pirate attack on Havana vary.[15] After the conquests of Mexico and Peru, many Spaniards left Cuba for the mainland, and in 1537 Havana contained only 40 Spanish *vecinos*, or householders, with their families. In addition, there were 120 Tainos and 200 slaves, both Taino and African. Havana's defenses consisted of three cannons, but they had been taken to other parts of the island. On March 16 a ship flying a French flag brazenly entered the harbor, apparently on a reconnaissance mission, and then headed west. There were three vessels in port, and the captains gave chase. They caught up with the corsair in Mariel, and here things went badly for the Spaniards. A sudden shift in wind drove the vessels aground, and the crews fled for their lives. Realizing that Havana was now defenseless, the French returned for the cargo the ships had left behind. For good measure, they burned down the settlers' thatched huts. It is often claimed that the slaves revolted and aided in the looting, but this seems unlikely since the French would have regarded them as valuable merchandise.

Perhaps emboldened by this success, another corsair returned to Cuban waters the following year and attacked Santiago. They were fended off by Diego Pérez, the valiant captain of the caravel *Magdalena*, and the French sailed on to Havana in May 1538. Little seems to have been done to fortify the port, for the corsairs disembarked without resistance. It is unlikely they found anything of value, since the settlers had barely recovered from the last attack.

A few weeks later, when Soto arrived with Isabel, their fleet was at first mistaken for yet more corsairs. As we have seen, Soto left Cuba within the year, but he began construction of a fortress to defend Havana, the predecessor of the Fuerza Real. Presumably it was undertaken under the direction of the capable Isabel, for it was completed by 1540. The Fuerza Vieja, as it came to be called, was situated approximately three hundred paces northeast of the present location. It was a square palisade forty-eight meters to a side, with a single tower ten meters high.[16]

Though unassuming, the Fuerza Vieja proved its worth during the third attack. In October 1543, Jean François de la Roque, who had been named by Francis I as governor of the newly explored territory of Canada, assaulted the port with four galleons. The *vecinos* manned the cannons that had been brought back to Havana and managed to repel the landing party, leaving twenty Frenchmen dead.[17]

The dynastic musical chairs of sixteenth century geopolitics continued, and the French and Spanish signed another peace treaty, only to declare war in 1552. This set the stage for a new round of attacks the following year. François Le Clerc, also known as *Jambe-de-bois*, or Pegleg, may have been the model for Long John Silver because of his wooden leg. Sailing out of La Rochelle, he ravaged the Canary Islands before sacking Santiago in 1544. The city was left in ashes, and this may have contributed to Governor Pérez de Angulo moving the capital to Havana.

The settlers thus had time to mount their defense. The Fuerza Vieja had been strengthened the year before, and guardposts had been established at the Punta, at the tip of the headland, and across the bay at El Morro. Juan de Lobera was named *teniente de guerra*, or military commander.

It was Pegleg's lieutenant, Jacques de Sores, who would attack Havana while returning from the fledgling French colony in Rio de Janeiro.[18] Sores was a Huguenot, like many of the corsairs, and he won the sobriquet *Ange Exterminateur* (Exterminating Angel) both for his piety and his ruthlessness. Capturing a Portuguese galleon off Tenerife, he executed thirty-eight Jesuits by throwing them overboard. His two ships were sighted at dawn on July 10, 1555, and the alarm was sounded. But rather than attack the port, the corsairs sailed past the bay and disembarked two hundred soldiers to attack Havana from the west. Pérez de Angulo panicked and fled with his family to his estate in Guanabacoa, and it was left to Lobera to organize the defense. While Lobera holed up with his men in the fort, Sores laid waste to Havana. There was a religious element to the attack, for he desecrated the church and used the priests'vestments as cloaks. Then the Exterminating Angel turned his attention to the Fuerza Vieja, firing upon it with artillery and trying to set fire to it. Lobera held out bravely for two days and managed to keep the French ships out of the harbor. Lobera was wounded by a shot from an arquebus, and when the palisade was breached, he had no recourse but to surrender. The defenders were imprisoned in one of the few stone structures in Havana, the house of the *vecino* Juan Rojas.

By then, Pérez de Angulo had recovered his courage and launched a surprise attack with a ragtag force of Indians and slaves he had gathered together in Guanabacoa. The corsairs fought them off, and in retaliation Sores killed the remaining prisoners, leaving only Lobera as a bargaining chip. He demanded 2,000 ducados as ransom, and when Pérez de Angulo failed to deliver, he burned down the city. Lobera was released, perhaps because of his bravery, and the corsairs sailed off on August 5. So complete was the destruction that when yet another corsair reached Havana a month later, the only loot to be had was a shipment of hides.

The Spaniards responded by replacing the cowardly governor and ordering the construction of the present Real Fuerza by a royal decree of 1558. And soon after, they dispatched Pedro de Menéndez de Avilés to exact vengeance. The Huguenots had a established the colony of Fort Caroline near present-day St. Augustine, and Menéndez de Avilés attacked it with five ships and six hundred men and slaughtered the defenders. The French fleet had been scattered by a hurricane, and Menéndez rounded up the shipwrecked survivors and put them to the sword, including the French leader, Jean de Ribault. On their graves, he left a sign that said: "I do this not to Frenchmen but to heretics." His brutality effectively halted further French incursions in the Caribbean, and he was rewarded with the governorship of Cuba.

Meanwhile, the Exterminating Angel fades from the history books. Perhaps he met the same end as many of his confreres, hanging from a Spanish yardarm, or perhaps he returned to La Rochelle with his booty and lived to a ripe old age.

Ironically, the depredations of the corsairs served only to strengthen Havana. Sores had left only three buildings standing: the church, the hospital, and the house of Juan Rojas, where Lobera was imprisoned. At the time, they were probably the only three structures made of stone.

Spanish settlements were strictly regulated by the Laws of the Indies, promulgated by Philip II in 1573. Towns were to be laid out in a strict grid like a Roman military camp, with the width of the streets and the exterior colors of the houses specified. Religious and civic buildings were to be grouped around the main square, which was to be rectangular, with minimum dimensions of 200 by 300 feet, with the corners aligned on the compass points. Out of necessity, these rules were largely ignored in Havana. The original main square was known as the Plaza de Iglesia, and would have been situated directly before the first church, known as the Parroquial Mayor. But in 1584, the area was requisitioned for the military, and so it became known as the Plaza de Armas. This necessitated a new square for civilian use such as markets and processions, the present Plaza Vieja. Havana thus developed in a polycentric fashion around these two main squares. A third, the Plaza de San Francisco, was laid out in 1628.

The Cabildo (town council) of Havana distinguished itself for contrariness in more ways than one. Royal orders were acknowledged in an elaborate ceremony in which the *vecinos* kissed the proferred document, but more than once the proviso was added: "We take notice but do not comply."

After the sack of Havana, the Real Fuerza was erected in record time, thanks to a donation of 12,000 pesos from the Viceroyalty of New Spain in Mexico. While the fortress was never assaulted, it served as a deterrent when Sir Francis Drake threatened the city in 1586 with a fearsome armada of twenty-two ships and two thousand men. Levies were called up around the island, a force of soldiers arrived from New Spain, stores of food and ammunition were laid in, and cannons bristled on the walls of the newly built fortress. But rather than attack, as the Habaneros were expecting, Drake sailed on.

The harbor was further strengthened when, in 1588, Philip II ordered the construction of El Morro on the rocky promontory across the channel.[19] The castle, which would not be completed until 1630, replaced

An early map of Havana showing the fortifications of the harbor, ca. 1602. (Courtesy of Emilio Cueto)

the guardpost that had been erected earlier. Designed by the celebrated Italian military architect Giovanni Baptista Antonelli, the polygonal walls contain two landward bastions with a deep moat. The battery guarding the channel is known as *Los Doce Apóstoles* (the Twelve Apostles). A watchtower with a lantern was built to guide mariners, but the current lighthouse was erected in 1844 by Governor O'Donnell. Today, El Morro remains the most visible symbol of Havana. It is to the city what the Eiffel Tower is to Paris, or the Coliseum is to Rome, framed in countless postcards sent back to Barcelona, Chicago, or Kiev.

The castle of La Punta was commissioned at the same time as El Morro, and upon its completion a chain made of huge cedar logs was stretched across the mouth of the harbor to deter further attacks. Havana was now one of the most fortified cities in the New World, with a population of four thousand. In recognition of this, the city was granted a coat of arms by the Spanish Crown in 1592: It displayed, above the ever-present sea, three castles—Real Fuerza, El Morro, and La Punta—and a golden key, which symbolized the city's role in unlocking new lands for settlement. In the Royal Letters Patent issued that same year, Philip II wrote: "I therefore desire and decree that from now on and henceforth forever the said town will be entitled San Cristóbal de la Habana of the said island of Cuba."

# CHAPTER 3

# The Time of the Mameyes

## Restoring Havana

The Havana of the 1600s would be recognizable today. You would find the harbor largely unchanged, though it would be filled with galleons of the Treasure Fleet rather than superannuated cargo ships. The Plaza de Armas had assumed roughly its present form, though it was used as a parade ground, full of soldiers with arquebuses rather than tourists with cameras. The principal streets of Habana Vieja had been laid out as well, together with its main squares.

The first two streets were Oficios and Mercaderes, reflecting Havana's passion for buying and selling. Oficios (trades) was the main street in 1584, connecting the Plaza de Armas with the Plaza de San Francisco. Originally known as Concepción, it was later named for the workshops of artisans, such as leather-workers, blacksmiths, carpenters, and others, that soon established themselves along its length. Running parallel to it, a block to the west, Mercaderes (merchants) soon reached the Plaza Vieja. It was Havana's first shopping district, where merchants laid out their wares.

Many streets were named after their physical characteristics. Empedrado (cobblestone) was the first street to be paved, and Tejadillo (tile) was so named because of the first house to receive a tiled roof. Prior to that, houses were generally covered with dried dung or palm leaves. Lamparilla (lamp) immortalizes the oil lamp lit by a pious woman every night on the corner of Habana Street. Aguacate Street took its name from an avocado tree that grew in the Convent of Belén.

Other streets were labeled by function rather than form. Picota (yoke) was the site of the whipping post for condemned criminals. Amargura (bitterness) recalls the grim religious procession of the Franciscan monks that passed each morning during Lent. Throughout Cuba, there are Amargura streets, where crucifixes were set up to mark the Stations of the Cross. Another popular street is San Pedro, which runs along the waterfront. It was given its name by sailors because of their devotion to St. Peter, patron saint of seafarers.

I found the oldest house in Havana on Obispo Street, just around the corner from the Real Fuerza. Located at numbers 117–119, it is generally overlooked by the tourists who walk the Hemingway Trail from the Hotel Ambos Mundos (where the writer often stayed) to the Floridita (where he regularly drank). A modest two-story building with blue balconies trimmed in yellow, it has an ox-eye window facing the street. The earliest references to it are in 1648, when it was the residence of Captain Antonio Carrillo, but most experts agree it was built the century before, perhaps following the sack of Havana by the Exterminating Angel.[1]

The earliest colonial dwellings differed little from the huts of the Tainos, with floors of beaten earth, walls made from palm tree bark, and thatch roofs. Apparently they were quite popular, for the Cabildo had banned such in dwellings by 1571. Though cool and dry, they were combustible and often went up in smoke even without the help of corsairs. The proscripted *bohios* were rebuilt with walls of *mamposteria*, which combined brick and crushed limestone, and red-tiled roofs. Many houses showed a marked Arabic influence, with open-air galleries overlooking an interior patio and elaborate carved ceilings known as *alfarjes*.

Fittingly, the one on Obispo is a bookstore run by the Historiador de la Cuidad de la Habana (literally, the city historian). This is a uniquely Cuban institution; every city has its own Historiador, charged with not merely recording the past but keeping it alive. In Havana, the first Historiador was Emilio Roig de Leuschenring. Born in 1889, he was a member of the avant garde Grupo Minorista and editor of the magazine *Social* before his appointment in 1935. Then, as now, Habana Vieja was crumbling. During the early years of the Cuban Republic, the city was expanding west at a rapid rate and the old colonial buildings were left in disrepair. Roig led a group of distinguished intellectuals, including Joaquín Weiss and Pedro Martínez Inclán, who focused attention on the problem. His first restoration project was the Palacio de los Capitanes Generales, where the Museo de la Ciudad de la Habana was established in 1942.

Early efforts to revitalize Habana Vieja were not without controversy. For example, restorers stripped the pastel-colored stucco that protected the limestone facades of many colonial buildings. Architectural purists applauded, but others bemoaned that it left Havana somewhat gray and somber. The effect is like that of the Roman Forum; looking at the ruins, tourists often assume the temples were of white marble, whereas in fact they were painted garish colors.

Roig was a prodigious writer, publishing countless monographs on diverse subjects and the first volume of a monumental history of Havana. But despite his passion for restoration, the Historiador was fighting a losing battle. At the time of the Revolution, only about five hundred of the three thousand buildings in Habana Vieja were considered in good condition.[2] In the 1950s, many of the colonial palaces had been turned into *ciudadelas*, shabby apartment buildings, and little had been done to counteract the effects of torrential rain and salt air. Yet like many cities in Latin America, Havana was on the verge of a building boom. An influential group of Harvard-trained architects led by José Luis Sert had submitted a plan for the city much like that of Le Corbusier for Paris. This would have devastated Habana Vieja, replacing old buildings with glass and steel high-rises, turning narrow cobblestoned streets into limited access highways, and reconfiguring plazas into parking lots. This urban nightmare also included an artificial island off the Malecón with casinos, malls, and hotels.[3] To a lesser extent, this was the fate of Lima, Caracas, and Santo Domingo, which retain little colonial flavor.

Inadvertently, Castro changed all that. The casinos shut down, the swank hotels filled with bearded *guerrilleros*, and the tourists were scared off. The subsequent elimination of the private sector derailed Sert's ambitious plans and overnight reduced the value of real estate to $4 per square meter. For better or worse, Habana Vieja was preserved like an exotic insect in a drop of amber.

Architectural preservation was decidedly not a priority during the early years of the Revolution, and Habana Vieja once more fell into somnolent disrepair. But the tide turned in 1982, when UNESCO designated Habana Vieja (including the surrounding fortresses) as a World Heritage Site. The current Historiador, Eusebio Leal, reached out to the public by offering guided walks of the old city on Saturday afternoons. Money from abroad began to trickle in, and efforts were undertaken to spruce up key landmarks, such as the Plaza de Armas. This made for some glaring contrasts, since one had only to walk a few blocks to see a building literally crumbling to the ground.

But Leal's portfolio changed immeasurably with the disintegration of the Soviet Union. In 1991, the Cuban economy went into free-fall with the loss of the huge sugar subsidies that had sustained it.[4] Castro declared the infamous Special Period, and Chinese bicycles replaced gas-guzzling Cadillacs on the Malecón. The future of Cuba would now be foreign tourism, and the U.S. dollar became legal tender in 1993.

This proved to be a blessing as Leal discovered another talent, for entrepreneurship. That year, the Office of the Historiador assumed responsibility for all tourism-related activities in Habana Vieja and brought in $4 million,[5] which was poured into restoration projects extending beyond the early face-lift of the Plaza de Armas. And that was just the beginning. In 2001, it earned $70 million and employed four thousand people. This funded seventy-six preservation projects, fourteen hotels, seventy-nine other tourist facilities such as restaurants, and even a slick magazine on historical topics called *Opus Habana*.

It is difficult to argue with success, and Leal has become a political superstar, sitting on the National Assembly as well as Cuba's Politburo, the all-powerful State Council. Yet despite his hectic schedule, he speaks before schoolchildren and occasionally leads his celebrated walking tours of the city. Most importantly, Leal has escaped the fate of many apparatchiks who fell afoul of Castro and were subjected to the "pajama plan," virtual house arrest in an obscure corner of the island. Perhaps one reason is that Leal has become a goodwill ambassador of sorts. He travels frequently to international conferences and has received the Aguila Azteca Award from Mexico and been inducted into the French Legion d'Honeur.

Like anyone in the spotlight, he has his share of detractors. The restoration of Havana Vieja is akin to gentrification, a familiar problem to American urban planners. When a creaky old building is transformed into a tourist hotel, where do the predominantly poor and dark-skinned residents go? Many are forcibly relocated to Alamar, a soulless housing project west of the city. Leal is sensitive to this and points to efforts such as the temporary prefabricated housing set up for the inhabitants of the Plaza Vieja during its restoration, but it has the air of a Potemkin village. It is estimated that up to thirty thousand people will be relocated in Habana Vieja alone.

Leal has also been criticized for excessively prettifying landmarks and creating a colonial Disneyland for tourists. Indeed, the immaculately whitewashed facades, with pastel-colored eaves and bougainvillea in flowerpots, can be oppressively quaint. One of the greatest charms of Habana Vieja is the eclectic, anarchic vitality of its architecture, with a neoclassical palace next to a sleek art deco apartment building, an ornate baroque church beside an art nouveau mansion. Leal's restorations can seem numbingly similar, as though tailor-made for the same guidebook. The effect is similar to that of Old San Juan, where the buildings have been turned into pricey condos. And there are occasional lapses in taste. How else to explain the bizarre homage to Princess Diana in a corner of the Plaza de San Francisco? Built in 1998, it is a walled garden replete with a stone plaque from Althorpe, Diana's childhood home, and a wrought-iron trellis spelling out *Jardin de Diana*.

Amazingly, Leal is respected even in hypercritical Miami, no mean feat for one of Castro's inner circle. But he has been called the architect of "tourism apartheid," since few Cubans can afford one of his chic cafés in Habana Vieja. A devil's advocate might point out that prior to the Revolution, ordinary Cubans would not have patronized expensive hotels like the Nacional either. But if foreign tourism has brought hard cash into the economy, it has also created severe tears in the supposedly egalitarian fabric of Cuban society. Apartheid or not, tourism is Cuba is big business, bringing in $2 billion a year.[6] In 2004, about 2 million tourists came to the island, including 200,000 Americans. It is estimated that if the travel ban was dropped, over 1 million Americans would visit the first year, credit cards in hand.

Yet little or no restoration has been undertaken outside of Habana Vieja and Centro Habana,* although there are plans to develop the fading Malecón. It is estimated that Havana loses three buildings every day. According to a Cuban government report, 1,400 structures must be abandoned each year,[7] and 20 percent of the 2.2 million Habaneros live in housing considered in "precarious condition." Despite this, about twenty thousand people move to Havana from the provinces each year. The city's infrastructure is equally in need of repair. According to one expert, it

---

* Centro Habana, which might be described as downtown Havana, is directly to the west of Habana Vieja and includes the Parque Central and the Paseo del Prado.

would take several billion dollars to upgrade Havana's failing water and sewage services.[8]

"I won't live to see the full restoration of the city," Leal told a reporter from the *New York Times*, which in November 2005 featured Havana on the front page of its travel section. "So much is left to be done, but this is a start."[9]

## LITTLE HAVANA

*[Obispo and O'Reilly] streets had always been his favorites; actually they are one, in two stretches of time: one to go to the bay, and the other to come back into the city.*

—José Lezama Lima, *Paradiso*

The breadth of Leal's fiefdom can best be seen at the Maqueta de Habana Vieja on Mercaderes Street, one block west of Obispo. *Maqueta* means "model," and this is a miniature Havana on a scale of 1:500.

Cubans are *maqueta*-mad, and a more complete one (encompassing the entire metropolis from Alamar to Cubanacán) can be found in the Vedado. But the *maqueta* on Mercaderes is limited to Habana Vieja, shaped like a lopsided baseball diamond, where the Real Fuerza is home plate. The playing field is bisected by Obispo and O'Reilly streets, which start at either end of the Plaza de Armas and stretch inland to Monserrate Street, the perimeter of the old city walls. The tiny houses are uncannily detailed, showing windows and even ventilation ducts on the roofs, and all that's needed is a choo-choo train with mock puffs of smoke. Buildings are color-coded according to when they were erected. Anything built before the nineteenth century is brown; between 1900 and 1959, beige; and after the Revolution, salmon-colored. The models are table height and illuminated by a spotlight, and there's a soundtrack with traffic noises and keening seagulls. It's all for the benefit of tourists, and for a dollar you can tower over the city as in *Land of the Giants* while a bored guide drones on heavily accented English.

From this perspective, it is easy to see how the city radiated away from the bay in the direction of the Almendares River. The seventeenth century was a profitable one. After the completion of El Morro and La Punta, Havana no longer had anything to fear from pirates. The treasure fleet continued to stop at Havana each summer on the way back to Spain, and the harbor was full of galleons most of the year. In fact, the *Carrera de*

*Indias* ran like clockwork until the 1730s, when the silver mines at last ran dry, reducing the size of the convoys. Individual ships would make the trip with military escorts, but continued to stop in Havana. Yet despite the wealth flowing through the customs house, Havana was never a sumptuous city. The ostentatious palaces of the sugar planters would not be built for another century, and Havana remained rough and ready, fueled by commerce rather than luxury.

From the Maqueta de Habana Vieja, if you follow Mercaderes south you soon reach the Plaza Vieja. Because of its proximity to the port, many of the early ship owners made their homes there. With Mercaderes to the east, it is bounded by Brasil, Muralla, and San Ignacio streets. At first, it was the site of processions, festivals, and religious ceremonies, but before long it acquired a commercial character, like much of Havana. At the center was a fountain of Carrara marble by the Italian sculptor Giorgio Massari, with four dolphins spouting water. Around it were market stalls with fish, poultry, fruit, vegetables, and fruit of every description. In 1835, Captain-General Tacón built a covered market named the Mercado Cristina in honor of the Spanish queen, which remained in use until 1908, when it was demolished to create a park. The Plaza Vieja's fortunes declined and, in 1952, during the final gasps of the Cuban Republic, an underground parking garage was built. Often cited as one of the worst architectural sins against Habana Vieja, it did away with the original cobblestones and raised the surface by one meter above street level.

Enter the Historiador, whose first task in 1995 was to destroy the garage and resurface the square. The restoration, completed only recently, once more made it one of the most beautiful squares in Havana. While the marble fountain had long disappeared, an exact replica was commissioned and once again the dolphins gurgle with water. The most impressive building in the Plaza Vieja is on the south side of the square. This is the Casa del Conde de San Juan Jaruco: now an art gallery, it was built in 1734 atop the foundation of an earlier house. The massive doors are secured by an unusual lock in the shape of an African girl with scarred cheeks, possibly tribal markings. Above the portico is a delicate wrought-iron balcony with louvers The windows are topped by brilliant *mediopuntos*, like fans of crystal.

If Havana's merchants were growing wealthy two centuries after the city was founded, they also grew pious. An explosion of ecclesiastical construction was spurred on by two remarkable bishops. The first was Diego de Compostela, who arrived in Havana in 1687. Bishop Compostela was

described as "an enchanting man, combining true saintliness with bound-
less energy. He went about on foot, treated everyone with unfailing courtesy, ate only one small meal a day and preached moving sermons in a
musical voice."[10] His legacy is the Convent of Belén, the largest religious
complex in Habana Vieja, on the corner of Luz and Compostela, to which
the bishop lent his name. Built in 1712, it was the first example of the ornate baroque style that was to dominate over the next century. For many
years an empty hulk, it is currently being restored and houses students
who come from abroad to study historical preservation.

In 1854, the convent was turned over to the Jesuits and became the
Colegio de Belén, which educated generations of the Cuban elite, including
Castro himself. Here it remained until 1925, when the school moved to a
spacious campus in Marianao, adjacent to the Tropicana nightclub. Although Castro has often spoken fondly of his Jesuit education, the school
was shuttered shortly after the Revolution and is now a military academy.

Bishop Compostela was succeeded by Geronimo Valdés, whose epis-
copacy lasted from 1706 to 1729. If not as diplomatic as his predecessor,
he was equally forceful, and founded the University of Havana in 1728.
This was first located in the Convent of Santo Domingo on Obispo,
which was torn down in the 1960s to build a banal government ministry
and is now the focus of yet another restoration. Only at the beginning of
the twentieth century did the venerable university move to its present location in the Vedado.

Bishop Valdés died at the age of eighty-three and was buried in the
Iglesia del Espíritu Santo, the oldest surviving church in Havana. Built in
1638, it was originally a chapel for the freed blacks and Indians living in
the poor Campeche district near the waterfront. Very little remains of the
original structure, which was rebuilt several times. The Espíritu Santo is
deceptively simple, with a high belltower and a triangular portal above the
plain facade, but the macabre vault beneath the altar has murals representing the dance of death. When the lateral nave was built in 1760, the wall
containing Bishop Valdés's tomb was demolished and his remains were
lost. He slumbered peacefully until 1936, when his coffin was discovered
beneath the floor. Now he lies buried beneath his statue by the nave.

## THE WALLS OF HAVANA

On the Maqueta de Habana Vieja, Espíritu Santo is approximately where
third base would be. If you proceed west on Acosta, with your back to the

waterfront, you quickly reach the outfield and the phantom walls that once surrounded Havana.

The Spanish had considered building a defensive wall as early as 1558, since the corsairs had attacked Havana not from the harbor but from the unprotected western flank. Bartolomé Sánchez, who built the Real Fuerza, received a royal decree to this effect but it was never carried out, perhaps due to lack of funding. The warlike Menéndez de Avilés, who became governor after his defeat of the Huguenots, erected a rough wooden palisade and posted guards along the landward side of the settlement. The issue of a more permanent defensive structure was not broached again until the construction of El Morro and La Punta. The royal engineer, Cristóbal de Roda (Antonelli's nephew), deemed it unnecessary, no doubt because he felt his uncle's vaunted fortresses could do the job. Another proposal that never saw the light of day was to dig a moat from one end of the peninsula to the other, making Havana an island.

Another effort was made in 1655 under Governor Montaño Blasquez, and the king ordered the treasury of New Spain to contribute the sum of 20,000 pesos. After various stops and starts, construction finally began on February 3, 1674. While it was hoped that the wall could be completed within three years, the last stone was not laid until 1740, 182 years after it was first proposed, at an estimated cost of 3 million pesos. The end result was a 1.4-meter-thick, 10-meter-high rampart with a perimeter of nearly five kilometers.[11] To the north, it began just below La Punta, and proceeded south along the crescent-shaped harbor until it came to the present-day intersection of Desamparados and Egido streets, where a semibastion called La Tenaza protected the shipyards of La Machina. From there, it turned right until it reached Muralla Street, the centerfield line on the Maqueta le la Habana Vieja. Here the wall followed Monserrate until it reached Avenida de las Missiones, and then slanted toward the foul line at La Punta. Despite the delay of nearly two centuries, it was an impressive piece of engineering, with nine bastions in addition to La Tenaza linked by curtain walls with sentry boxes. The original plan had called for a moat and a covered passageway around the entire wall, though this was omitted on the landward side. Indeed, the defenses of the harbor were significantly stronger. It was manned by a garrison of 3,400 men, with 180 artillery pieces of varying caliber.[12] At first, there were only two entrances: a small opening in the harbor, facing the docks, and a fortified gate called the Puerta de Tierra, at Muralla Street. Later, seven other gates would be added, that were open from sunrise to sunset. Their closing was signaled with a *cañonazo*, or cannon blast. The largest gate was at Monserrate, at the end of Obispo and O'Reilly streets.

But the walls failed to keep up with the growth of the city. When construction began, Havana huddled around the harbor and the fortifications enclosed large open stretches of fallow land. But as the threat of pirate attacks lessened, Habaneros were quick to move inland. By 1740, Havana extended well beyond the ramparts and was divided in two: *intramuros* (within the walls, or Habana Vieja) and *extramuros* (outside the walls). By the next century, the walls had lost their defensive function and became a popular place for a *paseo*, or promenade. Yet there was already severe crowding *intramuros* and traffic jams from over two thousand carriages and wagons. An outbreak of cholera in 1833 claimed three thousand lives, and already by 1863 demolition of the walls had begun.[13]

This was not completed until well into the twentieth century, and bits of the walls still remain. The only remaining gate is La Tenaza at Desamparados Street, commemorated by a dusty plaque. Argel Calcines, the editor of *Opus Habana*, explained that recent excavations at this site had uncovered the wall's foundations, which in many places still remain below the surface. The largest remaining portion is a few blocks north on Egido, known as the Cortina de la Habana. The neglected, weed-choked masonry gives little idea massive ramparts that once protected Havana's southern flank. Walking up Monserrate, through the neoclassical heart of Centro Habana, with the marble dome of the Capitolio to your left, it is hard to imagine the Spanish soldiers manning the walls through the long night after the *cañonazo*. Not until you reach the Presidential Palace do you see another trace of it, a lone sentry box at the corner of Refugio Street called the Baluarte del Angel. A second guardpost still stands a few blocks east on Cuba Street. This is all that remains of the harbor defenses, but it was landlocked when the Avenida del Puerto was built.

It is odd that this forlorn, stranded watchtower was left standing, and no one could tell me why.

## THE REDCOATS TAKE HAVANA

It is easy to dismiss the building of the walls around Havana as hubris, like a tropical statue of Ozymandias, but they were erected just in time.

Ever since Sir Francis Drake sailed past the harbor in 1586, the British had their eye on Havana. Cromwell's navy had conquered Jamaica in 1655 and heavily fortified Port Royal. From there, Admiral Myngs attacked Santiago de Cuba. But not until a century later would Havana itself be threatened.

It was during the Seven Years War that the sun stopped setting on the British empire as the redcoats seized France's colonies in Canada and India. When Carlos III sided with his Bourbon cousins in France, George II declared war in January 1762. British warships left Portsmouth two months later and approached Havana from the north, via the narrow channel through the Bahamas discovered by Antonio Alaminos over two centuries before. The British might have discovered this route from a pilot book found on a prize ship, since it was a closely guarded secret. It was the largest armada ever assembled in the Caribbean, with over fifty vessels, including ten ships-of-the-line. These were the aircraft carriers of their day, floating arsenals with ninety guns and crews of up to eight hundred. There were eleven thousand soldiers as well as several hundred black slaves. The attack was led by George Keppel, the third earl of Albemarle, together with his two younger brothers, William and Augustus Keppel.

Havana was a rich prize. By the 1760s, it had a population of about forty thousand, larger than either New York or Boston.[14] Taking Havana would severely disrupt Spanish shipping and cement British claims on the Caribbean. And from Havana, the British would be in a position to attack Veracruz as well as French possessions in Martinique. It was also a question of prize money. The Keppels were broke, and needed desperately to repair their family fortunes.

Perhaps it was the sheer audaciousness of the plan that ensured its success. With its trio of fortresses around the harbor and newly erected walls, Havana appeared impregnable. Governor Juan de Prado scoffed at rumors of an impending attack and ignored the warning of a merchant vessel that had spotted the fleet. On June 6, he was taken totally by surprise as Albemarle began to land troops to the east of the city at Cojimar and quickly overwhelmed the soldiers in the small fort guarding the mouth of the river. That night, Prado called a hasty council of war. The garrison, reduced by yellow fever the year before, numbered less than three thousand. There were also nine thousand sailors aboard ships in the harbor, and an ill-trained militia of a few thousand more.[15] The weakness in the Spanish defenses was the Cabaña, the narrow ridge overlooking the bay across form the Real Fuerza. From there, artillery could bombard the city, and Prado ordered his men to fortify it. The command of El Morro was given to Luis de Velasco, the captain of the warship *Reina*. Prado made a fatal tactical error by sinking three vessels at the mouth of the harbor to seal off the entrance. The Spanish warships were trapped inside and unable to engage the enemy.

Meanwhile, the British began to march on Havana and took the town of Guanabacoa. Guerrilla attacks were waged by a local magistrate, José Antonio Gómez de Bullones, known popularly as Pepe Antonio, with a lightly armed band of three hundred men. He has been raised to the status of a national hero, and his machete is on display at La Punta, but he hardly slowed down the British advance. Another landing was made at the mouth of the Almendares River, and Havana was now surrounded. But Captain Velasco still held El Morro, and weather and disease was taking its toll of the British. Torrential rains hampered the siege, and by July 25, over five thousand soldiers and three thousand sailors were ill with malaria and dysentery.

But reinforcements arrived from New York and Jamaica, and on July 30 the British stormed El Morro. The walls were breached by two mines, and marines poured into the fortress. Velasco fought valiantly until shot in the chest, and about two hundred soldiers were killed in the assault. Albemarle allowed Velasco to receive medical treatment inside Havana, but he soon died of his wound. After El Morro fell, there was little to be done. The British had taken the Cabaña as well and could simply bombard the city into rubble.

The desperation felt by the Habaneros is recalled in a popular saying. When things get tough, one can say *"Que ha llegado la hora de los mameyes"* (literally, the time of the mameyes has come). Mameyes are a tropical fruit with bright red flesh and black seeds, matching the crimson uniforms of the redcoats, with shiny black buttons.

On August 13, Prado surrendered, and the Union Jack flew over Havana.

The Keppels reaped a rich prize. Havana's coffers contained nearly $2 million, and the goods in the warehouses such as sugar, hides, and tobacco together with the ships in the harbor added another $1 million. The Spanish garrison had fought bravely and was permitted to leave with full honors of war, while Prado was sent home in disgrace and sentenced to death for his incompetence, though this was later commuted. Captain Velasco, the brave defender of El Morro, was given a unique honor. Ever since, there has always been a ship in the Spanish navy called *Velasco*.

Under the terms of surrender, the British troops that occupied Havana and Albemarle agreed not to attack the rest of the island. Indeed, the redcoats were stretched fairly thin and never ventured past Matanzas to the east and Mariel to the west. The Habaneros were not forced to become Protestants, as many had feared, and were given the right to return to Spain or else become British subjects. By the 1700s, the once-feisty Cabildo had become largely irrelevant and merely rubber-stamped decisions made by the governor. Albemarle stepped into these shoes and things went relatively smoothly. The only defiance was offered by Bishop Morell de Santa Cruz, who had succeeded Bishop Valdés. There was bad blood between the seventy-two-year-old firebrand and Albemarle from the start, and things came to a head when the British demanded that a church be reserved for Protestant worship. Bishop Morell refused and was ordered to board ship for Florida. According to legend, he refused to go and was carried by four British sailors on his throne in full regalia, wearing his robe and miter. The path they took to the waterfront was named Obispo (bishop) after this memorable passage.

It was all for naught, since the war ended in November. England agreed to return Havana in exchange for the peninsula of Florida. It is unlikely that Britain ever intended to annex the island, and many planters in Jamaica were leery of the competition. In January 1763, the British troops left Havana. Returning Spanish forces were led by Alejandro O'Reilly, an Irish soldier of fortune for whom O'Reilly Street is named. This is the source of a marvelous passage in José Lezama Lima's maddening, almost unreadable book *Paradiso*, which juxtaposes the defiant exit of Bishop Morell down Obispo Street with the triumphant entrance of the Irishman up O'Reilly Street: "The two streets are a little like the decks of playing cards. They are one of the wonders of the world." [16]

Though there is little today that brings to mind the brief British occupation of Havana, it had an indelible impact. Together with the British marines arrived a horde of merchants eager to sell their wares, initiating an unprecedented economic boom. Until then, Havana's trade had been limited to Sevilla and Cadiz, although smuggling between other islands in the Caribbean was rampant. That year, over seven hundred merchant ships entered Havana. In particular, a brisk trade was established with the British colonies in North America, soon to grow restive. Albemarle canceled many of the onerous taxes that had been imposed by the Spanish crown and reformed the corrupt judiciary, which was famous for talking bribes. Freemasonry gained a foothold in Cuba, and would become quite influential during the next century.

But the most important merchandise unloaded on the docks of Havana was the human variety. Albermarle granted Liverpool merchant John Kennion an exclusive monopoly to import slaves. It is estimated that up to 4,000 slaves were sold in Havana during the British occupation. It must be remembered that Cuba's vast sugarcane plantations would not be planted until the next century, and at the time there were only about 32,000 slaves on the island. British traders initiated the massive influx of African slaves into Cuba, and this remains Albemarle's darkest legacy.

Perhaps mindful that their coffers were rapidly filling up once more, the Spaniards made several important reforms. More Spanish ports were opened to trade, and commercial activity flourished within the Caribbean. The administrative functions of the Cabildo were taken over by an official known as an *intendente*, who represented the interests of the Spanish Crown. And anxious that it never be snatched away again, the Spanish continued to fortify Havana. In 1764, a massive rampart was built

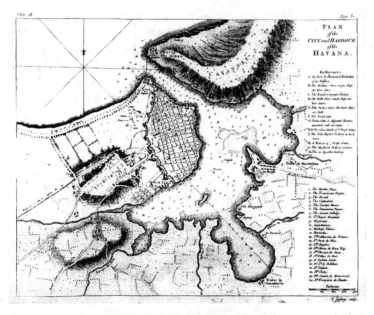

Havana as seen by the British, 1762. Note the city walls and the unprotected ridge of La Cabaña. (Author's collection)

on the ridge that had been taken by the British, named the Fortaleza San Carlos de la Cabaña in honor of the king. At the same time, two other forts were built: Atarés, just below the southern edge of the wall, above an *ensenada*; and El Principe, on a bluff to the west of the city, overlooking what is now the Vedado.

To reach La Cabaña, you take the tunnel that begins at the statue of Máximo Gómez near La Punta and passes underneath the bay, or else take one of the ferries that regularly cross the harbor. A vast defensive complex more than seven hundred meters long, it housed a garrison of one thousand three hundred men. From the walls there is a spectacular view of Havana. Each night at precisely 9:00 PM a curious ceremony takes place. Soldiers in eighteenth century uniforms, replete with powdered wigs, march in to fife and drum and elaborately fire one of the cannons, like the *cañonazo* that once heralded the nightly closing of the gates of Havana.

# CHAPTER 4

# Don Tabaco and Doña Azucar
## Holy Smoke

*In Havana I was born*
*And in all the world known.*

 —Andalusian riddle quoted in *Cuban Counterpoint*, by Fernando Ortiz

*If* you walk down Industria Street past the Capitolio, you can't miss the Partagás cigar factory. It's a four-story, cream- and chocolate-colored stucco confection built in 1845. Perhaps the most striking feature of the ornate facade is a parapet of undulating eaves topped by lions, bearing the words Real Fabrica de Tabacos.

If Havana is cigar Mecca, then the Partagás factory is the Great Mosque. Not surprisingly, most of the pilgrims are Americans. During the 1990s, the number of smokers in the United States nearly doubled to include ur-celebrities such as Madonna and Bill Clinton, and the cigar morphed from a smelly annoyance into a fashion icon. The factory was built by Don Jaime Partagás, a Catalan immigrant who first began rolling cigars in 1827. Flush with success, he bought land in the rich tobacco country west of Havana, which allowed him to weather the disastrous hurricane of 1844. He then established himself in the thriving commercial district of *extramuros*, just outside the crumbling city walls. Don Jaime died in 1868 under mysterious circumstances, supposedly caught in flagrante delicto with a rival's wife. Tour guides claim his ghost still haunts the factory, which now produces 5 million cigars a year.

The business eventually changed hands and was bought in 1900 by the Cifuentes family, who were most responsible for the worldwide fame of the Partagás brand. Ramon Cifuentes had to flee Cuba when the factory was nationalized in 1960, but in 1975 a court ruled that he retained rights to the Partagás brand in the United States and the Dominican Republic. Three years later he began producing cigars in Santo Domingo that are identical to the originals except that the word *Havana* is replaced by *1845* on the distinctive red and gold wrapper. Some connoisseurs say that due to superior quality controls, they are even better.

Ernesto López, the manager of the Partagás factory, welcomed the competition. "I can't change what happened because of the Revolution," he told writer James Suckling, "but I would love to spend time with Ramon Cifuentes in this factory."[1] In 1995, López celebrated the 150th anniversary of the Partagás brand with a bash at the Melía Cohiba hotel for three hundred well-heeled cigar buffs. A cedar-lined humidor autographed by Castro containing 150 special edition Partagás cigars was auctioned off for $67,000. Even in Cuba, the cigar remains the ultimate symbol of unrestrained capitalism.

A tour of the factory traces the journey of tobacco leaves from stem to stogie. The finest tobacco is grown in the Vuelta Abajo region of Pinar del Río, where Don Jaime raised his crop. A tobacco seed is the size of a pinprick, and each plant contains about 1 million. The seeds are sown each September in nursery beds and later replanted by hand to mature. Those leaves destined to be the wrappers of a cigar must be shielded from the sun and covered in long strips of cheesecloth. The mature tobacco plant is as high as a man, with fourteen to eighteen leaves. They are picked (once more, by hand) and left to dry in a curing barn for a month. Depending on their size and texture, they are sorted and begin the lengthy fermentation process, which can last up to two years. At the factory, the leaves are stored in huge piles called *burros*, in which they darken and release ammonia nitrate, which accounts for the piercing odor. When the process is complete, the leaves are carefully moistened and deveined.[2] There are no short-cuts in this enervating ritual; it is "as though each plant were a delicate lady," in the words of José Martí, himself an avid smoker.[3]

Only then are the leaves ready to become cigars. At the Partagás factory, this takes place upstairs, in a vast hall known as a *galera* (galley). This recalls the fact that many of the early cigar factories, including Partagás, utilized prison labor. However, the demand for cigars soon outstripped the prison population, and cigar rollers became the best-paid workers in Havana. The *galera* resembles nothing so much as a classroom, in which the cigar rollers (known as *torcedores*) sit at desks with the cinnamon-colored tobacco leaves spread out before them like schoolbooks.

At one end of the room is a raised platform where a man drones into a microphone, reading from the current issue of *Granma*, the official communist newspaper. This custom originated in prison dining rooms and in 1864 spread to cigar factories, where workers paid the *lector*, or reader, from their own wages. Don Jaime soon introduced it at Partagás, though the subject matter was less prosaic. Although traditionally the news was read in the morning, the afternoon was reserved for novels. Early favorites included *Don Quixote* and the *Hunchback of Notre Dame*. The result was that *torcedores* were among the first workers to form mutual aid societies and unions, and in 1865 they founded a weekly newspaper called *La Aurora*. Cigar rollers who fled to Key West and Tampa during the War of Independence were among Martí's strongest supporters. The Apostle of Liberty spoke often at cigar factories, which he described as "advanced pulpits of liberty."[4] It is no wonder that during the War of Independence, Spanish authorities banned the custom of reading as seditious.

Even today, *torcedores* are the aristocrats of the Cuban working class. The lascivious myth that Cuban cigars were rolled on the thighs of mulattas was started by a French journalist who might have seen the opera *Carmen* one too many times. In fact, women were not employed as *torcedores* in Havana until 1877. The most experienced cigar rollers, who can produce as many as two hundred *tabacos* a day, sit at the front of the *galera*. Their methods have changed little since Don Jaime's day. They begin by gathering together a bunch of leaves used as filler and wrapping them in a binder. This is the moment of truth, because if they are packed too tightly, the cigar will not draw properly. The leaves are then placed inside a wooden mold that gives the cigar its *vitola*, or shape. After about an hour, the mold is opened and any excess leaves are cut with a small knife known as a *chaveta*. The cigar is then encased in a wrapper, the immaculate leaf that grows beneath cheesecloth and gives the cigar much of its taste, and sealed with a drop of spirit gum.

The *tabaco* is now complete, and at Partagás a panel of twelve have the enviable task of tasting them. Before the Revolution, each factory produced its own brand, but now they are all controlled by the state-run agency Cubatabaco. For example, about half of this factory's output are

Partagás cigars. Roughly 25 percent are the famed Cohibas, and another quarter are lesser brands such as Ramon Allones and La Gloria Cubana.

The cigar rollers salute tourists by banging their *chavetas* against the wooden worktables. That is how they once cheered Martí, but now they are well-used to tourists and like nothing better than to mug for the tiny digital cameras that pop out of handbags. Among the oldest of the *torcedores* was a man named Orlando Ortega, who was hired by Ramon Cifuentes in 1951. Have things changed much for him?

"The workers have no fear of the owner," he said, "and we have a say in what we do. It was good then but it is better now."[5]

Don Jaime would be proud.

Who smoked the first cigar?

Most scientists agree that the tobacco plant, *Nicotiana tabacum*, is native to the Peruvian Andes and was first cultivated about 5,000 years ago. By 1492, it had spread from Patagonia to Alaska. Throughout the New World, tobacco was smoked, sniffed, chewed, and otherwise ingested every conceivable way. In particular, the Mayans prized its medicinal properties, and Bernal Díaz reported that the Aztec emperor Montezuma habitually enjoyed a smoke after dinner. Tobacco made its way to Cuba in the canoes of the Tainos, just in time for its fateful rendezvous with Columbus.

In his log book, the Admiral of the Ocean Seas notes that shortly after making landfall, he was given some dried leaves by the natives as a gift. Tobacco was apparently used as a peace offering, much as one might offer a cigarette to a stranger today. Its purpose was unclear until Columbus arrived in Cuba a few days later and sent two men to convey his respects to the Great Khan. They were Luis Torres, a converted Marrano Jew who spoke Arabic (what good that would have done him in China is unclear), and Rodrigo de Xerés, an Andalusian who had once visited a king in Guinea, probably on a slaving expedition. These unlikely ambassadors were the first Europeans to be smitten with smoke. In the words of Bartolomé de las Casas: "[They] met many people on the way going back and forth to their villages, men and women, and the men always carried a firebrand in their hand. . . ."[6]

Father de las Casas goes on the say that these firebrands were known as *tabacos*.

They were not cigars at all but rather tobacco leaves rolled in corn husks, probably about the size of one's forearm. Tobacco was central to the Taino religion, and their *behiques*, or shamans, used it to induce visions by inhaling it through Y-shaped tubes, like snuff. This ceremony was known as *cohoba*, and it is often thought that this was the Taino word for tobacco, but most likely it referred to a narcotic mixed in with the ground leaves. We do not know for certain the Taino word for tobacco. *Tabaco* referred to the "firebrands," yet the name stuck.

As for "cigar," there are several schools of thought. The Mayan word for tobacco was *sikar*, but pipe-smoking was more prevalent in the Yucatán. In Spain, *cigarra* referred to a cicada-like insect prevalent in Andalusia. Many Spaniards grew tobacco in their gardens at home, where the *cigarras* gathered. A more poetic theory is that cigars were named after summer houses in Toledo called *cigaralles*, where tobacco was enjoyed amid the chirping of the cicadas.[7] Like the origin of the name Havana, the etymology is shrouded in mist or, rather, smoke. But the Cuban connection remained, and cigars would become universally referred to as Havanas.

If Columbus brought back a few tobacco leaves to show his sponsors, Ferdinand and Isabel of Spain, they were unimpressed. At first, because of its role in the Taino religion, it was associated with the devil and described as an "evil practice." Rodrigo de Xerés brought back the habit from Cuba and took up smoking in his home in Ayamonte. For his pains, he was arrested by the Spanish Inquisition and spent three years in prison. Initially, the conquistadors disdained it, but as Father de las Casas saw, the colonists who followed after them soon grew fond of it. In Havana, the first tobacco merchants were freed black slaves who sold it to the mariners of the treasure fleet. This is echoed in the traditional English sign for a tobacconist, an African with a huge cigar. Tobacco became a staple on the long journey across the Atlantic, and the sailors spread it around the globe.

It reached Japan as early as 1542 and was soon flourishing in the gardens of the shogun's palace. The Spaniards established the trade route to the Philippines in 1571, and from there it spread to India, where it was much prized by the Great Mogul.[8] Jesuit missionaries brought it to China and the Portuguese to Africa through trading outposts such as Mombasa.

In Spain, the clergy soon overcame their scruples and were soon puffing away at the altar. This came to the attention of Pope Urban VIII, who in 1624 issued a bull threatening users in church with excommunication.

In Havana, Bishop Juan García de Palacios forbade priests to smoke in their vestries. These restrictions apparently had little effect, however.

The Tainos used *tabaco* as an antiseptic, and Spanish physicians soon prescribed it to sufferers of syphilis. But it was Jean Nicot, the French ambassador to Lisbon, who promoted it as a panacea after witnessing how a compress of tobacco leaves cured a man of a tumor. He introduced it at the court of Catherine de Medici in 1559. The "Nicotian Herb," as it became called, was the snake oil of its day. It was soon taken to cure any number of ills, from insomnia to the plague.

Within a generation, tobacco had conquered the world.

## FIDEL'S FAVORITE

In 1994, the publisher of *Cigar Aficionado*, Marvin Shanken, interviewed Fidel Castro at the Palacio de la Revolución in Havana.[9] This curiously frank interview caused a political firestorm in Miami, where the magazine was virtually banned from newsstands. But it was a journalistic match made in heaven. *Cigar Aficionado*, founded in 1992, is a glossy magazine thick with advertising pages, reflecting the revival of cigar smoking in the United States. As for Castro, he is the most famous cigar smoker since Winston Churchill.

Of course, Castro no longer smokes. As he told Shanken, he quit in 1985 out of solidarity with an antismoking campaign. But the publisher didn't buy it. Witness the following exchange:

*"You are saying that you do not smoke even in the privacy of your home by yourself?"*

*"No."*

*"Not even a puff?"*

*"No. No."*

*"Not even a little puff?"*

*"Not one."*

Castro claimed that it was not difficult for him to quit smoking, although he enjoyed cigars since the age of fifteen, when his father presented him with his first one over lunch. But he admitted that he still dreams about smoking Cohibas, as though enjoying them in his sleep.

Cohibas are often regarded as the finest cigar in the world. So the story goes, cigar roller Eduardo Rivero Irazurri created it for Castro's bodyguards in 1966, but it was only a matter of time before the *commandante en jefe* tried it himself. Castro liked it so much that he recruited Irazurri as his own personal *torcedor.* At first it was strictly for his own consumption and occasional gifts to heads of state, but the brand was commercialized in 1982. Only the finest leaves are used in a Cohiba, from the fields of El Corojo, and they are given a third fermentation. Castro's favorite was the Corona Especial, which measures six inches with a ring size of thirty-eight.*

It is no wonder that Castro misses his Cohibas. John F. Kennedy was similarly attached to his H. Upmann Petit Coronas[10] and could not bear to quit when the trade embargo went into effect. Supposedly, he ordered his press secretary, Pierre Salinger, to buy up all he could the day before. One can't help speculating how history might have changed if the two leaders had been able to settle their differences over a cigar.

## TOBACCO WARS

*We quarreled about Havanas—we fought o'er a good cheroot,*
*And I know she is exacting, and she says I am a brute.*

—Rudyard Kipling

Cigars have always been inseparable from revolution in Cuba.

Despite its popularity in the sixteenth century, tobacco remained ruinously expensive and soon threatened vested economic interests. In Havana, its sale by freed blacks was banned in 1557, perhaps because it had become so lucrative. In 1603, the death penalty was imposed on anyone selling tobacco to foreigners, but a brisk trade continued with English, French, and Dutch ships, often in open defiance of the authorities. In response to this, the King of Spain outlawed the growing of tobacco in the Americas in 1606, but it was like putting a finger in a dike. Smuggling remained rampant, particularly among the chain-smoking clergy. The ban was rescinded eight years later, although steep taxes were imposed. Apparently, it was deemed easier to profit from tobacco than to prohibit it. By the early 1700s, tobacco had become the dominant economic activity in Cuba, prompting the Spaniards to establish an official monopoly in 1717. Tobacco growers (known as *vegueros*) had to sell their product directly to the crown's purchasing agent in Havana, from where it was shipped to Sevilla.*

---

[1] The ring size is a measure of the diameter of a cigar in increments of 1/64th inch.
* Tobacco farms were originally known as *tabacales*, but by 1654 they were called *vegas*.

The dam finally burst, and the outraged *vegueros* occupied the church of Jesús del Monte on the outskirts of Havana. Soldiers surrounded the church, but there were massive protests in support of the farmers, and Governor Vicente Raja was forced to resign and return to Spain. Violence was averted, though the *vegueros* rose up once more in 1720. Though the new governor, Gregorio Calderón, made some concessions, the monopoly continued and the *vegueros* took up arms once again. Five hundred men marched on Havana, burning the tobacco fields of those who sold to the crown. This time the governor responded ruthlessly, killing nine farmers and hanging another twelve on the road from Havana to Jesús del Monte. This ended the revolt, and the monopoly grew stronger than ever. But tensions continued to simmer until they exploded in the next century.

On the ground floor of the Partagás factory is a cozy coffee bar, with leather armchairs and a walk-in humidor. Inside are display cases of the brands produced in the factory, including my own favorite, Montecristos. With a brown and white ring decorated with swords and a fleur-de-lys, Montecristos are the best-selling Cuban cigars in the world. The brand is relatively young, started as an offshoot of H. Upmann in 1935. While Cohibas are dark and intense, Montecristos are somewhat mellower, with a delicate aroma of roasted coffee. The name comes from the *Count of Monte Cristo*, by Alexander Dumas, often read to the cigar rollers.

Another cigar with a literary flavor is Por Larrañaga, much loved by Guillermo Cabrera Infante. In his pun-infested book *Holy Smoke*, the novelist recounts his delight at finding a box of pre-revolutionary Por Larrañagas bound in yellow silk ribbons in their distinctive, unadorned wooden box.[11] Though the brand has recently fallen on hard times, its pedigree stretches back to 1834. It was mentioned in Rudyard Kipling's poem that coined the infamous, often-quoted line, "A woman is only a woman, but a good cigar is a smoke."[12]

But if tobacco's ascendance was never in doubt, it took several centuries for the cigar to gain the upper hand. The early Habaneros probably puffed "firebrands" like those of the Taínos, dried leaves wrapped in corn husks. The galleons of the treasure fleet were not conducive to smoking, and so the sailors chewed the leaves they bought from the slaves on the waterfront. When Jean Nicot brought tobacco to France, it was in the form of snuff. Over the next two centuries, taking snuff would be the height of fashion in Parisian society. As Iain Gately explains in his informative book *Tobacco*, it was a peculiar habit. The powdered tobacco was blended with a bewildering variety of substances, such as musk and ambergris. A pinch was applied to each nostril, and it was customary to sneeze into an elegant handkerchief held at the ready.

The first tobacco factory was built in Sevilla in 1620, but it produced mostly snuff for export. The Spaniards preferred cigars, wrapped in leaves rather than corn husks, since maize (another gift from the Tainos) was looked down on and only used for feedstock. The cigars were called *puros*, to distinguish them from the adulterated snuff.

Across the English Channel, the pipe held sway. Tobacco was probably introduced by privateers such as Francis Drake, who encountered it in the Caribbean, but it was Sir Walter Raleigh who made it fashionable. His colonists in Virginia had encountered pipe-smoking Indians, the origin of Hollywood's ubiquitous smoke signals. Whereas the Tainos did not possess pipes, most North American tribes consumed tobacco in this manner. Raleigh persuaded Queen Elizabeth to take a puff, and pipe smoking was soon the rage in London. After Raleigh fell out of favor with the tobacco-hating James I, his last act in the Tower of London was purportedly to light a pipe. Christopher Marlowe, part-time spy and author of *Dr. Faustus*, took it to heart and said that "all they that love not tobacco and boys are fools."[13]

Cigars did not reach North America until the British occupation of Havana in 1762. Serving under Lord Albemarle was Colonel Israel Putnam, who would later switch sides and serve as a general in the Revolutionary War. He returned home to Connecticut with three donkey loads of *tabacos*, which soon became referred to as "Havanas." By 1810, according to the census, some 29 million cigars were manufactured per year in the United States.[14]

It took the Duke of Wellington to introduce cigars in England. During the Peninsular War of 1808 to 1814, his troops obtained puros from the occupying French forces, who often traded them for brandy. British cavalry officers were delighted and rapidly abandoned their pipes. In 1830, England imported 250,000 pounds of cigars.

The Spanish king Ferdinand VII finally ended the state monopoly on tobacco by royal decree in 1817. The Cuban cigar industry, poised to meet the explosive growth in demand, immediately flourished. Initially, cigar rolling was a cottage industry, taking place at home or in small workshops called *chinchales*. But by 1836, there were 306 tobacco factories like that of Don Jaime in Havana, employing 2,152 workers. During the next quarter century, the number would nearly double, with 498 factories and 7,687 workers assiduously rolling cigars.[15]

Cigars themselves have changed remarkably little since that time, but there were two important developments. The first was the cigar band, introduced in 1830 by a German immigrant to Havana, Gustav Bock. According to Cabrera Infante, the legend is that the band was developed to shield the fingers of ladies who wished to smoke without touching the tobacco, but most likely it was a marketing ploy to distinguish Bock's brand, Aguila de Oro. The second was the cigar box, introduced by Ramon Allones in 1845. Before that, bundles of cigars had been secured by ribbons. The development of color lithography created a new art form. Cigar boxes were soon decorated with an amazing variety of themes, ranging from loftily mythological to frankly commercial. The postcards of the day, they often contained typically Cuban motifs, such as royal palm trees or maps of the city. For many in the nineteenth century, the first glimpse of Havana was on a cigar box label.

As for the cigarette, we owe that to the Spaniards.* Among the poor, it was the custom to gather the butts of used *puros* on the street and wrap them in paper, which became known as *papelotes*. Later, lower-quality tobacco was shredded and reserved for cigarettes, as visiting Frenchmen called them. By 1840, cigarette smoking was common in Paris, and five years later, 6 million cigarettes were sold. In Havana, the most famous cigarette manufacturer was called La Honradez, located on the corner of San Ignacio and Cuba streets in Habana Vieja. It was owned by a Corsican named José de Susini, who bears the honor of having invented the first cigarette-rolling machine in 1866, which could produce sixty cigarettes per minute.

In the display case of the Partagás coffee shop is a box of Montecristo No. 4s. This is a Petit Corona, five inches long with a ring size of forty-two. The price for five is about $20. This is almost two months' wages for the average Cuban, though they can be obtained for about half that price

---

[1] Five hundred years later, the Spanish are still proud of this invention. The average Spaniard smokes 2,300 cigarettes a year, 850 more than the average European, according to the *New York Times*.

A view of Havana Harbor on a cigar box label, ca. 1910. (Courtesy of Emilio Cueto)

on the black market, which is to say any street corner. Most Cubans today without access to dollars smoke cigarettes or else inferior "national" cigars. But the point is moot to American visitors. As a Partagás employee balefully told me, all Cuban cigars are confiscated by ever-vigilant U.S. customs guards at the airport.

## THE TRIANGLE TRADE

If Cuba gave the world tobacco, then it received sugar in exchange.

Many of the conquistadors reported finding sugarcane growing in Taíno villages, which led to the conclusion that it was native to the Caribbean. In fact, Columbus brought it on his second voyage in 1493, and it spread quicker than the Spaniards. Sugarcane originated at the other end of the globe, on the volcanic slopes of New Guinea. A member of the grass family, it was one of the first plants cultivated by humans, nearly ten thousand years ago, and made its way west along the islands of the Indonesian archipelago.[16] The word for sugar comes from the Sanskrit *shakkara*, so most likely it was first refined into crystals in India—Alexander the Great encountered it in 325 B.C. From there, it followed the silk route to Persia and reached Europe with Islamic invaders. By 755, sugar cane was being grown near Córdoba.

Like tobacco, sugar was originally touted for its health benefits and used by apothecaries to hide the foul taste of medicines. The Portuguese were refining sugar in Madeira by 1432, and that is where Columbus encountered it. He planted it in Hispaniola, and Diego Velázquez brought it to Cuba, where the first sugar mill was built near Havana in 1523. But it had no export value, since there was a thriving sugar industry in the Mediterranean. That changed in 1570, when the Ottoman Turks conquered Cyprus, Crete, and much of North Africa. At the same time, demand for sugar rose as Europeans began to drink more coffee, tea, and cocoa. By 1600, prices had quadrupled.[17]

Since Spain was self-sufficient in sugar, it was England that looked to the New World to satisfy its sweet tooth. The first British settlers reached Barbados in 1627, and by the 1660s, the island was the world's greatest sugar producer.[18] What made slavery inevitable was the grueling manual labor needed to cultivate and refine sugar. Planting occurred in late summer, when the temperature was in excess of 100 degrees Fahrenheit. Cuttings were placed in pits about four feet square and a foot deep, dug with sharp sticks. The harvest was early in the year, when the canes were cut by machete into pieces about three feet long. The canes were crushed in mills, usually by wooden rollers driven by oxen, and the juice was boiled in open copper vats to extract the sugar. By 1675, black slaves in Barbados far outnumbered their white masters.

Sugar slavery did not originate in the Caribbean. African slaves had been sold in Europe as early as 1250, and Muslims developed a lucrative trade with captured Slavs (hence the word *slaves*). There were slaves at work in the cane fields of southern Spain, as well as Madeira and the Canary Islands, and Sevilla was a thriving slave market long before 1492. But the growing demand for sugar on the world market combined with a virtually unlimited supply of slave labor led to what became known as the Triangle Trade. The first leg was from Europe to West Africa, where slaves were purchased with trinkets, firearms, alcohol, and salt. The second was the hellish Middle Passage, where slaves were transported to the Caribbean in the holds of slave ships. There it is estimated that a slave could be sold for nearly eight times the cost of acquiring him. The now-empty holds were filled with rum, molasses, and sugar for the final leg home. Each side of the triangle was profitable, and although sometimes a third of the ships were lost, vast fortunes were made. According to the historian Henry Hobhouse, from 1690 to 1790, Europe imported 12 million tons of sugar, costing the lives of 12 million slaves. A chilling equation accounts for the Triangle Trade's profitability: *Each ton of sugar cost only one human life.*

African slaves sailed with Columbus and were brought by the conquistadors to the New World, mainly as servants. The rapid extermination of the Tainos necessitated a new labor force. Twelve slaves were brought to Cuba in 1513 to build the fortifications of Santiago de Cuba, and three hundred arrived in 1524 to work in the Jagua gold mines. A 1534 letter of Governor Guzmán mentions about a thousand slaves in Cuba at the time. But since the sugar industry remained economically insignificant, slavery did not achieve critical mass in Cuba until the end of the eighteenth century. When the British took Havana in 1762, they found six thousand boxes of sugar in the harbor.[19] It was the entire year's export, about five hundred tons. By comparison, this was about 1 percent of the annual production of Jamaica. There were only about one hundred sugar mills in Cuba, mostly in the vicinity of Havana. They had changed little since the sixteenth century, with the cane fed into the rollers by hand. Hugh Thomas estimates that at the time, there were only about 32,000 slaves on the island.

All that would soon change. Due to increased trade with North America, annual sugar exports from Cuba rocketed to about 10,000 tons a year in the 1770s, with five times the number of sugar mills. Among the many vessels to enter the harbor during the British occupation were slave ships, and up to 60,000 slaves were sold in Cuba from 1763 to 1789, as many as during the preceding two centuries. Before, the Spanish had granted an exclusive license to sell slaves to the South Sea Company of London. Now they entered the slave trade in earnest, purchasing trading stations from the Portuguese, and slaves were brought to Havana directly from Africa.

But just as the rise of the Ottoman empire had shifted sugar production from the Mediterranean to the Caribbean in 1570, another political maelstrom would make Havana the main axis of the Triangle Trade. The French seized the western half of Hispaniola in the 1600s, and it was now called Saint-Domingue. Only sixty miles from Cuba, it was by far the wealthiest colony in the Caribbean, producing 71,000 tons of sugar a year and over 30 percent of the world's supply of coffee. Over 90 percent of the population were slaves, and in 1791 they rose up against their masters. The bloody revolt and subsequent political turmoil led to a collapse of the sugar market, and Cuba seized the opportunity.

Between 1792 and 1806, 179 sugar mills were built near Havana.[20] French refugees brought with them a number of technical innovations, such as the so-called Jamaican train, which allowed the cauldrons to be heated by the cane left over after grinding. As early as 1797, the first steam-powered mill was used, and a machine called the *volvedora* was introduced to load the stalks into the grinders. Sugar production soared to 34,000 tons in 1805 and 160,000 tons in 1836.

In order to transport sugar, roads were built, and in 1823, a steamboat line was started between Havana and Matanzas. The first railroad in Latin America connected Havana and Guines in 1838, four years before Spain itself had a rail system. By 1860, there would be four hundred miles of railway in Cuba.*

It comes as no surprise that slavery grew at the same pace. In 1792, there were nearly 85,000 slaves in Cuba.[21] Havana became the largest slave market of the Caribbean, and up to 100,000 slaves would be sold there during the next decade. From the port, the unfortunate Africans were taken to barracoons, or slave barracks, located outside the walls near what is now Avenida Salvador Allende. It was a common diversion for elegant Habaneros to drive their carriages by the barracoons and throw scraps of food to the savages.

By 1827, the slave population had tripled to 287,000. Fourteen years later, there were 436,000 slaves, about 45 percent of the Cuban population.[22] Until slavery in Cuba was officially abolished in 1886, nearly 1 million men and women made the Middle Passage.

The city changed in other ways besides complexion.

Alejo Carpentier sets his novel, *Explosion in a Cathedral*, in Havana during the slave revolt in Saint-Domingue. Carpentier is perhaps the most enigmatic of Cuban writers. Born in 1902 to French parents recently immigrated to Cuba, he lived much of his life in exile. Briefly jailed by President Machado, he fled to Paris in 1927, and later lived in Venezuela. After the Revolution, he returned to Havana to run the state publishing house, producing a heavily abridged version of *Moby Dick*, and served as a loyal cultural attaché in Paris. There, he fell out with many intellectuals over Castro's policies and was derided as an apparatchik. Jean-

---

[1] Cuba was the seventh country in the world to have railroads. At the time of the Revolution, Havana had more railroads per square mile than any other Latin American country.

Paul Sartre snubbed him, and Cabrera Infante maliciously implied that he had not been born in Cuba, referring to him as "Alexis."

But a quarter century after his death, Carpentier's place in Cuba's literary firmament is secure, and he is regarded as the father of magical realism. A small museum dedicated to his work in located in the Casa del Conde de la Reunion, located on Empedrado Street in Habana Vieja. This elegant mansion, with a trefoil-arched doorway and a courtyard decorated with brilliant tiles, is depicted in *Explosion in a Cathedral.* The novel describes a bustling city in ferment, not just with commercial activity but with new ideas. The protagonists are three orphans whose lives are changed by the arrival of Victor Hugues, a Freemason inspired by the events of the French Revolution.

It is estimated that over thirty thousand French refugees arrived in Cuba during this time, many settling near Santiago de Cuba.[23] They had a lasting impact on Cuban art, music, and culture. In addition to the minuet and powdered wigs, they introduced the French custom of drinking coffee. Although coffee had been introduced in 1748, there had been relatively little cultivation on the island, and French planters established some of the first *cafetales* (coffee plantations) on the outskirts of Havana and farther west in Pinar del Río. As coffee grew in popularity, its price on the world market soared, and for a time it rivaled sugar. Exports in 1792 were under 80 tons, but by 1804 they were 550 tons. At one point, there were 192,000 acres in cultivation for coffee versus 180,000 for sugarcane.[24] But after 1840, the increasing profitability of sugar tilted the balance, and many of the *cafetales* were planted with sugar cane.

Yet for a time, Havana was coffee-crazy. The *Papel Periodico,* one of the city's early newspapers,* included a recipe for brewing this new drink. The first Parisian-style café was opened in the Plaza Vieja, and recently it has been restored as a smart brewpub. In 1804, the Café de los Franceses opened just beyond the city walls, and it soon became a gathering place for liberal intellectuals. The obsession with coffee continues to this day, though Starbucks has yet to reach Havana.

It was during this time that the Plaza de la Catedral was completed. Originally the site of a cistern for the Zanja Real aqueduct, it was the last square to be laid out in Habana Vieja. Officially called the Catedral de la Virgen Maria de la Concepcion Immaculada, the cathedral was begun by

---

[1] The first was the *Gaceta de la Habana,* published in 1782. The *Papel Periodico* was founded in 1790 and later changed its name to *Diario de la Habana.* It continued publishing until 1848.

the Jesuits in 1748 and completed in 1777. The sinuous, ornate facade with asymmetrical belltowers is a masterpiece of Baroque architecture and was described by Carpentier as "music turned into stone." Across from it is the Casa del Conde de Bayona, built in the 1720s and now housing the Museo de Arte Colonial. To the left is the Casa de Lombillo, the office of the magazine *Opus Habana*. In 1821, it was a post office, and set into the rough stone wall beneath the portico is a mailbox in the shape of a scowling Greek mask. The cobblestoned square is surprisingly intimate, with chairs and tables from a restaurant on the northwest side. It is a favorite of tourists, and there are cigar rollers, fortune tellers, and waiters passing out drinks.

Another account of Havana comes from Alexander von Humboldt. The celebrated German naturalist, who first visited Havana in 1800 toward the end of his five-year tour of Latin America, did much to introduce the city to European intelligentsia. Upon arriving, he declared, "The way Havana looks when you enter the port makes it one of the most pleasant and picturesque places." Yet he was decidedly ambivalent, griping about the mud on the streets and the porters who "elbowed passersby and made being a pedestrian annoying and humiliating." Despite these complaints, Humboldt is lauded as "the second discoverer of Cuba" and was honored in 1969 with a Cuban commemorative stamp on the 200th anniversary of his birth.

## POLITICS OF RUM

*There's nought no doubt so much the spirit calms as rum and true religion.*

—Lord Byron, *Don Juan*

Fittingly, the origin of the word rum (or in Spanish, *ron*) rivals that of tobacco for obscurity. The Malay word *beram* is often cited, though this was liquor made from tapioca and seems an unlikely etymological candidate. The process of distillation was well known to the Arabs, who gave us the word *alcohol*, so it seems probable that a variant of rum was drunk in the cane fields of Andalusia.

In Cuba, early planters most likely distilled sugarcane juice into a brandy, or *aguardiente*. This is still drunk today in much of Latin America, especially Colombia, and the Brazilian version is called *cachaça*. The molasses that remained in the kettle after the sugar crystals were boiled off was used to feed slaves. Once again, the intrepid British led the way by boiling this thick, brownish sludge a second time and allowing it to ferment. The resulting extract was a harsh, dark liquor called "kill-devil,"[25] drunk only by those too poor to afford anything else. We have the first accounts of it from Richard Ligon, who arrived in Barbados in 1647. Its effect on those who imbibed was to "lay them asleep on the ground." By 1667, it was called *rum** and proved popular as well as profitable. Barbados was soon producing 200,000 gallons a year.

If wine was drunk aboard Spanish galleons, rum will forever be associated with the Royal Navy. This began in 1655, when the British conquered Jamaica. Thereafter, Jack Tar was issued his famous "tot," or ration of one-half pint of rum, twice a day. Apparently sailors were wary of diluted rum, for they tested it by dripping some on a few grains of gunpowder. If the alcohol content was sufficiently high, the water evaporated and the gunpowder flashed when lit. This was the "proof," a measure that has remained on liquor bottles to this day.

As can be imagined, drunkenness aboard ships was common, and caused many fatal accidents, such as men falling from yardarms. Admiral Vernon, who attacked Guantanamo in 1740, attempted to remedy this. He ordered that each tot be mixed with one quart water (a ratio of four to one) and blended with lime juice to prevent scurvy. Vernon habitually wore a waterproof cloak made of a material called grogram, and his potation was soon called "grog." England also has Vernon to thank for the sobriquet *limey*.[26]

No doubt the British sailors who stormed Havana in 1762 brought their tots with them. In the decades that followed, the increased trade with North America and the expansion of the sugar industry created a booming market for Cuban molasses. It seems curious today that states like Massachusetts and Rhode Island were leading rum producers in the eighteenth century. Medford was chockfull of distilleries, and Paul Revere stopped there to fortify himself on his famous ride.

This spawned a peculiar variant of the Triangle Trade: Yankee slavers traded rum directly for slaves. In 1767, the going rate was 130 gallons of rum per man and 110 gallons per woman. From Africa, the slave ships proceeded to Havana, where they unloaded the slaves and took on hogsheads of molasses. The next stop was New England, where

---

[1] One etymological suspect is the Devonshire word *rumbullion,* which meant "a great tumult."

the molasses was exchanged for rum in order to purchase more slaves. And so on, until piety and politics turned many slavers into abolitionists in the nineteenth century.

The Triangle Trade created the fortune of many a Boston Brahmin. With his profits, merchant Peter Faneuil built Faneuil Hall, which became known as the Cradle of Liberty. Taxes on molasses shipped from Havana were one of the root causes of the American Revolution, and those who participated in the Boston Tea Party probably drank something stronger. Even after slavery ended, New England exported rum to Hawaii. Many of these distilleries continued in business until Prohibition finally did away with them.

The docks of Havana were thus awash in rum long before the slave revolt in Saint-Domingue, but the French refugees who fled the violence brought their distillation techniques with them. They found an eager student in Don Facundo Bacardi Massó, who was born in Sitges, Spain, and emigrated to Santiago de Cuba in 1829. He married the daughter of a French sugar baron and bought a tin-roofed distillery where he developed a charcoal filtering technique that created a smoother, mellower rum. A colony of fruit bats lived in the rafters, and the bat became the symbol of Bacardi y Compañia, founded in 1862.

Today Bacardi is a vast, transnational enterprise with headquarters in Bermuda. Selling more than 200 million bottles of rum a year, it is still controlled by six hundred of Don Facundo's descendants.[27] The company flourished during Prohibition, when American tourists flocked to Havana to drink in bars like Sloppy Joe's on Zulueta Street. Bacardi became synonymous with rum itself and an indispensable ingredient in Cuba libres. If Bacardi is to be believed, this cocktail was born during the Spanish American War when one of Teddy Roosevelt's Rough Riders added Bacardi to his Coca-Cola and drank to a free Cuba.

Another famous libation was developed at around the same time in the village of Daiquiri, not far from the Bacardi distillery. Rum sage Charles Coulombe maintains that the American engineer at the local iron mine ran out of gin one day and served rum to visiting friends. To hide the taste, he mixed it with lime juice and sugar, creating a variant of grog. The daiquiri would reach the summit of frozen artistry under Constante Ribailagua, bartender at the Floridita on Obispo Street. In

1932, he mixed one for a thirsty Ernest Hemingway, and the rest is literary history. The daiquiri has probably been featured in more novels than any other drink and was a favorite of John F. Kennedy, who enjoyed it with his H. Upmanns.

The holy trinity of Cuban cocktails is completed with the mojito, a fizzy version of the daiquiri with fresh mint. This is the signature drink at La Bodeguita del Medio, a bar on Empedrado Street near the cathedral, much frequented by Errol Flynn in his waning years. Apparently Hemingway liked mojitos as well, for on the wall above his signature is the famous inscription, *Mi mojito en La Bodeguita, mi daiquiri en El Floridita.* According to the journalist Fernando Campoamor, who drank more than one mojito with Hemingway, this is apocryphal and concocted as a marketing gimmick after the writer's death.

A stone's throw from the Floridita is the Bacardi Building, formerly the company's headquarters, built in the salad days of 1927. This sparkling gem of art deco architecture, with a polished marble facade and a terra-cotta tower topped by a bat, was one of Havana's first skyscrapers. When Castro marched triumphantly into Havana, a sign was hung above the entrance that said *Gracias, Fidel.* Even though Bacardi executives had raised money for Castro's 26th of July Movement, within two years the distillery in Santiago de Cuba was nationalized. But Bacardi had already moved offshore a few years earlier, perhaps hedging its bets, and hardly skipped a beat, growing into "the world's largest privately-held, family owned spirits company," according to its Web site.

In recent years, Bacardi has become as well-known for litigation as for rum, waging an expensive, politically savvy feud against Castro over trademarks. The Cuban government entered into a partnership with French liquor giant Pernod Ricard to market Havana Club, the brand of rum that features La Giraldilla on the bottle, and which is now produced in the old Bacardi distillery. Havana Club had been owned by the Arechabala family, who fled Cuba after the Revolution. Their office was located in the Casa del Conde de Bayona, facing the cathedral, the site of the famous Havana Club bar mentioned by Graham Greene in *Our Man in Havana.* When the trademark expired, Cuba re-registered it in the U.S. Patent and Trademark Office. Despite this, Florida lawmakers managed to get a bill passed that exempted nationalized trademarks such as Havana Club from the usual protections of international law.[28] The World Trade Organization later ruled against Bacardi, but the case remains mired in the legal trenches, with armies of lobbyists on either side.

Recently, Bacardi announced plans to sell Havana Club in the United States, perhaps auguring another contentious lawsuit.

Rum and politics are still familiar bedfellows.


## IN THE BARACOONS

In his whimsical yet incisive book *Cuban Counterpoint*, anthropologist Fernando Ortiz interpreted Cuban history through the interaction of tobacco and sugar. This is not so far-fetched as it may seem. During the first two centuries following the Spanish conquest, the export of tobacco was the island's leading commercial link to the world. Beginning in the eighteenth century, this role was supplanted by sugar. The cultivation of sugar propelled Cuba into the industrial age and brought about indelible changes in the fabric of Cuban life. But Ortiz extends his argument far beyond economic determinism. Sugar and tobacco are not merely abstract forces, but cultural entities with distinct personalities.

As we have seen, sugar and tobacco impacted Cuba in radically different ways. Ortiz describes the mutual attraction between Don Tabaco and Doña Azucar as one of opposites:

> Sugar cane lives for years, the tobacco plant only a few months. The one is white, the other dark. Sugar is sweet and odorless; tobacco bitter and aromatic. Always in contrast! Food and poison, waking and drowsing, energy and dream, delight of the flesh and delight of the spirit . . . . Sugar is she; tobacco is he.[29]

These contradictions shaped not just Cuba but Cubans themselves. While the cultivation of tobacco involves skill, the production of sugar requires brute force. Tobacco needs delicate care, while sugar demands backbreaking labor. The courtship of Doña Azucar thus led to a change in the means of production and created the need for slaves.

While it is uncertain if Spanish-style slavery was more humane than British-style, the Spanish were certainly more familiar with the institution. In 1492, there were up to 100,000 slaves in Spain, subject to a detailed legal code that the conquistadors brought to the New World. In the British colonies of North America, slaves had no rights whatsoever and were legally indistinguishable from chattel. In Cuba, they could marry and acquire and dispose of property. Significantly, they could even buy their own freedom. This was known as *coartación*, which has been described as a slave "breaking his chain link by link."[30] The custom appears to have originated in Havana as early as the 1520s. A slave could secure his freedom by paying a sum of money to his master as a down payment and then paying the balance in installments. This could also be done to free a child or a relative.

From the earliest days of city, freed slaves lived alongside the Habaneros and, as we have seen, were the original tobacconists. Many worked in Havana's booming shipbuilding trade and became established in a number of other professions, such as cooking, laundering, carpentering, tailoring, and, of course, cigar-rolling. In 1762, there were as many as 20,000 freed blacks in Cuba.[31] Many of them owned slaves themselves. They served in the militia, with special regiments for *morenos* (blacks) and *pardos* (mulattoes). Relations between different races were relatively free and easy, although this would change after the slave revolt in Saint-Domingue, when many whites feared lightning might strike twice. It is an old chestnut that the mulatta was the Spaniard's greatest invention, and this theme has myriad variations in Havana's bawdy humor. But it appears that masters tended to free their illegitimate children, for there was a steady increase of free mulattoes, increasing 200 percent between 1774 and 1841.

Slaves in the city, amounting to a quarter of the slave population, lived very differently from their counterparts in the country. Many were domestics, living in close proximity to their masters. In colonial palaces, slaves often lived in the *entresol*, a sort of mezzanine between the first and second floors, and large households had dozens of slaves ranging in hue from ebony to near white. Many masters rented out their slaves, creating an extra source of income. If some masters were kindly and paternal, others were cruel and vicious. In many old houses can be seen iron rings set in the walls for slaves to be tied, and near the castle of La Punta was a whipping post where they could be sent for punishment.

Nearly a third of the slaves worked in sugar plantations, known as *centrales*. During the six-month harvesttime, slaves were literally worked to death, sleeping as little as four hours a day. Since weak slaves could not cut sugarcane, they were fed plentifully. Vast, boiling cauldrons were filled with plantains, malangas, sweet potatoes, yucca, corn, and salt cod or fresh meat—this is the origin of the *ajiaco*, a sort of Cuban gumbo. Accidents were common: An overseer stood by the sugar grinders with a cutlass to cut off the arm of a slave should it become caught. Cholera and other diseases were rampant. The replacement rate was as high as 10 percent each year, guaranteeing the need for a fresh supply. Recalcitrant slaves (mostly recent arrivals from Africa, who had yet to be "seasoned") were regularly beaten, restrained in stocks, or forced to wear tin masks and pronged collars. Any who fled were hunted down by the same wolfhounds that had mutilated the Tainos, and soldiers were posted near the *centrales* to crush any attempted uprisings. Unlike in American cotton plantations, the backbreaking work of the sugarcane harvest could rarely be done by women, so nearly all the slaves were men. At night, they were imprisoned in the barracoons until a bell announced the start of a new day, well before dawn.

The barracoons were stinking, filthy barracks with floors of beaten earth that offered little protection from the pestilential heat and rain. Some housed as many as four hundred slaves. But it was here that they were able to create a space of their own. Cuban slaves were acquired at various ports along the west coast of Africa from Senegal to Angola, but the majority appear to have been from the Congolese and Yoruban nations. Slaves were often placed in barracoons according to tribes, and they were able to retain their folk traditions, religious practices, and languages.* The overseers encouraged dancing and singing, since this was good for morale, and to this we owe rumba, mambo, salsa, and much of modern pop music.

In Havana, the cultural function of the barracoons was served by the *cabildos*,** social clubs started by freed blacks. The *cabildos* had elected offices and were organized along ethnic lines, and for newly arrived slaves they functioned as mutual aid societies. In 1755, Bishop Morell de Santa Cruz was so impressed that he granted them official church status. His objective was for the *cabildos* to provide religious instruction, but the result was quite different.

It can be argued that the *cabildos* permitted the blacks to retain and strengthen their own beliefs, but what emerged was something altogether new. The link between the traditional Yoruban deities and the Catholic saints is easily established. The symbol of Changó is the ax, and so he was identified with St. Barbara, who is usually pictured with a hatchet. Cuba's patron saint, the *Virgen de la Caridad del Cobre*, was the favorite of sailors,

---

[1] Many African words entered the Cuban dialect, such as *jimagua* (used more frequently than the Spanish word for twin, *gemelo*) and *quimbombó* (okra, also loved in Dixie).

** The name was taken from the town council of Havana, the Cabildo.

and so she became linked with Oshún, the goddess of rivers. And since Babalu Ayé triumphs over death and disease, he became St. Lazarus. These beings became known as *orishas*, the foundation of the syncretistic religion of Santeria, which has spread from Cuba to the United States and continues to grow.

In *Cuban Counterpoint*, Fernando Ortiz described this cultural mixing as "transculturation," comparing it to a stew in which each ingredient contributes its own flavor. Each year on the Feast of the Epiphany (January 6), the *cabildos* took to the streets of Havana. This riotous celebration began in the traditional black neighborhood Jesus María in Habana Vieja, by the docks, and made its way north along Oficios Street. A famous engraving by Federico Mialhe showed the dancers in tribal costumes with fringed skirts and horned masks decorated with peacock feathers and multicolored beads. Music is supplied by horns and bongo drums. There are young and old, men as well as women, and a dog scampering between their legs. Along the street, more soberly dressed whites (and blacks) look on with evident amusement. The procession ended at the Plaza de Armas, where representatives of each *cabildo* would solemnly approach the Palacio de los Capitanes Generales to greet the captain-general,* who tossed a few coins to the crowd.

## CHINATOWN

Another transculturation took place with the arrival of Chinese immigrants to Cuba.

The slave trade was officially abolished by Britain in 1808, and Spain reluctantly followed suit in 1820. Although the Royal Navy occasionally boarded slave ships, smugglers operated with little difficulty and the Triangle Trade continued until the American Civil War. But Cuban planters saw the writing on the wall and looked about for new sources of cheap labor. Following the example of the conquistadors, they imported Indians from the Yucatán, many of them full-blooded Mayans. At midcentury, thousands of them worked under contract in the *centrales*, but they found conditions too harsh and most of them returned to Mexico or settled in

---

* After the British invasion, the Spanish governors were generally military men and used this title.

Habana Vieja west of the Plaza Vieja, which became known as the Barrio Campeche.

The planters looked farther afield and settled on China. Chinese laborers, or "coolies," had been brought to Trinidad as early as 1806. In 1844, 204 coolies arrived Cuba from Xiamen in Guan Dong (Canton) on the Spanish ship *Oquendo*. During the next twenty years, nearly 140,000 more would join them.[32] Most were from mainland China and shipped out via the Portuguese colony of Macao, but up to a third were from the Philippines, Hong Kong, and Indochina. Conditions aboard ship were brutal, and it is estimated that 12 percent died on the trip or shortly after arrival. Many of them were press-ganged and had little idea where they were going, but on arrival they were taken directly to the *centrales*, where they worked side by side with the slaves and were kept in barracoons of their own. Most coolies were on eight-year contracts and received the equivalent of 20 to 30 cents a day. They may have been treated even worse than the African slaves, since they had no value to the planters after their contracts expired. Others worked in similar conditions to build the railways. Predictably, many tried to escape or committed suicide, and the majority of those who survived returned to China. The Chinese government finally halted the emigration in 1873.

But those who remained left Havana a potent cultural legacy. Many settled along the Zanja Real and cultivated small plots of land, where they grew the first mangoes in Cuba. There were Chinese battalions in the War of Independence, and on the corner of Linea and L streets is a black marble slab commemorating their bravery. It bears the words of patriot Gonzalo de Quesada y Aróstegui: *"Nunca hubo un chino cubano traidor, nunca hubo un chino cubano desertor"* (There was never a Chinese traitor or deserter). By the early twentieth century, Havana had the largest Chinatown in all of Latin America, known as the Barrio Chino. Its epicenter is the corner of Cuchillo and Dragones streets. The narrow streets are clogged with tourists (with *jineteras* in pursuit), signs are written in Chinese, and paper lanterns hang above the entrances of the many restaurants. The first Chinese restaurant opened in Havana in 1858, establishing the unparalleled tradition of the Cuban Chinese restaurant. For a few dollars you can get *maripositas* (wontons), a heaping plate of fried rice, and a smoked pork chop, a meal that is as Cuban as, well, anything else.

In recent years, the government has attempted to refurbish the Barrio Chino for tourists, and the People's Republic of China funded the

Ming-style, 62- foot-wide Portico Chino, or Dragon's Gate, at the inter-section of Dragones and Amistad. But nearly all the ethnic Chinese left after the Revolution, and the Barrio Chino is a mere shadow of what it was. Writing in the 1920s, Carpentier described a thriving community with several Chinese-language newspapers and radio stations, mutual aid societies, and businesses of every description. On the corner of Zanja and Galiano streets was the Teatro Chino. Here Chinese operas were per-formed starring the famed Wong Sin Fong. Nearby was the seedy Shang-hai Theater where Fredo Corleone took his guests in *Godfather II* to witness the famed Superman show. The five-story Pacifico Restaurant on San Nicolas was a favorite of both Hemingway and Castro, though it is doubtful they ever shared a bowl of wonton soup.

Perhaps by coming into contact with African slaves, the Chinese had their own version of Santeria. This can be seen in the *Chino de la Charada*. One of the most reproduced images in pre-revolutionary Ha-vana, this is a picture of a Chinese mandarin with a series of figures around his body, accompanied by numbers. For example, on his sleeve is an elephant, with the number nine. On his shoulder is a tortoise, with the number six. The Chinese brought their passion for gambling to Cuba, and the *Chino de la Charada* was a code for picking winners. In particular, it was the key to the *bolita*, a lucrative lottery that still flour-ishes illegally in Miami. If you were to dream about an elephant and a tortoise, let's say, you might choose a number containing ninety-six. Each *orisha* has a corresponding number—Changó is four and Oshún is five—giving such dreams a religious significance.

One of the many names for Castro is *El Caballo*, or the horse. This refers not to sexual prowess but to the *Chino de la Charada*. Astride the mandarin's head is a horse, with the number one.

## BABALU

December 17 is the feast day of St. Lazarus. From all over Havana, up to fifty thousand pilgrims trek to Rincón, about twenty miles south, to visit the Iglesia de San Lazaro. This is called the Procesión de Milagros, and many crawl the last few miles on their hands and knees, while others sweep the ground ahead of them with palm fronds. Behind the small, well-cared-for church surrounded by flowering hibiscus is a mossy foun-tain where they bathe their hands and feet to give thanks to Babalu Ayé, perhaps the best-loved *orisha* in Cuba.

The *Chino de la Charada* sold many a lottery ticket. (Author's collection)

St. Lazarus was a bishop who lived in Marseilles during the last days of the Roman Empire, but better known are the two Lazaruses of the New Testament: the one who rose from the dead, and the beggar who suffered from leprosy. It is these two who were transculturated into Babalu Ayé. Known as the "Father of the World," he is usually pictured dressed in rags, wracked with pain and disfigured, accompanied by two small dogs. Babalu Ayé is invoked to ward off diseases, so it is fitting that nearby is the sanatorium of Los Cocos, for sufferers of AIDS. Pope John Paul II visited it in 1998, as did Jimmy Carter in 2002.

With its growing popularity outside of Cuba, Santeria has entered the realm of pop culture, but the term is often misused. It refers to the *santos* (saints), as the Yoruban *orishas*, or deities, are often called. But the Congolese slaves followed the secretive *palo de monte* rituals, which have little to do with the *santos*, while those from the Niger Delta established the Abakua secret societies, whose initiates are called *nañigos*. Thus Santeria is only a part of the picture. Also, it has become a business of sorts. Santeria priests, or *babalaos*, have charged as much as $4,000 to foreigners wishing to be initiated.[33] One suspects that the commercialized, feel-good Santeria described in self-help books and tourist brochures has little to do with the real thing.

There are many stories about the *orishas*, and it is easy to read them like Greek myths, which they loosely resemble. But the *orishas* are not gods like Zeus or Athena, and the Western bipolarities of good and evil are largely irrelevant. *Santeros* (followers of Santeria strive to attain *ashé*,[34] described as a state of order and balance in the universe. When a person experiences imbalance in his life, he consults a *babalao* to learn how to restore harmony. The *orishas* empower believers to attain this balance.

Another difference with Western religions is that many *santeros* see no difficulty in being practicing Catholics, or following other traditions such as *palo de monte*. Of course, Santeria is not limited to blacks, and the pilgrims visiting Rincón are a racially diverse group. Whereas before the Revolution many white, middle-class Habaneros practiced Santeria in secret, now they do so more openly.

The Cuban government has varied in its approach to Santeria but, due to its popularity, it cannot be ignored. During the early years of the Revolution, all forms of religious expression were discouraged, but this changed during the 1990s. According to journalist Andres Oppenheimer, the government tried to co-opt Santeria in order to promote tourism and undermine the growing influence of the Catholic church. How well it has succeeded in this effort is debatable. The reverse may well have taken place, since many communist party members have become initiates.

But to many, Babalu Ayé will always be identified with the song immortalized on *I Love Lucy*. In 1937, Desi Arnaz Jr. played in a nightclub with Xavier Cugat's band in Miami Beach and soon had the crowd hopping in a conga line. "Babalu" became Arnaz's signature song and, through the new medium of television, reached millions of Americans. "Babalu" was written by composer Margarita Lecuona in the 1920s, and describes a *bembé*, a Santeria ritual. The celebrant asks for *un cabo de tabaco* (a cigar butt) and *un jarrito de aguardiente* (a glass of cane brandy), both traditional gifts to the *orisha*.

It is the ultimate transculturation: from Don Tabaco and Doña Azucar to Babalu Ayé and *I Love Lucy*.

# CHAPTER 5

# Priests and Poets

## On the Prado

*As it was a public holiday, I accepted an invitation to take a ride in a volanta.*
—The Reverend Abiel Abbot, 1828

Leaving Habana Vieja, if you enter the Parque Central and turn right, you have before you one of the most spectacular vistas in Havana. It is the Prado, a majestic boulevard nearly a mile long that stretches from the park to the Malecón. On Neptuno Street, two black lions of cast iron guard the entrance to the raised walkway of inlaid marble, lined with Spanish laurel trees and streetlights decorated with griffins. There is traffic to either side, and the cars appear to be heading into the water, for the Prado looks directly across the harbor at the lighthouse of El Morro.

The Prado was once the commercial hub of Centro Habana, teeming with stores, hotels, and cafés. On the corner of Virtudes Street was the American Club of Havana, locus of the expatriate colony, and across from it was the Wonder Bar, frequented by Dr. Hasselbacher in *Our Man in Havana*. On Neptuno was the Miami Restaurant, a favorite of Martín Fox, owner of the Tropicana nightclub. Farther down was the Teatro Fausto, a movie theater; the first Cadillac dealership in Cuba; and the offices of Pan American. The Prado was famed for all-female orchestras, such as the Orquesta Anacaona (composed of Chinese mulattas), which played in the cafés. At the water's edge was once a *glorieta*, a neoclassical pavilion used for concerts, though it was regrettably torn down in the 1930s. While most of the remaining buildings are of stolid limestone, with broad porticoes facing the street, there are occasional arabesques of art nouveau, such as the old Hotel Regis, and the tiled facade of the Arab Cultural Center on Trocadero. Most are shuttered or anonymously empty, except for a swish boutique selling high-end cosmetics that would not be out of place on the Champs Elysées. Much of Centro Habana has a tired, dusty feel to it, as the wave of restoration has not yet swept across from Habana Vieja. It takes a leap of the imagination to picture the Prado thronged with pedestrians carrying shopping bags, rather like the Ramblas in Barcelona, which it resembles.

First known as the Alameda Extramuros, it was the first street built outside the walls. During the nineteenth century, it was renamed the Alameda de Isabel II in honor of the Spanish queen, and in 1904, it became the Paseo Martí. But to Habaneros, it was always the Paseo del Prado, perhaps echoing the boulevard in Madrid between the Cibeles Fountain and Atocha Station. Early in the nineteenth century, the Prado became *the* fashionable place to see and be seen, as wealthy families promenaded in their *volantas*, ethereal-looking carriages on oversized wheels drawn by a single horse with a mounted coachman.* Engravings from the period show the coachmen dressed in elaborate livery, with a top hat, waistcoat, and black leather gaiters. In 1828, the Reverend Abiel Abbot, a native of Andover, Massachusetts, visited Havana and described the Prado as:

> about a mile long and wide enough for carriages to drive by side by side so close to each other that acquaintances can exchange greetings, which the ladies can do with a gesture of their fans. . . . There are pavements and benches all along the way. . . . and the whole length of the [Prado]is planted with beautiful trees. Five bands placed at various points along the way play exquisite music.[1]

Two years later, another visitor to Havana was Eugene Ney, the son of Napoléon's favorite general.[2] Having different interests from the Yankee pastor, Ney notes that beautiful women were at the windows of the houses along the way, eager to see the show. The *paseo* took place between five and six in the early evening. The *volantas* passed in single file in either direction, beginning at a fountain decorated with a statue of Neptune and

---

[1] A *quitrin* was the deluxe version of the *volanta*, with a leather top that could be slid open or shut, depending on the weather.

passing a statue of Carlos III, near the Plaza de Toros, or bullring. This was located on the southeast corner of the Campo de Marte (now the Parque de Fraternidad, south of the Capitolio). In case the flirtations grew indecorous, a squad of cavalrymen kept order. For the *paseo*, the Habaneros dressed to the nines in the latest fashions from Paris: the men with frock coats, cravats, and white breeches, and the women in gowns of crinoline or muslin. From there, the *volantas* proceeded to the Plaza de Armas, where yet another concert was given by a military band. Ney describes the latter much as it is today, with flowers and fountains and stone benches to rest in the shade.

A well-appointed carriage was not just a status symbol but a necessity, the Frenchman adds, since Havana had the dirtiest streets ever seen and no gentleman would be caught dead on foot. The need for an expensive *volanta* reflects the vast fortunes created from slaves and sugar, which were transforming Havana. In the three centuries since its foundation, the city had changed from a frontier settlement to one of the largest cities in the Americas, with a population of 130,000. Now the descendants of the hardy *vecinos*, the early Habaneros who fended off attacks from corsairs, delighted in luxury and refinement.

A promenade on the Prado, 1853. In the background is the Fuente de la India. (Courtesy of Emilio Cueto)

Another visitor was Countess Merlin. Born in 1789 to an aristocratic Cuban family, she married a French general and lived much of her life in France, but returned to Havana in 1840. The account of her stay, in the form of letters to her family, paints an intimate portrait of life in Havana and earned her the title of the "Cuban Sheherazade."[3] In Havana, the countess stayed with her wealthy uncle Juan Montalvo, in the mansion known as the Casa de Mateo Pedroso, now the Palacio de Artesanias on Cuba Street. Countess Merlin recalls that the household had one hundred black slaves and a French cook. She delighted in the same *paseos* on the Prado that Abbot and Ney took, but noted that it was the one opportunity for women to leave the house. Black women had considerably more freedom, "strutting along in the middle of the street, swinging their hips, with their headscarves, their bracelets, and a cigar between their lips." Slavery was so prevalent that she declared: "There are no people in Havana, only masters and slaves."[4]

The Prado bears the undeniable stamp of Miguel Tacón y Rosique. Serving as captain-general from 1834 to 1838, he has a mixed reputation. Though regarded as a despot, Tacón literally made the trains run on time, inaugurating the first railroad, and embarked on an ambitious program to beautify Havana. In addition to remodeling the Prado, he paved Obispo and O'Reilly streets (until then, only Empedrado Street had been paved) and established the first police force and fire department. His brother Francisco was the Spanish ambassador to Washington, D.C., and he was influenced by Pierre L'Enfant's neoclassical design for the new capital.[5] In addition to remodeling the Prado—Tacón added the raised marble walkway and streetlights—he built a broad avenue running west from the city gates to the castle of El Principe. Named the Alameda Carlos III, it soon became known as the Paseo de Tacón.

But Tacón's greatest project was the grandiose opera house at the southern end of the Prado, predictably called the Teatro Tacón. Behind its Doric exterior, it was as luxurious as anything in Europe, painted white and gold with an enormous crystal chandelier and magnificent armchairs. A stagehand at the theater was an Italian inventor named Antonio Meucci. In 1849, in order to communicate backstage, he devised a way to transmit speech through copper wire; Meucci later moved to the United States and is regarded by some as the inventor of the telephone. During the early days of the twentieth century, Habaneros were crazy for opera, and Enrico Caruso and Sarah Bernhardt performed there. The theater is now contained within the Centro Gallego, which was built around it in 1915, and is known as the Gran Teatro.

Despite this architectural legacy, Tacón was bitterly resented. A sixty-year-old widower when he arrived in Havana, he was an ardent Spanish patriot who had fought Bolivar's forces in Colombia and Peru. His mandate was to keep the island under Spanish control by any means, and he brutally repressed any stirrings of independence, censoring the press and ruling with an iron fist. Perhaps because of his experience with the rebels, he mistrusted the Cubans and excluded them from positions of power, preferring the company of Spanish merchants, who made him extremely wealthy. Tacón's high-handedness did much to polarize the *peninsulares* (Spanish-born) from the *criollos* (native-born, or creoles).

It was a breach that would not be healed until the twentieth century.

Not unlike the Iron Curtain in the 1980s, the Spanish imperial system was under significant strain in the early 1800s. It broke down altogether in 1805, when the Spanish navy was decimated at the Battle of Trafalgar. Communication between Spain and its colonies became increasingly difficult, and in the following year, Cuba relied entirely on non-Spanish vessels. But the unthinkable happened in 1808, when Napoléon forced Ferdinand VII to abdicate and placed his brother Joseph on the Spanish throne. Two years later, a provisional junta was established in Caracas, and Spanish officials were deported. The same occurred in Buenos Aires and Bogotá, and within a few years only Cuba and Puerto Rico remained of Spain's once-grand empire.

Why did Cuba not gain its independence earlier? The Venezuelans had urged Cubans to join in the revolt, but the Havana junta rejected the proposal, earning the title of *la siempre leal isla de Cuba* (the ever faithful island of Cuba). But this loyalty had more to do with self-interest than love for Spain. The memory of the slave revolts in Saint-Domingue was still fresh, and many Cubans feared the same would happen were Spanish authority to disappear. The Spanish minister Calatrava summed it up rather smugly: "The fear which the Cubans have of the blacks is the most secure means which Spain has to guarantee her dominion over this island."

This anxiety seemed justified when in 1812 a far-reaching slave revolt was organized by a freed black named José Antonio Aponte, a carpenter in

Havana. Deeply religious, Aponte saw himself as a latter-day Moses, and hoped to lead his people out of captivity.[6] In addition, Aponte was a leader of his Yoruban *cabildo*, and much of the conspiracy was conducted under the guise of Santeria rituals. Aponte made contact with other *cabildos* around the island and even secured the support of Haitian revolutionaries. But two of his coconspirators confessed under torture, and Aponte was arrested by the shrewd captain-general. There were minor uprisings around the island and a few sugarcane fields were burned, but they were ruthlessly put down. Aponte was hanged and his head was exhibited in the Plaza de Armas.

In 1823, another conspiracy was uncovered, even more dangerous. It was organized by José Francisco Lemus, an ex-soldier. He called his organization the *Soles y Rayos de Bolivar* (Suns and Rays of Bolivar). Just as Aponte had used the *cabildos* to hide his conspiracy, Lemus organized secret cells within Masonic lodges. He planned to establish an independent Republic of Cubanacán (a Taino name for the center of the island) and found support among many intellectuals disenchanted with events in Spain. But Spanish spies had infiltrated the cells, and just a few days before the planned uprising, Lemus and his lieutenants were imprisoned. Some of his supporters were able to flee, including the precocious poet José María Heredia, who had joined the revolt through a Masonic lodge in Matanzas.

From that point on, Cuba was garrisoned with forty thousand troops. In effect, martial law was declared, a condition that would continue until the War of Independence. A decade after the *Sol y Rayos de Bolivar* conspiracy was betrayed, Tacón arrived and continued the repressive policies of his predecessors. Despite the vast wealth that flowed into Havana and the promenades along the Prado, there was a deep undercurrent of bitterness toward the *peninsulares*. A visitor to the island commented: "The loyalty of Cuba is indeed a royal fiction. As well might a highwayman praise the generosity of a rich traveler who surrenders his purse, watch, and diamonds, at the muzzle of a pistol." [7]

Beneath the gracious surface of life in Havana, the waters were roiling.

## VARELA'S CONVERSION

*I keep vigil when all sleep and toil when all repose.*

—Father Felix Varela

In January 1998, Pope John Paul II visited Havana. For Americans, the impact of this groundbreaking visit was muffled when the news anchors of the three major U.S. networks left Havana to cover the sordid Monica Lewinsky sex scandal, but the attention of the world remained riveted on Havana as the pope celebrated an open-air mass with Castro in attendance. The delicate maneuvering between high pontiff and *commandante en jefe* had begun two years earlier, when Castro visited the Vatican. Each wanted something: Castro hoped to enlist the pope's support, while the latter hoped to invigorate the ailing church in Cuba. To some extent, both succeeded. The pope spoke against the embargo, saying that "no nation can live in isolation," and Cuban Catholics received a spiritual shot in the arm. One year after the pope's visit, I found the churches full, teeming with young people.

But the pope also praised "freedom of expression" and "freedom of association," scarce commodities in Cuba. He did so by invoking Father Felix Varela, the nineteenth century priest who is a symbol of political as well as religious freedom, and described him as "the foundation stone of Cuban national identity."

The message was not lost on Castro, a keen student of Cuban history. Varela's remains are enshrined in the University of Havana, and he is regarded as a secular, not a religious, figure—a precursor of the Apostle of Freedom, José Martí. Yet Varela's principled, nonviolent resistance to tyranny and his reluctant embrace of exile have made him an ambivalent figure in the pantheon of the Revolution and an inspiration to dissidents.

Varela was born in Havana to a stalwart Castilian military family in 1788. Orphaned at the age of six, the boy was raised by his grandfather Don Bartolomé Morales, commander of the Spanish garrison in St. Augustine, Florida. The massive, brooding fortress of San Marcos was Varela's childhood home, and he might well have chosen a military career had he not felt the call of the priesthood. At the age of fourteen, he returned to Havana to enroll in the Seminario de San Carlos y San Ambrosio, adjacent to the cathedral.

The seminary had been run by the Jesuits until their expulsion in 1767 and was Cuba's most progressive seat of higher learning. The University of Havana, founded in 1728, was mired in stodgy Aristotelian scholasticism. In contrast, students in San Carlos received a thorough grounding in literature, ethics, and law. Varela was fortunate to have as a mentor Bishop Juan José Diaz de Espada. This formidable figure gathered around him a host of independent thinkers who brought much-needed educational reform. Varela was ordained by Bishop Espada in 1811 and promptly joined the faculty of San Carlos.

At a time when violent revolution was sweeping the entire continent, Varela launched its intellectual equivalent in Havana. Encouraged by the bishop, the young professor galvanized the seminary with new courses in social sciences and physics. A fluent writer and talented orator, Varela developed an eclectic philosophy that stressed critical analysis and the scientific method. In addition, he was a talented violin player and helped found the Philharmonic Society of Havana. Varela soon took the momentous step of teaching courses in Spanish. (Until then, all courses had been in Latin.) In 1820, Bishop Espada proposed that he teach a course in the new and controversial field of constitutional law. Before long, Varela's classes were packed with students, among them José María Heredia.

In just a few years, the physically frail Varela had become an intellectual giant. Had his career ended then, he would have been known as Cuba's most influential philosopher, the man who "first taught us to think." But because of his expertise in constitutional law, he was ordered by Bishop Espada to lead the delegation pleading Cuba's case in Madrid. There Varela advocated limiting the autocratic powers of the Spanish captain-generals, who ruled Cuba as private fiefs, and maintaining ties between Spain and the newly liberated republics in South America. His most radical idea was to eliminate slavery, and he proposed a plan to reimburse the owners and diversify the Cuban economy. In this regard, Varela's ideas were far ahead of his time and were well-received. This made him a marked man when the Spanish king Ferdinand VII overturned the Constitution of 1812 with the help of French troops. Varela and the other Cuban delegates barely escaped, coming under fire from a French warship. Nor could he return to Cuba after the crackdown on the *Sol y Rayos de Bolívar* conspiracy, though Varela had no part in it and condemned armed rebellion. In December 1823, he arrived in New York.

Exile was difficult for Varela. Other Cubans had arrived in New York after the aborted conspiracy, including his former student Heredia. But the cold weather threatened Varela's precarious health, and he spoke no English. Moreover, his experience as a delegate left him disillusioned, and he now realized Cuba had no alternative but to cut its ties to Spain. The die was cast when Varela published a magazine called *El Habanero*, which was smuggled into Havana and widely circulated. Overtly political, it sought to mold public opinion with statements such as: "The indepen-

dence of Cuba is not an object of choice but a necessity." *El Habanero*
caused an uproar. The Marqués de Vives, the captain-general who had so
ruthlessly quashed the conspiracy, felt threatened and sent an assassin
named "One-Eyed Morejon" to murder Varela in New York. According
to one account, the asthmatic priest encountered the thug and calmly
talked him out of it.[8]

In all, seven issues of *El Habanero* were published, and Varela's biographers disagree as to why it was discontinued. It had been officially
banned, and Vives imposed strict penalties on anyone found reading it.
But most likely Varela was horrified by the idea that he might incite his
readers to violence. Although he kept abreast of events in Cuba and continued to support the cause of independence through his writing, Varela
focused his prodigious energy on pastoral duties. Nonetheless, the Spanish crown still regarded Varela as dangerous and condemned him to death
*in absentia*.

The conversion of Varela from the intellectually precocious law professor
in Havana to a parish priest in New York is nothing short of astounding.
Varela lived thirty years in the United States, nearly half his life, and became a leader of New York's growing Catholic community as the vicar
general of the archdiocese. Working tirelessly in the hospitals, he risked
his own life when a cholera epidemic swept through the city. Later he acquired a church building on Chambers Street with the help of John Del-
monico, the celebrated restaurateur. Varela named it the Church of the
Transfiguration, and it was to become a beacon for the poor Irish immigrants who had begun to arrive in great numbers.*

Varela genuinely loved the United States, but through his writings
runs a melancholy strain of homesickness. Among the "frozen lakes" of
New York he dreamed of "the garden of the Antilles where all is vital. I
see leafy trees, restless streams, thick-topped mountains, and flowering
plains." In 1834, a general amnesty was announced, and Varela was invited to return despite the death sentence. But his old mentor, Bishop
Espada, had died and the constitutional law course at San Carlos had

---

[1] The church still stands today, in what is now New York's rapidly gentrifying Chinatown, and a plaque describes Varela as a "forerunner in the field of social welfare."

been abolished. Rather than compromise his principles, Varela declined the offer.

In 1850, his health declined, and he spent the last three years of his life in St. Augustine, where he had grown up when it was still a Spanish outpost. Varela died on February 25, 1853, a month after José Martí was born.

⌐

Varela's star has steadily risen since then. In 1911, his remains were exhumed and taken to Havana with much pomp. They were placed in a marble urn atop a pedestal in the Great Hall of the University of Havana, where they remain today. A statue of Varela was erected on the corner of Zanja and Dragones streets, in the heart of the Barrio Chino. In 1953, the politically charged year after Batista's coup ended the Cuban Republic, the centenary of Martí's birth and Varela's death were celebrated together. Varela's works were reprinted in Havana after the Revolution, and the Cuban government created the Order of Felix Varela, the highest honor given for achievement in the cultural sphere.

But Varela's name would become linked to another struggle altogether. On the eve of the pope's visit to Havana, a dissident named Oswaldo Payá started the Varela Project, a grassroots, nonviolent movement to change Cuba from within. According to the Cuban Constitution of 1976, a petition of ten thousand signatures was sufficient to call for a national referendum. In 2002, Payá took the unprecedented step of presenting eleven thousand signatures to the Cuban National Assembly and called for a plebiscite on human rights issues such as those mentioned by John Paul II: free speech and free assembly. The Varela Project was championed by Jimmy Carter, who visited Havana that same year and praised Payá in a speech broadcast nationwide. In December, Payá was permitted to travel to Strasbourg to receive the European Parliament's prestigious Sakharov Prize, given annually to those who defend human rights and democracy. By 2003, Payá claimed to have thirty thousand more signatures.

Like Varela himself, Payá is an atypical revolutionary. As a teenager in Cuba, he demonstrated against the Soviet invasion of Czechoslovakia in 1968 and was sent to a work camp in the Isle of Pines. There he developed a strong religious faith and came to the conclusion that the system could only be changed through nonviolent means. Payá refused to leave Cuba during the Mariel boatlift in 1980 and instead founded the faith-based Christian Liberation Movement, today the most popular dissident group in Cuba. Despite harassment from Castro's Orwellian security services, he gathered signatures from around the island without access to mass media, relying on word of mouth. Shrewdly, Payá distanced himself from hard-line exiles in Miami and refused to endorse the U.S. embargo, which made it difficult to claim that he was a CIA agent, a standard accusation against dissidents. Instead Payá framed the struggle in a different light: "This has finally become a duel between power and spirit in Cuba," he told reporter Tim Padgett.[9]

Castro's response was equally shrewd. He held massive demonstrations in support of the regime and organized a referendum of his own, which declared socialism to be "irrevocable." Then he arrested seventy-five of Cuba's top dissidents, fifty of whom were Payá's lieutenants, sentencing them to lengthy prison terms. Many were brutalized by "rapid action brigades," mobs who gathered outside their homes.

It can be argued that the Varela Project accomplished little more than landing its supporters in jail. But the gauntlet was thrown down, and Castro dared not imprison Payá, perhaps due to fear of the international reaction. Meanwhile, the Christian Liberation Movement continues to grow, and Varela's example of nonviolent, faith-based resistance may prove more revolutionary than ever. In 2005, the Ladies in White, the wives of the seventy-five imprisoned dissidents who hold weekly protest marches through Havana, received the Sakharov Prize.

Whatever the outcome in Cuba, Varela eventually may be remembered for something else. In 1985, the wheels of the Vatican began turning in the process of canonization. In 2003, Monsignor Octavio Cisneros presented a document to church leaders known as a *positio*, the first step in beatification, which makes a candidate eligible for sainthood.[10]

"I think what made him special was his openness to do what he had to do at the moment when it had to be done with the grace of God," said Cisneros.

Currently, investigators are researching Varela's life to identify a miracle, which is necessary for beatification. Yet another miracle is necessary for canonization. The process often takes hundreds of years. This should be comforting to the Cuban government, which must find the prospect of Saint Felix Varela uniquely embarrassing.

## HEREDIA'S FRACASO

*When will the novel of my life end, so that reality can begin?*

—José María Heredia

Varela's most celebrated pupil in Havana was José María Heredia. His ringing, lyrical verses, full of classical allusions and symbolic metaphors, do not translate well, and he is not likely to be read outside of a college course on Latin American poetry. But like his mentor, Heredia continues to inspire Cubans today.

In *Novela de mi Vida* (Novel of My Life), novelist Leonardo Padura fictionalizes the first encounter between poet and priest. Heredia, then a precocious adolescent, interrupts Varela's violin playing to show him a poem. I came to know Padura, one of Cuba's finest contemporary writers, through his detective novels in which inspector Mario Conde solves crimes in a bleak, dangerous Havana. These gritty narratives offer stinging social commentary—in one novel, Conde investigates corruption on the part of a government official—yet Padura is published by UNEAC, the Cuban writer's union. He described *Novela de mi Vida* to me as "a dialogue between past and present." It contrasts the story of a troubled exile who returns to present-day Havana with Heredia's own life. It is an apt comparison, for Heredia was the first of many Cuban writers in exile.

Heredia was born in Santiago de Cuba in 1803, the son of Dominicans who emigrated to escape the slave revolt. His father was a magistrate who served in various outposts of the Spanish empire, including Caracas, Mexico, and Pensacola. Heredia was of delicate health and led a bookish, peripatetic childhood. He studied law in Havana, where he encountered Varela, but from an early age, he was stricken with the poetic muse. His early efforts were overheated, plaintive sonnets dedicated to Lesbia or Belisa (in reality, Isabel Rueda y Ponce de León, his first love). Heredia's world was that of the gallant promenades on the Prado and evening concerts in the Plaza de Armas, and Isabel must have been one of the delectable charmers gazing out the window as his *volanta* passed by. Those poems and a play, *Eduardo IV*, established Heredia's reputation in Havana's literary circles while he was still a teenager.

It was through a Masonic lodge called the *Orden de los Caballeros Racionales* (Order of Rational Gentlemen) that Heredia learned of José Francisco Lemus and became embroiled in the *Sol y Rayos de Bolívar* in 1823. The extent of his participation remains unclear. Heredia enlisted in the militia in Matanzas, where his uncle was a lawyer, and may have received military training, but there was never a more unlikely conspirator. Most likely his involvement resembled his flirtations on the Prado, brief and illusory. But when arrests were made in Matanzas, Heredia was denounced and a warrant issued for his arrest. Heredia remained in hiding for several months, and the result was *La Estrella de Cuba* (The Star of Cuba), a stirring anthem of revolution that paints the conspirators as heroes betrayed by cowards. When the dust settled, he escaped to Boston, dressed as a sailor. He was not yet twenty years old.

From there, Heredia continued to New York, where he was reunited with his former professor, Varela. Like him, Heredia spoke no English and was unaccustomed to the cold. The young poet supported himself by giving Spanish lessons and may have collaborated in writing *El Habanero*. Following a sightseeing trip to Niagara Falls, Heredia wrote what remains his best-known poem, *Oda al Niagara*. That these cataracts, forever tagged as a 1950s honeymoon destination, inspired such a rousing elegy seems faintly comical today. But Heredia used the majestic waterfall as a symbolic backdrop for man's helplessness in the face of nature's brute force. Even in the face of such splendor, however, Heredia could not help but long for Cuba's royal palms. The poem was astonishingly influential in Latin America and is still regarded as the finest example of Romanticism in the Spanish language.

Through such poems, and his connection with the *Sol y Rayos de Bolivar*, Heredia had become a celebrity and was able to obtain a passport for Mexico in 1825. Many of his coconspirators had fled there, and perhaps Heredia hoped to continue the struggle and eventually return to Cuba. But nothing came of it, and Heredia became a magistrate, much like his father. His muse, once so fecund, had left him and he no longer wrote poetry.

By 1836, Heredia was down and out. He had lost favor with the Mexican government and was struggling to make a living. After much soul-searching, he decided to accept Tacón's offer of amnesty and see his ailing mother in Havana. To this end, he wrote a letter to Tacón renouncing his sympathies for the independence movement, and received permission to return.

It was a painful visit. His letter had been disseminated, and he was reviled as a traitor by the same literary circles that had once lionized him. Worst of all was the rejection of his childhood friend Domingo Del Monte, who refused to see him but sent him a letter calling him a "fallen angel," a phrase from one of Heredia's early poems. Heredia stayed in Havana less than three months and returned heartbroken to Mexico.

The last three years of Heredia's life were spent mostly trying to make ends meet. He found humiliating employment as the editor of a government-sponsored newspaper. His health failed him and he died of tuberculosis in 1839, at the age of thirty-five.

If Heredia's brief, star-crossed life seems a cautionary tale as to the involvement of Cuban poets in politics, it would not be heeded. It is a story that would repeat itself again and again, from Juan Clemente Zenéa, executed by firing squad in 1871, to Heberto Padilla, imprisoned and forced to recant his views in 1971, to Reinaldo Arenas, who found himself reviled when he fled Cuba in 1980. Unlike Varela, who found vast reserves of spiritual strength in exile, Heredia was destroyed by it. It is this failure—neither profound nor heroic, but ultimately banal—that fascinates writers in Cuba today.

Critic Pedro Henríquez Ureña called him *el poeta del fracaso* (the poet of failure).[11] But "failure" is an inadequate translation of *fracaso*, which has particular resonance in Cuba. A *fracaso* is a failure, to be sure, but an unredemptive one. One cannot draw solace from a *fracaso*, which is generally one's own fault. Though self-inflicted, it is not a suicide. A *fracaso* comes from placing oneself in the path of trouble, of bad luck, of an immovable obstacle, of another *fracaso*. They often tumble into each other, like dominoes. In a *fracaso*, things fall apart, they crumble, they disintegrate. There is no remedy to a *fracaso*, and no moral lesson to be drawn from it. Therefore, *fracasos* often repeat themselves, again and again. The victim of a *fracaso* is not to be pitied but mocked, because *fracasos* can often be quite funny, even to the victims themselves: ¡*Coño, que fracaso!*

If Heredia remained a "fallen angel" to his contemporaries, his reputation would soar a generation later. In a famous speech given in New York in 1889, Martí cited Heredia as an inspiration, compared him to Bolivar, and proclaimed him "the first poet of Latin America." If Heredia is not Cuba's greatest poet, he has certainly become the best-known one, eclipsing Martí himself. Yet like Varela, he fits uneasily into the pantheon of the Revolution. Many of his poems cut a little too close to the bone nearly two hundred years later. In *Himno del Destierro* (Hymn of Exile), written while Heredia was en route from New York to Mexico in 1825, he longs for Cuba to be *libre y pura* (free and pure). It is easy to see why Martí identified with him, since he was another poet who lived much of his life in exile.

Despite his literary stature, there are no monuments to Heredia on the Prado, where the languid, lovely Habaneras in their *volantas* inspired his love poems, nor anywhere else in Havana that I could find.

# CHAPTER 6

## The Apostle of Freedom
### Martí in Havana

*I am sorry to be behind bars, but my imprisonment is very useful to me. It has given me plenty of lessons for my life, which I foresee will be short, and I will not fail to make use of them.*

—José Martí, age sixteen, in a letter to his mother

*I*n March 1949, two U.S. sailors defiled José Martí. After a night of carousing at the nearby Floridita, they relieved themselves on his statue in the Parque Central. Flanked by royal palms, the monument depicts Martí pointing in the direction of the bar, as if demanding a daiquiri for himself. The ugly Americans were thrown in the hoosegow, creating a diplomatic incident. This incident is immortalized in the Museo de la Revolucion (formerly the Presidential Palace) a block from the Prado. Beneath a grainy snapshot of the drunken seamen clambering up Martí is this caption:

*The Yankee marines were closely connected to gambling and the proliferation of vices in Cuba's capitalist society.*

It just goes to show that in Havana, you don't mess with José Martí.

The Apostle of Freedom, as he is officially known, is everywhere you turn. Havana's airport is named after him, as is the national library and myriad other institutions throughout the island. Perhaps the most enduring image of him is the statue in the Parque Central that survived the onslaught of the U.S. Navy. Sculpted by José Vilalta de Saavedra from

Carrara marble, it was unveiled in 1905 by Cuba's first president, Tomás Estrada Palma. The most monolithic Martí is in the Plaza de la Revolución, a lamentably stylized version fifty-nine feet tall, built in 1958. Martí sits in repose, and behind him is a 330-foot obelisk topped with radio antennas and inevitably circled by buzzards. Supposedly its design was based on an advertisement for Schenley's whiskey that appeared in the 1939 World's Fair. The most recent one was erected by the Protestidromo* on the Malecón. It is a bronze, broad-shouldered Martí holding a small child (presumably Elian González) and pointing reproachfully at the horizon. As if these weren't enough, there is a bust of Martí in front of virtually every primary school on the island, usually made of white plaster, and many more Martís look out at you from stamps, coins, and billboards.

Ironically, few of them resemble the man himself. His most famous photograph, taken shortly before his death at the age of forty-two, reveals a physically frail man—he was just over five feet tall and suffered from a variety of ailments. Martí wears his habitual black frock coat, as if in mourning for Cuba. He is balding, with wispy dark hair framing a high, domed forehead, and a bushy mustache that nearly eclipses his chin. Most memorable, though, are his eyes, almond-shaped beneath slender eyebrows, with a mocking cast to them. As diverse as they are, the images of the Apostle throughout Havana are all frightfully solemn and miss one essential detail: Martí had a wicked sense of humor.

If Martí the revolutionary icon is omnipresent, little remains of the man in Havana, perhaps because he lived most of his life in exile.

Martí's parents were Spaniards. His father was from Valencia, an artillery sergeant at the fortress of La Cabaña, and his mother from Tenerife in the Canary Islands. The house where he was born in 1853 is on the western edge of Habana Vieja, across from the railway station and the surviving fragments of the city walls. Today it is a museum with a number of Martí's personal effects, such as letters, a lock of his hair, and a tailored replica of his famous frock coat. Built of yellow stucco with blue trim, it gives an idea of what a typical middle-class home in Havana was like mid-

---

[1] This is a futuristic stadium built for mass demonstrations in front of the U.S. Interests Section during the Elian González crisis in 1999.

The monument to the Apostle of Freedom at the Parque Central, erected in 1905. (Author's collection)

century, with shotgun rooms clustered around a narrow courtyard. Known as Pepe, Martí was the couple's first child and only son. They were to have seven daughters, two of whom died in infancy.

Martí spent the first four years of his life in that house. The growing family moved when his father became a policeman in the district of the

Templete, near the Plaza de Armas. At the age of nine, Martí had a seminal experience that he would later describe in his poetry. During a trip to the countryside with his father, he witnessed Africans being unloaded from a slave ship and was horrified to see the corpse of one who tried to escape, hanging from a ceiba tree.[1] His hatred of slavery was strengthened when Martí fell under the sway of Rafael María Mendive, his teacher at the San Pablo School located on the Prado. Mendive was himself a poet and took a personal interest in the boy, offering to support him when his father threatened to pull him out of school.

Passionately influenced by Cuba's struggle for independence, Martí was arrested for having written an unsent letter accusing a friend of being a traitor. At the age of sixteen, he was condemned to six years hard labor at the San Lazaro stone quarry. This damaged his health, and for the rest of his life Martí suffered from hernias caused by the chain that ran from his ankle to his waist. He also wore an *anillo de hierro* (iron ring) forged from his manacles with *Cuba* engraved on it, which, together with the frock coat, entered Cuban political mythology. After a year, his father used his connections to get him transferred to the Isle of Pines, where he lived under house arrest in the home of a family friend. A few months later, Martí was permitted to leave the country and continue his education in Spain.

This experience was the basis for *Political Prison in Cuba*, a searing indictment of the colonial regime that Martí soon published in Madrid. Still chilling a century and a half later is his description of a twelve-year-old boy worked to death in prison. Martí earned a law degree at the University of Zaragoza and in 1875 went to Mexico, where his family was now living. Martí tried to establish himself in Mexican literary circles, but when his parents decided to return to Havana, he joined them under the false name of Julián Pérez. It was not a very convincing disguise, being a combination of his middle name and his mother's maiden name, but it appears that his father's friends kept him out of trouble. Yet despite his long absence from the city, he soon grew depressed with what he saw there. Spain had clamped down harshly on dissenters, and the revolt was petering out from exhaustion. Martí left after only a month and a half.

He then found employment as a schoolteacher in Guatemala, where we see another side of Martí, that of a lover and poet. Despite his infirmities, Martí was somehow irresistible to women, and he began an affair with Maria Granados, a daughter of Guatemala's ex-president.[2] But Martí was already engaged to a Cuban woman, Carmen Zayas-Bazán, whom he married the following year. After the wedding, Maria drowned, and Martí wrote about it in his melancholy poem *La Niña de Guatemala*.

Now with a family of his own to support, Martí returned to Havana after the end of the war in 1878. His wife was expecting a child, and at her urging he attempted to make a go of it as a lawyer, but had little success. Like Heredia, Martí felt uncomfortable in Havana after several years of exile. "I was not born to be happy in this land," he lamented. Before long, the lure of conspiracy proved irresistible. Martí was quickly betrayed and deported.

This time he decided to try his luck in New York, where he met Charles Dana Anderson, the powerful publisher. Anderson invited Martí to contribute to his literary magazine *The Hour*, launching his journalistic career. Before long, Martí was writing articles on everything from current events to art exhibits, written in Spanish, French, and halting English. Regarding New York, it was love at first sight. Recording his first impressions, he wrote: "I am, at last, in a country where everyone looks like his own master. One can breathe freely, freedom being here the foundation, the shield, the essence of life. One can be proud of his species here."[3]

Martí admired the diligent, hardworking New Yorkers and renounced the "lazy life and poetical inutility" of Europe, and perhaps his own life up until that point.

If he had one complaint, it was the women. Martí complained that he found no solace among the fair sex of New York, and deplored "their calculated coldness, their contempt of passions, their dry, practical notions of life."

Despite this, Martí would make New York his home for the next fifteen years. He would not return to Cuba until 1895, and then only briefly.

## GRITO DE YARA

Martí had come of age during the uprising that became known as the Ten Year War. It began on October 10, 1868, when Carlos Manuel de Céspedes freed the slaves on his plantation in eastern Cuba and added them to his army of 147 men.[4] This is referred to as the *Grito de Yara* (Shout of Yara) after the nearby town where Hatuey had been executed by the Spaniards more than three centuries earlier. Ten days later, Céspedes and his followers had forced the surrender of the Spanish garrison at Bayamo and raised the flag of rebellion.

The taking of Bayamo inspired Cuba's national anthem, "La Bayamesa," which was written by Pedro Figueredo, one of Céspedes's lieutenants:

*Al combate corred Bayameses,*
*Que la patria os contempla orgullosa;*
*No temáis una muerte gloriosa,*
*Que morir por la Patria es vivir.*

[To battle, Bayameses
As your country proudly looks on.
Fear not a glorious death
To die for your country is to live.]

By the end of the year, Céspedes had twelve thousand men at arms and the rebels had taken Holguin and Camaguey.

Initially, things looked bleak for the *peninsulares*. Captain-General Francisco Lersundi had only about seven thousand troops, many of whom were ill and could not be mobilized immediately. The timing of the revolt was propitious, since Spain had troubles of its own. The reactionary government of the Spanish queen Isabella II had been overthrown, and military defeats in Santo Domingo and Peru had drained the treasury. But Lersundi remained loyal to Isabella II and counterattacked. His forces engaged the rebels in January and took back Bayamo. Céspedes's rebels still controlled much of eastern Cuba, so the Spaniards built a thirty-mile defensive line called the *trocha* to cut him off. It consisted of earthworks, wooden palisades, and forty-three small forts running from one end of the island to another at its narrowest point, from Morón to Júcaro.[5] Remains of it can still be found near Ciego de Avila. As the war dragged on, neither side could gain a decisive advantage.

Two outstanding military leaders emerged whom Martí would later come to know well. The first was Máximo Gómez, a Dominican soldier who enlisted as a sergeant in Céspedes's army. His mounted statue now guards the entrance to Havana Harbor, behind the castle of La Punta.

The second was Antonio Maceo, a mulatto groom born in Santiago de Cuba. Known as the Titan of Bronze, he has a statue of his own, at the other end of the Malecón. Maceo was the leader of the many blacks who joined the rebels, known as the *mambises*. According to Fernando Ortiz, this word comes from the Congolese *mbi* and was used by the contemptuous Spaniards to describe the slaves in Santo Domingo. The term spread to Cuba and was later used by the blacks themselves as a point of honor. It is estimated that only about a quarter of the rebels had guns. Many fought barefoot, with machetes or spears.*

As for Céspedes, his statue stands serenely in the Plaza de Armas, and he is often referred to as the Father of the Nation." At the time of the revolt, he was a prosperous forty-nine-year-old landowner who had participated in various Masonic conspiracies in his youth. Though freeing his slaves was considered revolutionary, Céspedes did not advocate the abolition of slavery, but rather a gradual emancipation in which owners were to be indemnified. Moreover, perhaps to maintain the support of the wealthy sugar planters, Céspedes was reluctant to bring the war to western Cuba. When the rebellion flagged, Céspedes was blamed by the more radical elements and ousted from command. In 1874, he was ambushed by the Spaniards at a farm in San Lorenzo and died, revolver in hand.

After Céspedes's departure from the scene, Gómez and Maceo breached the *trocha*. They penetrated into the Sancti Spiritus area, where they burned plantations and freed the slaves. But political disunity doomed their efforts. Maceo, a brave and brilliant commander, was dismissed because many refused to serve under a mulatto. Gómez, though a meticulous organizer and keen strategist, was resented for being a foreigner.

By then, exhaustion had started to set in among the rebels. The death toll had been staggering, with over fifty thousand Cuban lives lost. Many fled the violence, with up to a hundred thousand settling in the United States. This was to be the first of many mass migrations across the Florida Straits. Miami was little more than a coconut grove, so the refugees went to Key West, Tampa, and Jacksonville, or like Martí to New York. Spanish casualties were even greater, over two hundred thousand, with yellow fever taking a greater toll than the *mambises*. But fresh troops had been sent from Madrid and now numbered seventy thousand. Even if the revolt could not be stamped out, the *peninsulares* now had the upper hand.

᳒

During the Ten Year War, despite Gómez's raid beyond the *trocha*, the fighting was mostly limited to the east. Havana was thus spared the worst effects of the war, with one important exception.

---

[1] Ironically, the term *guerrilleros* referred not to the rebels but to paid mercenaries employed by the Spaniards to hunt down the *mambises*.

Militias had been established in 1762 to defend Havana against the British. Now, Lersundi reorganized them to combat the rebels. Fears of a slave revolt had led authorities to encourage Spanish immigration, and these new arrivals formed the Voluntarios, as they were called.[6] For the most part, they were middle-class *peninsulares* with ultra-conservative, racist views. Financed by Spanish merchants, their ranks swelled and regiments were established throughout the island. At their peak, they numbered perhaps sixty thousand.

Lersundi was replaced as captain-general in January 1869 by Domingo Dulce, who favored negotiating with the rebels. The Voluntarios staged violent demonstrations throughout Havana and forced his resignation. It was the Voluntarios who forced the arrest of Mendive, Martí's mentor. An armed mob attacked the Villanueva Theater, where liberals often gathered, resulting in several deaths. Mendive was later linked to these demonstrations and arrested, although it is unlikely he was in the vicinity.

The greatest abuse occurred on November 27, 1871. The Voluntarios claimed that a group of medical students had entered the cemetery and profaned the grave of one of their number. At four o'clock the next morning, eight medical students were executed without a trial in the presence of fifteen thousand Voluntarios. Their death is commemorated in a Grecian-style monument at the base of the Prado, on the site of Tacón's jail, and November 27 is observed as a national holiday.

The mob rule imposed by the Voluntarios helps account for Martí's distaste for Havana during his return in 1877, a year before the war's end. After Captain-General Dulce was sent packing, his replacement was careful to accommodate the rogue militias. For much of the war, the militias ruled the city and dictated a hard line to the Spanish government.

But in 1877, the latest captain-general, Arsenio Martínez Campos, faced down the militias and declared a general amnesty. Before long, peace negotiations began, resulting in the Pact of Zanjon in February 1878. Along with the cease-fire came political reforms, including the end of slavery. Slaves were obliged to work for their masters for a period of six years under the *patronato* system, and slavery was finally abolished in 1886.

Maceo, who still had one thousand five hundred men under his command, demanded a meeting with Martínez Campos at the town of

Baraguá, near Santiago de Cuba. Maceo told the astonished captain-general that there could be no peace without independence and the unconditional liberation of the slaves. But after ten years, there was little fight left in the rebels, and Maceo capitulated a few months later and was allowed to leave on a Spanish cruiser. After the fall of the Soviet Union, Castro adopted Maceo's continued resistance as a political symbol when he declared an "eternal Baraguá."

Martí returned to Havana shortly after Maceo departed and became embroiled in what became known as the *Guerra Chiquita* (Little War). It was yet another uprising, begun in August 1879 by Calixto García. Yet like Maceo's uprising, it was stillborn. Most of the conspirators were betrayed, like Martí himself, and García was quickly captured.

The next revolt would begin outside of Cuba.

## MARTÍ IN NEW YORK

A statue of Martí rivaling those in Havana is found in New York on the Avenue of the Americas at the entrance to Central Park. The massive bronze sculpture was erected in 1965 during the Cold War, when relations between Cuba and the United States were even frostier than today. It depicts Martí mounted on a rearing horse, falling backward as he is shot. There is no attempt to be realistic: The Apostle is dapper in his trademark frock coat, which he is unlikely to have worn in combat, and he is unarmed. On his birthday, January 28, the Cuban Cultural Center of New York places flowers on the sculpture.

It is a fitting tribute to Martí, who became an out-and-out New Yorker at the age of twenty-seven. He arrived in 1880 and soon made contact with other conspirators. Spanish agents were hot on his heels, and had him watched by Pinkerton's Detective Agency. Martí's political activities were a point of contention with his wife, Carmen, who joined him with their infant son in March. He complained to his friend Manuel Mercado that she did not share his enthusiasm for politics. In one telling passage from Martí's diary, he wrote: "What do you want, my wife? For me to do the work that will be applauded on earth . . . [or] serene and doing the work whose applause we will not live to hear?"[7] A familiar domestic complaint. After a stay of only a few months, Carmen returned to Havana.

The role of an apostle's wife is not easy, and Carmen has been depicted by many biographers as a bit of a shrew, nagging Martí to get a job rather than liberate Cuba. This is not completely fair, and their quarrel may have had to do with something else altogether. For much of his time in New York, Martí stayed at a boardinghouse on 51 East Twenty-ninth Street, run by another Cuban woman named Carmen and her invalid husband, Manuel Mantilla. Martí began an affair with her almost immediately. In November (ten months after Martí's arrival) she bore a daughter named María.* Martí apparently tried to patch things up with his wife, without success. She returned to New York in 1882 and remained for two years, and then again in 1891 for just two months. But after the ailing Mantilla died in 1885, Martí lived openly with Carmen and helped raise the little girl.

After the failure of the *Guerra Chiquita*, Martí was elected president of the Cuban Revolutionary Committee in New York and was soon planning another uprising. Gómez and Maceo had both fled to Honduras, and in 1884 they arrived in New York to meet with him. At first, things went well, and the three men spent days closeted together in the boardinghouse. It was decided that Martí would accompany Maceo on a trip to Mexico, and when he offered various suggestions, an impatient Gómez abruptly cut him off: "Look, Martí, just follow orders." Stunned, Martí took his leave. Two days later he withdrew from the movement with a letter saying: "A nation is not founded, General, the way one commands a military camp. . . ." Martí was criticized for taking his toys and going home, but the split with the soldiers revealed an important fault line. Martí became convinced that the revolution should have civilian, not military, leadership, and that an independent Cuba not be run by caudillos.[8]

For the next several years, Martí produced copy rather than conspiracies. In addition to his freelance work for Charles Dana Anderson, Martí contributed hundreds of articles to Latin American newspapers such as *La Nacion* in Buenos Aires and *La Pluma* in Bogotá. Known as his *Cronicas*, they paint a fascinating picture of New York during the Gilded Age. Martí covered everything from political events, to baseball games, to the inauguration of the Brooklyn Bridge in 1883. His initial fascination with the nascent metropolis he called the "Iron Babel" never wavered. He described the new elevated railroad as a "dark monster" and Coney Island as "brimming with people, filled with luxurious hotels."[9] But his enthusiasm

---

[1] It is all but certain that she was Martí's. María Mantilla's son was the actor Cesar Romero, forever known as the Joker in the campy television series *Batman*.

became tempered with caution as he witnessed the dark underbelly of capitalism. Behind the gaiety of the amusement park were "damp streets, where men and women are heaped together writhing," and during a cholera epidemic he saw children with "eyes like caves." If Martí was thrilled by the diligence and energy of New Yorkers, he was also disgusted by their indifference to poverty and crass materialism.

Martí's articles were immensely influential in Latin America and provided for many the first glimpse of the "Colossus of the North." In his efforts to appeal to readers in countries as diverse as Argentina and Colombia, he crafted a Latin American identity of shared values and culture that still resonates today and declared, "I am a son of America." Martí was among the first to utilize the term latino, prefiguring its modern usage.

Martí also engaged in a number of other journalistic ventures including a children's magazine called *La Edad de Oro* (The Age of Gold) backed by a wealthy Brazilian. After four issues, the prickly Martí fought with his benefactor and the magazine folded. He also translated a number of books and even wrote a hack novel called *Amistad Funesta* (Fatal Friendship) under the unlikely pen name of Adelaida Ral. This was clearly intended to pay the rent, since Martí wrote it in only seven days. It met with little acclaim, like many another literary debut.[10]

Martí was equally well-known as a poet, though he published only two slender volumes of verse in his lifetime: *Ismaelillo* and *Versos Sencillos.* Hailed as a proponent of *modernismo,* he was a direct influence on many poets, such as Ruben Dario. Martí's verses were put to music in 1928 by Joseito Fernandez and later popularized in the United States by Pete Seeger. The result was "Guantanamera," which has become the unofficial anthem of the Cuban diaspora because of the haunting melody and unforgettable lyrics:

*Yo soy un hombre sincero*
*De donde crecen las palmas . . .*

[I am a sincere man
From where the palm tree grows][11]

The song still brings tears and applause when played in Cuban restaurants throughout the world.

José Martí in New York. (Author's collection)

Like other immigrants, Martí made a life for himself in New York. But by the end of the 1880s, he was ready to jump back into the fray. Before him was a daunting task. Few of the promised reforms in Cuba had taken place, and the Spaniards had put in place an effective web of informers and police spies to stamp out dissent. The exile groups abroad were deeply divided, and the heroes of the Ten Year War were long in the tooth. Maceo had set himself up as a farmer in Costa Rica, and Gómez had returned to Santo Domingo.

One of the most pressing issues was money. Martí looked for financial support among the cigar rollers in Florida, who had imbibed liberal ideas through the custom of reading instituted by Don Jaime Partagás fifty years before. Martí headed south and in November 1891 gave an important speech at the Liceo Cubano in Tampa. With his frock coat and aristocratic manners, Martí must have seemed faintly comical to the rough-hewn *torcedores*, and they must have been skeptical as he began to speak in his low, mellifluous voice. Perhaps they shuffled their feet until something he said struck a chord deep within him. He spoke not of revenge against Spanish oppressors but justice; not of prejudice but brotherhood among all Cubans:

> Let us rise up for the true republic, those of us who, with our passion for right and our habit of hard work, will know how to preserve it. . . . And let us place around the star of our new flag this formula of love triumphant: "With all, and for the good of all!"[12]

Martí was a spellbinding orator, combining poetic hyperbole with shrewd logic and carefully honing his message for each audience.

With the financial support of the cigar rollers, who agreed to donate 10 percent of their earnings to the cause, Martí founded the Cuban Revolutionary Party in 1892. Just as he had been a literary chameleon, he became a protean politician skillful at bringing together diverse groups, such as freed slaves, exiled merchants, and aging revolutionaries, under one banner. Martí literally willed the new movement into being, with two guiding principles. First, he recognized that blacks would be an important part of the new Cuba. He dispelled the old fears of a Haitian-style revolt by saying: "Others may fear [the black man]. I love him." Second, Martí was convinced that one of the greatest dangers facing Cuba was that the United States would intervene before freedom was gained from Spain. Nothing short of unconditional independence for Cuba was acceptable.

Once the movement was established, Martí swallowed his pride and went to Santo Domingo to enlist Gómez. Nearly sixty, the gruff Dominican must have been reluctant to go back to war. But Martí's organizational abilities won him over, and their past disputes were put aside. Martí then proceeded to Costa Rica and convinced Maceo to leave his prosperous farm and join him as well.

Martí soon began to plan his secret war in earnest. These were years of feverish activity and constant travel as he handled many details personally to avoid betrayal. By the end of 1894 he was ready, having chartered three ships, the *Baracoa*, the *Amadis*, and the *Lagonda*, to take weapons and nearly a thousand men to join the rebels in Cuba. In January, disaster struck: The three ships had been impounded by the U.S. government, anxious (for the time being) to avoid offending Spain. But it was too late to turn back, and the revolt began on February 24, 1895, when insurgents seized the town of Baire, north of Santiago de Cuba.

## MARTÍ IN DOS RÍOS

By then, Martí had already embarked for Santo Domingo, the first leg of his journey. The journal that he kept during this time is known as the *War Diaries*, and it is regarded by many as his most powerful piece of writing. In contrast to Martí's usual style, which is flowery and ornate, its simple, direct sentences would make Hemingway envious. Traveling through the Dominican countryside to Gómez's farm, he is invigorated and eats a hearty meal of "white rice, chicken with arrowroot, sweet potato, and squash."[13]

Interestingly enough, the plan was for Martí not to accompany Gómez but to return to New York and continue his fundraising and political activities. But he learns that a newspaper article in New York has already placed him in Cuba and realizes that if he goes back he will lose face. More likely, Martí intended to go all along. His enemies often derided his lack of battlefield experience, and he may have wanted to prove them wrong. The crossing to Cuba could have been penned by Conrad. The skipper of the German freighter *Nordstrom* agrees to take them for $1,000 and, pursued by a British frigate, drops them off three miles from Cuba in a fierce gale. Martí describes as he and Gómez set out with four other companions:

> They lower the boat. Heavy downpour as we push off. Set the wrong course. Confused and conflicting opinions in the boat. Another downpour. Rudder lost. Back on course. I take forward oar. . . . We strap on our revolvers. Head toward clearing. Moon comes up red from behind a cloud. We land on a stony beach. I the last to leave the boat.[14]

They land at Playitas, a desolate spot near Baracoa. One can literally feel the stinging rain on their faces and the slick rocks beneath their boots.

On his way to join the *mambises*, Martí crosses rivers up to his waist and hikes up a hill carrying weapons and a heavy pack. He and his companions sleep in caves and on dry leaves. There are more delicious dinners: stewed pork, malanga, and jerked beef with plantains, washed down with Málaga wine and coffee sweetened with cane juice.

In a sense, he rediscovers the Cuban countryside, which he had not seen since he was a child. Martí, the consummate city dweller describes "jagged, bosomy, peaked mountains" and a "pool of water where hummingbirds drink."[15] He delights in the hospitality of the *guajiros*\* and catalogs the local flora and fauna.

Novelist José Lezama Lima called the *War Diaries* "the greatest poem ever written by a Cuban." It makes for delightful reading, particularly since the writer is a sickly, middle-aged man with no military training. But the excursion soon comes to an end, barely six weeks after it started. Martí and the others landed on April 11, and by May 5 they had rendezvoused with Maceo's forces. The last diary entry is May 17. On May 19, the rebels were set upon by a Spanish column of six hundred men commanded by Colonel Ximenez de Sandoval in an area called Dos Ríos, between the Contramaestre and Cauto rivers. After a brief skirmish, Gómez signaled for his forces to retreat. Disobeying orders, Martí charged ahead on a white horse, pistol in hand, accompanied only by a recruit named Angel de la Guardia. Spanish snipers in waist-high grass along the riverbank felled Martí with three shots. De la Guardia managed to flee. According to some accounts, Martí was killed instantly; others suggest he was finished off by a Spanish scout with a Remington rifle.

When he heard the news, Gómez dispatched a column to rescue Martí, whom he hoped was still alive, but it was too late. The body was buried in a common grave the next morning in the town of Remanganaguas. When Colonel Sandoval learned of Martí's death, he ordered him exhumed for proper burial a few days later. Because the body had decomposed in the humid earth, no autopsy was performed. Martí was buried May 27 in Santiago de Cuba.

---

\* Cuban peasants or countryfolk. One theory of the word's origin is that U.S. soldiers so admired the bravery of the farmers that they called them "war heroes." But Martí uses the word in his journal, which predates American intervention. Possibly the prefix *gua-* is Taino is origin. It may also refer to the Canary Islands, whose inhabitants are called *guanches*.

The mythmaking that would transform Martí into the Apostle of Freedom began almost immediately after his death. One school of thought, echoed by writers such as Guillermo Cabrera Infante, was that Martí deliberately sacrificed himself for the cause. It is true that Martí was preoccupied with death, and his verses are rife with sepulchral imagery, such as the death by drowning of *la niña de Guatemala* and his prophecy that he will die "with [his] face to the sun." The manifesto that he issued with Gómez before sailing to Cuba contains the phrase *Victoria o el Sepulcro* (victory or the tomb) perhaps the inspiration for Castro's *Patria o Muerte* (fatherland or death.) But the author of *War Diaries* clearly loved life too much to squander it prematurely.

Still, Martí's death served as a rallying cry for the duration of the war. If the movement now lacked a leader, it had a convincing martyr. A drawing in the Havana newspaper *El Figaro* showed Martí crucified, with Cuba prostrate at his feet.[16]

But there are many Martís. His collected works comprise twenty-six volumes, constantly being reedited by the Centro de Estudios Martíanos (Center of Martí Studies) in Havana. The sheer volume and variety of his writing, from newspaper columns to romance novels, permits virtually any interpretation of his views. Moreover, Martí himself was an idiosyncratic and contradictory thinker. He left no definite political program for the new Cuba other than broad ideas such as equality among the races and independence from Spain and the United States. For example, during the early years of the Cuban Republic, Martí became a symbol of unity. A generation later, during the Machado years, Martí the nationalist was applauded. Batista quoted him in a speech after his military coup in 1952, as did Castro during his trial for the attack on the Moncada barracks. Following the Revolution, Martí the anti-imperialist emerged, defined by the famous quote, "I have lived in the monster and know its entrails,"[17] which he wrote in a letter to a friend just days before his death.

Yet Martí is quoted just as frequently in Miami as Havana. Throughout exile communities, there are schools, streets, and libraries named after him, and the U.S.-funded effort to broadcast into Cuba, directed by right-wing Cuban exiles, is called Radio and TV Martí. It is hardly surprising that Martí's words—sometimes taken wildly out of context—are used to support virtually any political premise. For example, Martí is often depicted as a socialist due to quotes such as:

> *How can a person who inherits wealth be thought more noble than one who creates it?*

Martí also admired Karl Marx, writing:

> *He deserves to be honored, for he placed himself on the side of the weak.*

Yet almost in the same breath he says:

> *Socialist ideology has two main dangers. One stems from confused and incomplete readings of foreign texts, and the other from the arrogance and hidden rage of those who, in order to climb up in the world, pretend to be frantic defenders of the helpless so as to have shoulders on which to stand.*[18]

Friend or foe? To be sure, Martí had personal experience of political repression and prized freedom of expression above all else. One guesses he would quickly fall afoul of the regime in Cuba today. Yet he would be equally repulsed by U.S. efforts to interfere in Cuba's internal politics. What would he make of the trade embargo and the committee set up by President Bush in 2004 to speed Cuba's "transition" to democracy?

Similarly, Martí is often portrayed as blatantly anti-American, yet he lived quite comfortably in the "monster" for fifteen years. He had a carefully nuanced view of America, and his critique of New York's glittering excess is still valid today. Above all, he feared the specter of annexation, the very real possibility of the United States gobbling up Cuba. In this he was prescient, but it did not blind him to America's virtues, saying: "We love the country of Lincoln as much as we fear the country of Cutting."

Yet there is something ineffably Cuban about Martí, not the glorified Apostle but the man himself, much more interesting and immediately recognizable a century later. It is his peculiar combination of idealism and expediency, of lofty poetry and hack novels, of personal flaws and betrayals together with selfless commitment to a cause, of personal eccentricities

---

[1] Colonel Francis Cutting was one of the founders of the American Annexationist League.

combined with obsessive single-mindedness, and above all his *fracaso*, even greater than that that of Heredia.

One of the great "what-ifs" of Cuban history follows if Martí had survived by obeying Gómez's orders to stay behind the lines. Perhaps Martí could have negotiated an end to the war and prevented U.S. intervention. Perhaps he would have been elected president, a Cuban George Washington, and established the republic "with all and for the good of all" that he dreamed of. But Martí's failure was not his premature death at Dos Ríos. Rather, it was letting himself be transformed into the Apostle of Freedom—a stiff, pious scarecrow Martí would have mocked. From the grave, Martí could no longer control his carefully constructed political persona. What elevates this to a *fracaso*—perhaps the most sublime *fracaso* of all—is that in the years to come, the lifeblood of his spirit, his words, would be manipulated to create visions of a Cuba he himself would no longer recognize.

# CHAPTER 7

# Remembering the Maine
## At the Hotel Inglaterra

*Please remain. You furnish the pictures and I'll furnish the war.*
— William Randolph Hearst to Frederic Remington

*I*f Martí's statue in the Parque Central is heading to the Floridita, then it appears to have just left the Hotel Inglaterra.

The grande dame of Havana hotels lies directly behind him, across the Prado. Last buffed in 1982, it is still open for business. During a recent stay, I found it somewhat shabbier than the latest renovated hotels to open in Centro Habana, such as the Telegrafo and the Saratoga. But the Inglaterra is in a class of its own, steeped in momentous events, outsize characters, and wild conspiracy theories.

Its origins stretch back to a coffeehouse built by a Spaniard named Juan Escauriza in 1843 near the city gates.[1] In 1856, it was combined with the adjacent building on the corner of Prado and San Rafael streets, and soon became the city's trendiest watering hole, located next to the Teatro Tacón. The restaurant on the ground floor was called the Café Louvre, and with outdoor tables it became known as the Acera del Louvre. It drew not just theatergoers but revolutionaries. The first of many plots to be hatched here was during the Ten Year War in 1868, when the Voluntarios stormed the café and assaulted the students meeting there.

The Inglaterra also acquired a reputation as the best hotel in Havana and soon welcomed increasing numbers of *norteamericanos*. At midcentury, about five thousand Americans visited the island each year, including future presidents Ulysses S. Grant and Grover Cleveland. An 1884 advertisement notes that the Inglaterra boasted:

> *Every modern improvement, baths, stables, &c. Attentive waiters and a splendid cuisine. Well furnished and ventilated rooms and apartments. Music every night on the park opposite the hotel.*[2]

Business was booming and the hotel was enlarged in 1891. Another floor would be added in 1915, giving the Inglaterra its present appearance. It seems rather demure beside the bombastic Centro Gallego, but the coffee-colored pilasters and iron balustrades lend the facade a pleasing symmetry. Even if the paint is peeling, the windows are fronted by elegant wooden louvers, and the portico recalls the Palacio del Segundo Cabo in the Plaza de Armas.

When the War of Independence began in 1895, the Inglaterra received a new species of visitor: the foreign correspondent. Martí was nothing if not media savvy, and a few days before his death he had been interviewed by Eugene Bryson, a reporter from the *New York Herald*. The outbreak of hostilities in 1895 drew worldwide attention, and newspapermen flocked to Havana.

Among the first, curiously enough, was Winston Churchill. He was then a twenty-year-old second lieutenant in Her Majesty's Fourth Hussars. Having little to do until his regiment shipped off to India, Churchill prevailed on the British ambassador to Spain to let him go to Cuba. Armed with press credentials from the *London Daily Graphic*, Churchill and a brother officer arrived in Havana on the steamship *Olivette* on November 30, 1895.[3] Stood up by the Spanish official who was to have met him, he checked into the Hotel Inglaterra and for a few days did little else than discover a passion for Cuban cigars, which was to last all his life. When word came that rebel commander Máximo Gómez had been sighted near Sancti Spiritus, Churchill set out by rail to see the action. He joined Spanish forces as an observer and soon came under fire from the *mambises*. The rebels nearly captured a well-laden Spanish convoy and killed eighteen soldiers.

Despite this close call, Churchill was contemptuous of the Cubans. In the *London Daily Graphic* he wrote that they "neither fight bravely nor do they use their weapons effectively. They cannot win a battle or hold a single town. Their army, consisting to a large extent of colored men, is an undisciplined rabble."[4] His vacation over, Churchill himself soon beat a retreat back to England by way of Tampa. His views should not be taken for more than they were, those of a young subaltern eager to please his Spanish hosts. Yet he was severely criticized upon his return home. The *Newcastle Leader* wondered "what motive could possibly impel a British officer to mix himself up in a dispute with the merits of which he had absolutely nothing to do," and Churchill was not permitted to wear the medal given him by the Spaniards.

The battle near Sancti Spiritus reveals the initiative seized by the insurgents in the first months of the war. Martí's death did not affect the military strategy. Learning from the failures of the Ten Year War, Gómez was determined to take the fight to the prosperous center of the island, and punched through the fortified *trocha* with a thousand cavalrymen. Harassing Spanish columns and setting fire to cane fields, he was soon threatening Matanzas. Meanwhile, Maceo traversed the spine of the island and wreaked havoc in the western province of Pinar del Rio. By the end of 1895, there were about 25,000 rebels throughout the island. The Spanish garrison had twice that number of soldiers, but many were ill with yellow fever. As seen in Martí's diary, the *guajiros* (Cuban peasants) openly sided with the insurgents, who enjoyed widespead support throughout Cuba. The beleaguered Spanish troops kept to their fortified positions and rarely ventured out into the countryside. Gómez was soon within twenty miles of Havana.

In early 1896, the rebels had the initiative, and the war might have taken a different turn had it not been for the new Spanish captain-general, Valeriano Weyler. He was a severe, ascetic professional soldier who had served in Washington, D.C., as a military attaché during the Civil War and admired the scorched-earth tactics of General Sherman. Weyler later fought in the Ten Year War and, like Gómez, learned its lessons well. His first task was to stem the rebel advance and protect Havana. With fresh reinforcements, he pushed back Gómez and tried to trap Maceo by building a new, modernized *trocha* to cut off Pinar del Rio, with land mines and electric floodlights. Weyler completely overhauled the Spanish defenses, creating mobile cavalry regiments and establishing more effective lines of communication. But his most radical innovation was the policy of *reconcentración*.[5] Aware of the support the rebels received in the countryside, like a "fish in the sea," Weyler ordered that the *guajiros* leave their farms and relocate to enclosed military zones. There was severe repression, and anyone found outside these "concentration camps," as they became known, was summarily executed. In principle, food was to be provided by the Spanish troops, but inefficiency and corruption combined with destruction caused by the fighting led to mass starvation among the *guajiros*. The result was a slaughter not seen on the island since the extermination of the Tainos. Prosperous farmlands grew barren, entire communities vanished, and several hundred thousand Cubans perished. Weyler became known as the Butcher.

Yet he was effective. If Gómez (now seventy-three) and his forces remained at large in central Cuba, Havana was no longer at risk. Maceo managed to cross the western *trocha* but was killed in a minor skirmish with Spanish troops near Punta Brava, together with Gómez's beloved son, Panchito. A bloody stalemate was achieved by the time Weyler returned to Spain in 1897. Spain had sent 200,000 soldiers, and the woefully outgunned rebels had sustained many losses. Weyler's replacement was the more conciliatory Captain-General Blanco, and Spain made promises to grant the island limited autonomy.

It is often claimed that Cubans eventually would have secured their independence without U.S. intervention, but that hardly seemed likely after three years of brutal warfare. Although Cuba had been devastated, Spain seemed willing to hold on to it at any cost.

There is a grim footnote to Churchill's visit to Cuba. It has been suggested that his trip was not a romp but rather a fact-finding mission for the British military. While this is unsubstantiated, the Butcher's strategy would be put to good use—just as brutally—by the British in the Boer War. Throughout the twentieth century, it has proved the most effective way of fighting insurgents, as Castro showed in the Escambray Mountains in central Cuba, where in 1961 the local farmers were once again forcibly relocated in order to isolate counter-revolutionaries.

The War of Independence coincided with (and furthered) the rise of "yellow journalism." In New York, there was a frenetic circulation race between the *Journal*, owned by thirty-three-year-old William Randolph Hearst, and the *World*, run by the blind and aging Joseph Pulitzer. The fighting provided great copy, and soon both papers were full of accounts of scantily dressed Cuban Amazons fighting in the jungle with bloodthirsty Dons, as the Spaniards were called. In particular, Weyler's depredations captured the public's outrage. The *Journal* described him as a "fiendish despot . . . pitiless, cold . . . an exterminator of men." Before long, there were calls for U.S. intervention.

Hearst was the prototype for Citizen Kane, and I find it difficult to picture him as other than Orson Welles. In fact, he was surprisingly bashful and ill at ease among people. While his stated objective was to sell newspapers, he had a genuine sympathy for the Cuban rebels. In his office, he kept a jewel-encrusted sword from Tiffany with the inscription *Viva Cuba Libre*, which he hoped to personally give Gómez. In 1897, Hearst dispatched his ace reporter, Richard Harding Davis, to Cuba on his yacht *Vamoose*. Davis was a dashing man about town as well as a novelist. He had traveled widely and knew Cuba from a brief visit to Jennings Cox, the supposed inventor of the daiquiri. With him was Frederic Remington, the equally famous illustrator of cowboys and Indians, whose drawings would give readers their first glimpse of the war. This celebrity duo encountered a storm in the Florida Straits and had to return to Key West, where they cooled their heels for a month. Finally, they arrived in Havana aboard the same steamship *Olivette* that had delivered young Churchill nearly two years earlier.

Ensconced in the Hotel Inglaterra, they saw even less action. Weyler's crackdown had left Havana bleak and shuttered. Many of the victims of *reconcentración* wound up in Havana and lived in doorways, begging for food. As in the Ten Year War, mobs of rowdy Voluntarios roamed the streets hunting down rebel sympathizers. It is estimated that up to ten thousand Habaneros were arrested and sent to hellish Spanish prisons in North Africa. Davis obtained permission to leave the city, but Spanish authorities kept close watch on him. He was given a guided tour of the *trocha* and witnessed the execution of a rebel by firing squad in Santa Clara. But although the *Journal* claimed their men had reached the front lines, that was as close as they came to the fighting, which was on the other side of the island. Disgruntled, Remington cabled his boss:

*Everything quiet . . . There will be no war. I wish to return.*

Hearst is said to have replied:

*Please remain. You furnish the pictures and I'll furnish the war.*[6]

This exchange, which has been the bane of every foreign correspondent since, is probably apocryphal. Hearst himself denied it, and he had no reason to, since he admired a good turn of phrase. Remington and Davis returned empty-handed, and war between the United States and Spain was still a year off.

The two were to be hoist on their own petards. On the way home from Havana, Davis was smitten by a beautiful young Cuban woman named Clemencia Arango, who had been deported by the authorities. In his story, he wrote that she had been brutally strip-searched by Spanish customs guards. Remington's illustration showed her nearly naked, being pawed at by bearded ruffians. An embarrassed Señorita Arango later explained that the search had been conducted politely by matrons. Pulitzer's *World* gleefully seized upon this, and Davis resigned in disgrace.

Another denizen of the Hotel Inglaterra was Fitzhugh Lee, the nephew of Robert E. Lee. The U.S. government kept a wary eye on developments in Cuba, and in April 1896, newly elected President McKinley sent Lee as consul-general to Havana. A West Point graduate, he had fought Comanches in Texas and rose to the rank of brigadier general in the Confederate army. Now sixty-two, fat and mustachioed, he lived at the hotel and cut a raffish figure in a white linen suit and Panama hat.

Cuba had been an issue in the presidential campaign, eerily foreshadowing contemporary Florida politics. Although McKinley wanted to avoid war, his predecessor, Grover Cleveland, had been attacked for "doing nothing about Cuba." His choice of consul-general was therefore surprising, since Lee openly pushed for U.S. intervention and regaled credulous reporters like Davis with tales of Spanish atrocities. Lee further stoked the flames by warning of obscure conspiracies and imminent danger to American citizens in Havana, and urged a show of force. McKinley finally relented due to pressure from Lee and another firebrand in his administration, the assistant secretary of the navy, Theodore Roosevelt. In December 1897, the battleship USS *Maine* was ordered to Key West, from where it could be sent to Havana on short notice.

Lee's fervid warnings were looked at askance by McKinley, but the situation changed a month later. On January 12, protests shook Havana against the concessions offered by the Spanish government to the rebels in an effort to end the grueling war. Either by panic or design, Lee reported that American lives were threatened by mobs, though this was patently untrue. The headline in the *World* announced, "THE RIOTS IN HAVANA MEAN REVOLUTION," and Hearst's *Journal* declared, "NEXT DOOR TO WAR IN CUBA." Lee also spread rumors of a German armada in the Caribbean.

On January 24, McKinley obtained permission from the Spaniards for the *Maine* to visit Havana "purely as a mark of friendship." The battleship was soon steaming south and dropped anchor the next morning in Havana Harbor. Despite Lee's alarm, there had been no more protests, the Germans failed to materialize, and all was quiet for the next three weeks. The *Maine's* captain was received cordially and even attended a bullfight in Regla with Spanish general Parrado.

Then at nine-forty on the night of February 15, Walter Scott Meriwether (yet another foreign correspondent, from the *New York Herald*) was on his way to the Inglaterra when he heard a powerful blast. According to his account, it shook the entire city, shattering windows and knocking out electrical lights.[7] Meriwether went to the balcony of his room and looked across Habana Vieja to the harbor. The sky was lit by flames and brightly colored lights shot out of the water like rockets.

The *Maine* had exploded.

In 1898, "Remember the *Maine!*" was a battle cry rivaling that of the Alamo. Largely forgotten today, the ship changed the course of history as few ever have.

The *Maine* was among the first steel battleships commissioned by the U.S. Navy. Completed just three years before in the Brooklyn Navy Yard, it was 319 feet in length and measured 57 feet across the beam.[8] It boasted formidable firepower, with four ten-inch guns mounted fore and aft on armored turrets. At the helm was Captain Dwight Sigsbee, a graduate of Annapolis who had fought in the Civil War at the battle of Mobile Bay. The first and only captain of the *Maine*, he commanded a crew of 354 officers and men. At the time of the explosion, Sigsbee was in his cabin. Through the wreckage, he made his way to the poop deck. There was a fire amidships and the battleship was already listing to port. Through the glare, he could see the bodies of men in the water and heard their cries for help. Boats from the Spanish cruiser *Alfonso XII* and the Ward Line steamer *City of Washington* soon arrived to rescue them. Only three lifeboats from the *Maine* were undamaged, and Sigsbee and the other survivors cast off as the ship settled into the oily water.

That night, 2 officers and 258 men were killed. Eight more would later succumb to their injuries. The next morning, a cloud of black smoke hung over the smoldering wreckage in the middle of Havana Harbor.

The battleship sank in forty feet of water, but a mast and part of the mangled superstructure remained above the surface. The explosion took place directly below the enlisted men's quarters, explaining their high casualties and the survival of the officers. Many of the sailors were black, a fact that would figure in later conspiracy theories. There could be little doubt that the forward magazine had exploded, and the fireworks seen by Meriwether from the Inglaterra was ordinance set off by the heat. But the cause of the explosion remained unknown.

President McKinley was understandably cautious and had yet to see the explosion as a casus belli. Sigsbee noted the assistance offered his men by the Spanish and preferred to reserve judgment until an investigation could be held. The voluble Lee had no such doubts, and blamed it on sabotage by "unknown conspirators." As for Hearst, his *Journal* surpassed 1 million in circulation for the first time with the headline on February 17: "THE WARSHIP MAINE WAS SPLIT IN TWO BY AN ENEMY'S INFERNAL MACHINE." The publisher is said to have declared: "This means war!"[9]

## FILIBUSTERS

The sinking of the *Maine* provided a convenient excuse to invade Cuba, for Americans had long coveted the island. Thomas Jefferson wrote: "I

A postcard showing the "wrek" of the *Maine* in Havana Harbor. (Author's collection)

confess that I have ever looked on Cuba as the most interesting addition that could be made to our system of states."[10]

In 1808, still unwrapping the Louisiana Purchase, the third president sent an envoy to Havana to inquire about purchasing the island. Jefferson appreciated Cuba's strategic position at the entrance to the Gulf of Mexico, but his main concern was that it not enter into the hands of his former masters in Britain. His interest was looked on favorably by Cuban slaveholders, since Spain was already tightening the lucrative Triangle Trade, but faltered from fears of another invasion by the redcoats.

This theme would resurface in 1823. John Quincy Adams, then secretary of state under President Monroe, likened Cuba to a ripe apple. A slaveholding Cuba could destabilize domestic politics, so he preferred it to remain a Spanish colony for the time being. But should the apple fall from the tree, America would be there to catch it.

The next president to pick up the gauntlet was James Polk. In 1848, the Treaty of Guadalupe Hidalgo added California and Texas to the Union, and Cuba seemed next. The term manifest destiny was used to imply that the superior Anglo-Saxon race would soon dominate its Hispanic neighbors. Ironically, it was coined by New York journalist and Democratic Party hack John L. O'Sullivan, whose brother-in-law was Cristóbal Madán, a Cuban planter who supported annexation for the purpose of maintaining slavery in Cuba.

Polk was unwilling to wait for the apple to fall and set about trying to buy it. He ordered his ambassador to begin negotiations with the Spanish government and tendered an offer of $100 million for the island, lock, stock, and barrel. It was hardly a good price, since Cuba brought Spain nearly $10 million a year in taxes. The Spanish foreign minister replied contemptuously, saying he would rather see Cuba sink into the ocean. Polk's successor, Franklin Pierce, later upped the ante to $130 million, with little effect. Annexationists in Havana were equally impatient to join the Union, and soon took matters into their own hands.

Today, the term *filibuster* refers to a congressional delaying tactic, but it comes from a Dutch word for freebooter, or pirate.[11] The most famous filibuster of all was the doomed and somewhat quixotic Narciso López. López was born in Venezuela in 1797 and fought against Bolivar. Returning to Spain, he made a career as a bureaucrat and was sent to govern Trinidad, on Cuba's southern shore. It was here that López made contact with annexationists such as Madán, and he began to organize a military expedition to seize Cuba for the United States.

He found eager allies in O'Sullivan and other proponents of manifest destiny, and recruited veterans of the Mexican War. To lead the troops, López tried to hire Robert E. Lee, who respectfully declined. Though middle-aged, López then assumed command himself. In May 1850, he managed to take the port city of Cardenas, east of Havana. López's plan was to seize railroad cars and use them to attack nearby Matanzas, but when Spanish reinforcements arrived, the filibusters quickly sailed back to Key West.

López tried again a year later with an army of 435 volunteers. This time, he chose for a landing site the village of El Morillo in Pinar del Río, west of the port of Mariel. His strategy presaged that of Martí and, later, Castro. He hoped to establish a base in the mountains, recruit local support, and march on Havana. But the Spaniards were quickly alerted and dispatched General Manuel Enna, who methodically hunted down the filibusters. López himself was captured after a month and taken in chains to Havana.[12]

Most of the survivors were shot by firing squad, while others were sent to North Africa and later ransomed, much like the prisoners at the Bay of Pigs a century later. On September 1, 1851, López was garroted outside the castle of La Punta before a somber crowd. His last words were: "It was not my intention to injure anyone, my object was your freedom and happiness."

A street was named after López in Habana Vieja. It is barely a block long, between the Templete and the Hotel Santa Isabel, intersected by a street named after his nemesis, General Enna. But Cubans have a more vivid reminder of the filibusters. As a colony, Cuba had no flag of its own. Strangely enough, the banner that López flew would become the flag of the Cuban Republic. It was designed by José Tuerbe Tolón, the editor of the annexationist newspaper *La Verdad* in New York, and sewn by his wife, Emilia.

## ROOSEVELT GOES TO WAR

*All the great masterful races have been fighting races.*

—Theodore Roosevelt

During the Civil War, Cuba was put on the back burner. But after Reconstruction, a newly resurgent and belligerent America yearned to flex its muscles.

No one was spoiling for a fight more than Theodore Roosevelt. Moreover, it seemed to make little difference to the young police commissioner of New York against whom the war was fought. In 1895, there was a minor dispute with Britain over the Venezuelan border, and Roosevelt wrote to a friend:

> *Let the fight come if it must. I don't care whether our sea-coast cities are bombarded or not; we would take Canada. . . . Personally, I rather hope the fight will come soon. The clamor of the peace faction has convinced me this country needs a war.* [13]

President McKinley appointed him Assistant Secretary of the Navy with some trepidation, since Roosevelt was a well-known "jingo," or warmonger. McKinley was swayed by Senator Henry Cabot Lodge, Roosevelt's mentor and a fellow member of the snooty Porcellian Club, Harvard's answer to Yale's Skull and Bones. Roosevelt knew that sea power would be decisive in this war, whenever it came, and set about modernizing the U.S. Navy, commissioning more battleships like the *Maine*.

Roosevelt took its loss personally and claimed that it was sunk by "dirty treachery" on the part of Spain. [14] Two courts of inquiry were soon held on the explosion, by Spanish and American officials. Predictably, the Spaniards ruled that it had been caused by the accidental detonation of the forward magazine. The Americans concluded that it had been set off by an external explosion, possibly caused by a submerged mine. This was based on the finding that the hull seemed to have bent upward from the ocean floor, though the report stressed that the evidence was inconclusive. This was enough for Roosevelt, who reacted to McKinley's caution by saying the president had the backbone of a "chocolate éclair." [15]

Meanwhile, the war drums continued to beat. Some of Roosevelt's statements from this period could have been lifted from *Mein Kampf*. In a speech at the Naval War College, Roosevelt told the assembled cadets:

> *All the great masterful races have been fighting races; and the minute that a race loses the hard fighting virtues, then . . . it has lost its proud right to stand as the equal of the best. . . . No triumph of peace is quite so great as the supreme triumphs of war.* [16]

The future president was influenced not just by manifest destiny but also the writings of Brooke Adams (yet another member of the Porcellian Club), a Social Darwinist who bemoaned the decline of manly virtues.

Roosevelt saw the sinking of the *Maine* as an opportunity not just to deploy his new navy, but to save civilization from itself.

The fever that gripped Roosevelt and many others was fueled by gleeful propaganda from the yellow journalists. Hearst sent several senators and their wives on an uproarious "fact-finding mission" to Havana, putting them up at the Inglaterra. The *Journal* even planned to sponsor a platoon of giants, such as boxer John Sullivan, to "overawe" the diminutive Spaniards. This hoopla was combined with astounding cynicism, and one senator who went on Hearst's junket declared that war would stimulate American industry, particularly the railroads. McKinley made an effort to stem the tide by secretly offering to buy Cuba, this time for $300 million. Like the others, this offer was hardly taken seriously. In the end, McKinley bowed to political pressure. One sop to the Cubans was the Teller Amendment, which stipulated that the United States had no intention to gain sovereignty over Cuba and ultimately would "leave the government and control of the island to its people." [17]

On April 20, 1898, barely two months after the destruction of the *Maine*, the United States declared war on Spain.

Roosevelt did not want to be left out. A month before, he had attempted to obtain a commission in the New York National Guard. Despite his connections, this request was denied, not surprising for a deskbound forty-year-old with no military record. Undaunted, Roosevelt prevailed on the secretary of defense to make him a lieutenant colonel in the U.S. First Volunteer Cavalry, which became known as the Rough Riders. He promptly ordered a uniform from Brooks Brothers "without yellow on the collar and with leggings," and set out for San Antonio, where cowboys were being recruited at the bar of the Menger Hotel, across from the Alamo.

It was an easy sell. At the time, the U.S. Army consisted of fewer than 30,000 officers and men, mostly stationed at forts along the receding frontier. McKinley proposed to recruit 125,000, but over 1 million volunteered. Among those receiving commissions were Fitzhugh Lee himself and another aging Confederate warhorse, "Fighting Joe" Wheeler. While Roosevelt trained with the Rough Riders, a naval blockade around Cuba was ordered. The first shot in the war was fired by Admiral Dewey, who on May 1 destroyed the Spanish fleet in Manila Bay without loss of a single ship or sailor. Meanwhile, another Spanish fleet under Admiral

Cervera managed to reach Santiago de Cuba, a grievous tactical mistake, since it was soon bottled up by American warships.

An effort was made to contact the Cuban rebels by sending Lieutenant Andrew Rowan secretly ashore to contact Calixto García, who was based near the Sierra Maestra. Rowan soon found the bewildered rebel commander, who had no clue of the upcoming invasion and insisted that Gómez should have been informed.*

The Rough Riders reached the embarkation point of Tampa on June 3, and a week later they joined the 5th Army Corps under General Shafter en route to Cuba. The first wave consisted of 16,000 men, together with 90 journalists. Among them was Hearst's new foreign correspondent, the novelist Stephen Crane, author of The *Red Badge of Courage*. On June 10, a division of marines met little resistance at Guantanamo Bay, where they remain to this day. The Rough Riders would not reach Cuba until June 22, landing at Daiquiri.

General Shafter marched directly on Santiago de Cuba, sixteen miles away. A minor skirmish at the village of Siboney resulted in the first U.S. casualty. The Spaniards soon fled, and "Fighting Joe" Wheeler declared, "We've got the damned Yankees on the run!" [18]

The Rough Riders continued on the road to Santiago de Cuba, fending off sporadic attacks from the Spaniards. Despite his bluster, Roosevelt was scarcely more suited for war than Martí. A famous photograph taken during a lull in the fighting shows him standing proudly before an American flag, surrounded by his men. They are a shaggy lot, bearded and unkempt, grinning at the camera. Roosevelt, immaculate in his puttees and Brooks Brothers uniform, stands ramrod straight, his chest thrust out, his thumbs cocked in his belt. His broad-brimmed hat is crammed down over his forehead, almost obscuring his thick spectacles.* Unlike the others, he scowls pugnaciously, perhaps like the cowpokes he met on western dude ranches.

The only land battle of the war was fought on July 1, on the heights guarding the approach to the city. A visit to San Juan Hill is de rigueur for tourists in Santiago de Cuba, but those expecting Iwo Jima will be disappointed. It is a gentle slope easily ascended in a few minutes, but

---

* This is the source of the odd book *Message to Garcia* by the Babbit-like businessman Elbert Hubbard. An early best seller, it extolled the initiative of the plucky young officer.
* Roosevelt was terribly nearsighted, and brought six pairs of glasses for the campaign.

here the Spaniards established their first line of defense. It was then called Kettle Hill, perhaps because of a huge iron cauldron at the summit used to boil sugarcane. García's rebel army was in the vicinity, but they do not appear to have participated in the fighting. It has been suggested that the *mambises* were hedging their bets, but more likely they were simply not informed of the attack. The defenders were vastly outnumbered, yet they managed to hold off the Americans for most of the day. After several volleys cleared the trenches, the Rough Riders entered the fray. Roosevelt appears to have acquitted himself with bravado, killing a Spanish soldier with a pistol. One contretemps occurred in the heat of battle. Two black troopers had been sent back from the front lines to begin digging in, and Roosevelt threatened to shoot them, accusing them of cowardice. It is difficult to imagine the reaction of the two soldiers when confronted by the diminutive Harvard man. Most likely they were "Buffalo Soldiers," the legendary Indian fighters of the frontier, and explained that they were under orders. Roosevelt hastily apologized.

While the charge up San Juan Hill has entered military lore, it was in fact a Pyrrhic victory. The American dead numbered 223, with 1,243 wounded and 79 missing. This was effectively 10 percent of the U.S. fighting force, and Santiago de Cuba was still strongly defended. If the Spaniards had launched a counterattack the next day, the Americans could have taken severe losses and their advance might have been halted.[19] The invasion took place during the fetid rainy season, and already some Rough Riders were suffering from yellow fever and malaria. But the Spanish had no more stomach for war.

On July 3, Admiral Cervera's fleet was obliterated as it tried to run the blockade.* Two weeks later, Santiago de Cuba surrendered. Madrid quickly sued for peace, and by the end of the month the war was over.

The Cuban apple had finally fallen from the tree.


## LOS NORTEAMERICANOS

*Nobody wants to annex [Cuba] but the general feeling is that they ought to be taken by the scruff of the neck and shaken until they behave themselves.*

—Henry Cabot Lodge

---

* Unlike the modern American ships, with stainless steel plating, the Spanish ships still had wooden decks, and were easily set on fire by artillery shells.

The Spanish American War* lasted just three months, but American involvement with Cuba was just beginning.

In January 1899, General John Rutter Brooke formally accepted the keys of Havana from Captain-General Jimenez Castellanos, the last of a long line. Things began badly when Gómez and other rebel leaders were not invited to the ceremony marking the transfer of power. American troops patrolled the streets, sharing police duties with the rebel army, which would not be disbanded for several months. The two occasionally clashed, resulting in fistfights and more hard feelings. In contrast, the departing Spanish troops were treated with great civility, and the vanquished Spanish commander, Admiral Cervera, was fêted as a hero in the United States. But relations between Americans and Cubans only got worse.

The *norteamericanos* soon learned the extent of destruction caused by the war. A census taken in 1899 showed that the Cuban population was 1,500,000. Based on previous estimates, it was calculated that 300,000 Cubans had died.[20] This was almost 20 percent of the previous population, a loss comparable to that of Russia in World War II and significantly higher than America's in the Civil War. Probably the figure was even higher, since many victims of *reconcentración* remained unaccounted for. The countryside was devastated, with many towns in ruins and farmlands laid waste. In 1895, there were over 1,100 sugar mills in Cuba; now there were 207.[21] The psychological toll is even more difficult to calculate: Lives were shattered, families were divided, and for those who had left, there was nothing to come home to.

Havana fared better, having escaped the fighting. The census showed that it now had 250,000 inhabitants, occupying six square miles. Nonetheless, General Brooke reported that he found "desolation, starvation, and anarchy."[22] The city was overcrowded with displaced *guajiros*, livings in tenements or shanties called *yaguas*, made from palm tree bark like the huts of the Tainos. There was difficulty in obtaining fresh water and danger of more starvation. Occupying troops distributed 6.5 million food rations by August 1899.

The Americans set about rebuilding with dispatch, and Havana experienced a building boom. The antiquated water system was replaced

---

* This unfortunate name persists, implying it had nothing to do with Cuba. There it is referred to as the *Guerra de Independencia* [War of Independence].

with new pipes and modern sewage disposal, and new houses had hot and cold running water for the first time. Public buildings were repaired, streets were paved, and dock facilities were improved. New telephone lines were installed, and by 1900, Havana was connected to towns within seventy-five miles. An electric trolley was running by 1901 connecting Habana Vieja with new suburbs, such as El Vedado to the west and El Cerro to the south. Throughout Cuba, roads were constructed, bridges were built, and railroads were laid. To handle increased maritime traffic, waterways were cleared, harbors were dredged, and ports were expanded.

One corollary to this was the increasing Americanization of Havana. The economic devastation created dazzling business opportunities, and many U.S. soldiers remained to seek their fortune. Most foreign correspondents had moved on, but the Hotel Inglaterra was now full of carpetbaggers, speculators, and investors, described as a "second army of occupation." [23]The real estate market had plummeted, and by 1905, 13,000 *norteamericanos* had bought land in Cuba. Contemporary accounts show that Havana was full of American advertising, particularly for beer. In 1898, an English-language newspaper was founded, the *Havana Post*. A fixture on the breakfast tables of the American colony, it would continue publishing until 1960. The custom of celebrating Christmas was introduced, complete with Santa Claus and frosted Christmas trees, and gradually replaced the more traditional *Dia de los Reyes*. A profusion of U.S. businesses opened, including the Texas Bar near the Prado and the American Grocery on O'Reilly Street.

This was America's first experience of "nation-building," and it proved profitable. Imports from the United States tripled between 1898 and 1902, and the Reciprocity Treaty of 1903 guaranteed American products a privileged place in the Cuban market. While the Teller Amendment specifically prohibited America from maintaining sovereignty (as in Puerto Rico), many thought that Cubans would voluntarily ask to join the Union. This was certainly the expectation of General Brooke and his successor in December 1899, General Leonard Wood.

But before long, America grew reluctant to shoulder the White Man's Burden. McKinley was soon eager to take his leave, and instructed Wood:

> *I want you to go down there [and] give them a good school system, try to straighten out their courts, put them on their feet as best you can. We want to do all we can for them and get out of the island as soon as we safely can.* [24]

One reason was that the United States was now fighting a vicious counterinsurgency war in the Philippines, which would last until 1902. Due to rigid censorship, most Americans did not know of the brutal treatment and wholesale slaughter of Filipinos on the other side of the world. There were 4,200 American dead and 2,800 wounded, but over 20,000 rebels were killed and 200,000 civilians perished from many of the same tactics that the Spanish employed in Cuba.

Roosevelt himself apparently felt distaste for Cubans and had nothing more to do with the island. After the Rough Riders were demobilized, he became governor of New York and then McKinley's running mate in the 1900 election. When McKinley was killed by a Polish anarchist a year later, Roosevelt ascended to the presidency. His greatest legacy is perhaps the Panama Canal, which he wrested from Colombia and justified by describing Colombians as "contemptible little creatures." [25] Roosevelt's reputation has continued to rise in the twentieth century and he now has his own island in the Potomac River.

Despite America's eagerness to leave, there was a price to pay for Cuban independence. The Platt Amendment was the brainchild of Secretary of State Elihu Root and under U.S. pressure was inserted into the new Cuban constitution in 1902. Specifically, it gave the United States the right to intervene "for the preservation of Cuban independence" or to protect "life, property, and individual liberty." Other provisions prohibited Cuba from entering into foreign treaties without U.S. consent and limited public debt. Perhaps the most bitter pill to swallow was the U.S. right to maintain military bases on Cuban soil. The result is the American naval base at Guantanamo Bay, leased in perpetuity for the sum of $2,000 a year. Although it has little strategic value for the U.S. Navy, after 2001, it served as a detention facility for suspected members of the Al Qaeda terrorist group. Originally the United States intended to establish other bases at Cienfuegos, the Bay of Nipe and Bahia Honda, but it was limited to one due to Cuban protests. Although the Platt Amendment was annulled in 1934, it has continued to poison the murky well of U.S.-Cuba relations, and the Helms-Burton Act of 1996* reflects much of its wording.

---

* Also known as the Libertad Act, it strengthened the U.S. trade embargo against Cuba.

## THE PRESIDENT'S SHOES

The Avenida de los Presidentes (also known as G Street) is a broad, tree-lined boulevard that begins in El Vedado beneath the castle of El Principe and funnels down into the Malecón. It is named for the statues of presidents along the grassy median, including Benito Juarez and Salvador Allende. At the corner of Calzada was a statue of Tomás Estrada Palma, Cuba's first president, but it was torn down by a mob in 1959. If you stand beneath the elaborate plinth, all you can see is a pair of massive bronze shoes.

Estrada was a planter from Bayamo who fought in the Ten Year War and served as president of the rebel government. Captured by the Spaniards in 1877, he was imprisoned in Barcelona. When the war ended, he went to Honduras and then upstate New York. Retired from politics, Estrada became a Quaker and founded a school for boys in Central Valley called the Instituto Estrada Palma. He might have lived out his days as a schoolmaster had Martí not recruited him to join the movement. After the latter's death, Estrada led the Cuban Revolutionary Party and ably represented the insurgents in New York, providing Hearst's reporters with copious press releases. A naturalized American citizen, Estrada actively encouraged U.S. intervention.

But having lived in exile for nearly a quarter century, Estrada was not well known in Cuba. The obvious choice for president was Gómez. Initially slighted by the Americans, he had returned triumphantly to Havana after the Spanish surrender and installed himself in the Quinta de Molinos, the summer residence of the captain-generals. But the incorruptible old Dominican was weary and had no interest in politics. He threw his support behind Estrada and lived out his days in quiet dignity until his death in 1905.

Because of his fondness for America, Estrada was eminently acceptable to General Wood, who filled the election commission with his supporters and assured his election in December 1901 as the unopposed candidate of the Republican Party. The Cuban Republic was officially proclaimed on May 20, 1902.

The seventy-year-old president quickly acquired a reputation as an able administrator, and continued the rapid program of economic development started by the Americans. He was also scrupulously honest, perhaps the only Cuban president to merit that accusation. Yet some of his associates lacked his restraint and gleefully plundered the new newly minted treasury by giving themselves lavish salaries and selling public offices. In particular, the Congress elected in 1904 was plagued with scandal, and Estrada was powerless to stop it.

Despite this, the first years of the Cuban Republic were hopeful ones. The birth rate increased sharply, and between 1899 and 1907, the population under five increased 162 percent. This points to one of the undoubted achievements of the U.S. occupation, the eradication of yellow fever. General Wood, a doctor, appointed a commission headed by Walter Reed to seek a cure. Their work was based on the earlier research of a Cuban doctor of Scottish descent named Carlos Finlay, who posited that the disease was spread by mosquitoes. Reed's efforts were successful, and the number of cases of yellow fever dropped from 1,400 in 1900 to none in 1902.

Another reason for the increase in population was a massive migration of Spaniards to Cuba. This seems surprising given the bitterness of the war, yet between 1902 and 1910, 200,000 Spaniards arrived on the island. [26]To process these immigrants, an Ellis Island-like facility called Triscornia was built across the harbor in Casablanca. One million would arrive by 1930, a demographic flood that would change the face of Havana. The new arrivals quickly dominated certain sectors of the economy, such as the retail trade, and the skinflint *gallego* at the corner store, or *bodega*, became a stock Cuban character. Spaniards had their own banks, schools, and mutual aid societies, which provided members with insurance and medical care. The best examples are the lavish Centro Gallego and Centro Asturiano* beaming at each other across the Parque Central.

Yet electoral chicanery would be Estrada's undoing. Opposing the Republicans was the Liberal Party headed by José Miguel Gómez. As the presidential election approached, the Liberals complained of fraud and withdrew. Estrada was thus reelected in December 1905, once more without opposition. All was quiet for a few months, but by August 1906 the disgruntled Liberals had raised the flag of rebellion in Pinar del Río and prepared to march upon Havana. Armed with machetes and weapons of the *mambises*, they comprised a formidable army of 24,000. Since the Americans had not organized a standing army, Estrada had at his disposal

---

* These ornate buildings were social clubs benefiting natives of Galicia and Asturias, respectively.

only 600 soldiers and a few rural guards. Under the terms of the Platt Amendment, he formally requested U.S. intervention.

President Roosevelt, with problems of his own in Panama, greeted this request with annoyance and declared:

> At the moment, I am so angry with that infernal Cuban republic that I would like to wipe its people off the face of the earth. All we have wanted from them was that they would behave themselves and be prosperous and happy so that we would not have to interfere. And now, lo and behold, they have started an utterly unjustifiable and pointless revolution. [27]

Roosevelt stalled by sending William Taft, his secretary of war, to Havana. His strategy was to force the Cubans to come to terms, but Estrada outfoxed him by abruptly resigning. With no alternative, Roosevelt sent 2,000 marines to Havana, where they established themselves at Camp Columbia, their old barracks on the heights of Marianao. The second American occupation of Cuba had begun, and would last until 1909. The marines would return in 1912 to quell racial unrest and again in 1917 to prevent another uprising by the Liberals.

Estrada left Havana by train for Matanzas to retire once more from politics, and died in 1908. He is almost universally reviled in Cuba as a turncoat, as seen in the destruction of his statue on the Avenida de los Presidentes. Yet this is hardly fair, given his dedication to the cause of Cuban independence stretching back to the Ten Year War. Martí certainly admired both his courage and integrity. Estrada's reputation was ruined in America as well—Roosevelt considered him a coward and blamed him for invoking the Platt Amendment. Yet in his defense, Cuba's first president had little choice under the rules of the game established by the American proconsuls. The purpose of the Platt Amendment had been to maintain U.S. control over Cuba, but it proved to be an onerous responsibility.

## WHO SANK THE MAINE?

The question of who sank the *Maine* is moot to the thousands of New Yorkers who pass the somber memorial to its crew each day on Central Park South, a stone's throw from the statue of Martí meeting his death at Dos Ríos.

Another monument to the *Maine* was built by the Cuban government in 1925 on the Malecón, near the Hotel Nacional. At the base are massive cannons from the sunken battleship. From it rise two Corinthian columns upon which perched a bronze eagle with a wingspan of thirty feet. The eagle was as unlucky as the *Maine* herself. The paint was hardly dry when it was felled by the vicious hurricane of 1926 (which also toppled La Giraldilla from the belltower of the Real Fuerza), and it now hangs in the former residence of the U.S. ambassador. The eagle was replaced in 1928 only to be shattered by a mob after the Bay of Pigs invasion in 1961. Its head now adorns the cafeteria of the U.S. Interests Section, while its wings can be seen in the museum in the Palacio de los Capitanes Generales. Castro later dedicated a plaque on the pedestal that states:

> *To the victims of the Maine, who were sacrificed by imperialist voracity in its eagerness to seize the island of Cuba.*

During the 1960s, Pablo Picasso offered to replace the eagle with a dove of peace, but it never alighted, another victim of the Cold War. The columns remain empty.

A "victim" implies a crime, and doubts about the explosion lingered on. The *Maine* remained at the bottom of Havana Harbor until 1911, when a steel cofferdam was erected around her and the water was pumped out. Investigators once more examined the wreckage and reviewed the report of the earlier court of inquiry. They confirmed the findings that the ammunition magazine had been detonated by an external explosion but offered no additional proof. Presumably it was caused by a floating mine or a torpedo.

Is this the "conspiracy" warned of by Fitzhugh Lee or the "treachery" that justified U.S. intervention for Roosevelt? Like the fictional detective Nero Wolfe, let us assemble the suspects in this century-old and still-unsolved murder mystery. Of all of them, the Spaniards had the weakest motive. Tension had been high between the two governments, and Spain had every reason to keep the United States from intervening. The *Maine* had been welcomed with all decorum, and sailors from the nearby cruiser *Alfonso XII* were among the first to rescue the survivors, as Captain Sigsbee himself noted gratefully. The accidental detonation of a torpedo seems equally unlikely, given the high volume of traffic in the harbor.

Could a rogue Spanish commander, with characteristic fatalism, have wanted a war? This scenario is implausible given the mismatched combatants. Weary and divided imperial Spain could hardly prevail over the superpower-to-be in its own backyard. The catastrophe visited upon

Spain by the brief war, resulting in the loss of its entire overseas empire, inspired a popular saying: No matter how bad things get, *más se perdió en Cuba* (more was lost in Cuba).

What of the Cubans? Many exiles, such as Estrada, actively worked for intervention, and the destruction of the *Maine* certainly accomplished that. Moreover, beleaguered rebel commanders, such as Calixto Garcia, welcomed the arrival of American troops. But despite the motive, no suspect emerges. Had the plot been discovered, it would have had disastrous consequences for the insurrection, perhaps an entente between the United States and Spain. And if the *mambises* had the means to sink armored battleships in Havana Harbor, they would certainly have struck earlier—against the Spanish fleet.

Aficionados of conspiracy theories naturally point the finger at Citizen Hearst, though there is no evidence to implicate him. However, there are means and motive. The Machiavellian publisher certainly had the wealth to obtain a suitable bomb, and enough henchmen, such as Davis and Remington, to detonate it beneath the *Maine*. His objective was evident enough: increased circulation for the *Journal*. But Hearst was also a patriot, and it seems unlikely he would have killed nearly the entire ship's crew as a promotional gimmick.

Could a mysterious, unnamed tycoon have been behind it? As had been predicted, the war brought staggering economic benefits to American industry, opening up vast markets not just in Latin America but in Asia as well. The collapse of the Cuban economy provided easy pickings for American capital during the subsequent occupation of the island, creating dynastic fortunes that continue to this day. Yet however tempting it is to suspect the emerging military-industrial complex of 1898, no culprit steps forward.

Despite the two courts of inquiry, most Americans eventually gravitated from conspiracy theories to the conclusion that the explosion originated internally. The investigators had agreed that the forward ammunition magazine on the port side of the ship had exploded. This magazine was separated from a coal bunker by a single steel bulkhead. If improperly stored, coal could ignite by spontaneous combustion, as had occurred in other ships. The bunker had been filled three months earlier at Newport News, Virginia, enough time for spontaneous combustion to take place. This would suggest negligence on the part of Captain Sigsbee or the U.S. Navy itself. At the time, the crime of the *Maine* could well have been a cover-up on the part of the naval investigators.

In 1976, Rear Admiral Hyman G. Rickover undertook an exhaustive study of the findings using state-of-the-art technology. [28]He found no evidence of an external blast from a torpedo or floating mine and concluded: "The evidence is consistent with an internal explosion alone."

After the second court of inquiry, the gash in the *Maine*'s hull caused by the explosion was sealed. When the cofferdam was opened, the barnacle-encrusted battleship floated to the surface of Havana Harbor. On February 16, 1912, she was towed four miles out to sea and sunk for the last time.

# CHAPTER 8

# *Republic of Rumba*

## *From the Capitolio to the Malecón*

*You can stare at the pretty señoritas because such staring is a compliment, not a crime.*

—Basil Woon, *When It's Cocktail Time in Cuba*

Heading south from the Hotel Inglaterra, with the Centro Gallego to your right, you soon come to the Capitolio. While it's Havana's largest building (in fact, it's the fifth biggest edifice in the world), it gets lost in the marble jungle of Centro Habana. Its location seems an afterthought, sandwiched between the Prado and the Barrio Chino. The French architect Jean Nicolas Claude Forestier, who gave Havana its neoclassical sheen in the 1920s, proposed to remedy this by enlarging Brasil Street and creating a majestic approach from the port. The Capitolio would then have been visible from ships entering the harbor, much like the lighthouse of El Morro. But this never came to pass, and Habana Vieja was spared yet again.

The site of the Capitolio was once a swamp outside the city walls where Habaneros dumped their garbage. Nearby was the Campo de Marte, a parade ground, and the city's bullring. In 1843, it was the location of the Estación Villanueva, the terminus of Cuba's first railroad, connecting Havana and Bejucal. With the expansion of the railways during the American occupation, the station was moved to its present site across from Martí's birthplace. In 1910, construction began at the abandoned rail yard on what was to be the Presidential Palace. This decision was soon reversed by President-elect Menocal, who decided to build the palace at its present location on the other side of the Prado at Refugio Street. The Capitolio, home of the Cuban legislature, would be built in the former swamp.

But Menocal's administration was known for payola rather than public works, and the Capitolio remained unfinished. Following World War I, pent-up demand skyrocketed the price of sugar from 7.3 cents per pound in November 1919 to 22.5 cents in May 1920. The resulting sugar boom brought previously unimaginable prosperity to Cuba in what became known as the "dance of the millions." The jig was soon up, however. In June 1920, the price began to drop, and by December, it had plunged to 3.75 cents.[1] Planters who had borrowed lavishly now found themselves bankrupt, and the run on deposits closed all but a handful of banks. Cuba's financial system was resurrected only by a massive infusion of U.S. capital, led by J.P. Morgan with a loan of $50 million. Cuba thus passed within a year from *vacas gordas* to *vacas flacas* (literally, fat cows to thin cows).

Meanwhile, the abandoned construction site was used for a variety of purposes. A flea market was established, and near it the big top of the Pubillones Circus, with twelve lions whose roars interrupted opera performances at the nearby Gran Teatro. One of Cuba's first neon signs was erected, an enormous green frog advertising Campana Gin. There was also a macabre exhibit on the effects of syphilis, with a sign at the entrance that said:

*Aqui el que entra bailando rumba sale todo desconflautado.*
(Whoever comes in here dancing rumba leaves deflated.)[2]

It was not until the election of Gerardo Machado in 1925 that construction of the Capitolio began. The cupola went up in record time, and the building was inaugurated with much fanfare in 1929. It cost $20 million, over one-third of the national budget.

It is often repeated that the Capitolio was a slavish copy of the U.S. Capitol. In fact, it owes its design to an earlier inspiration, the Pantheon in Paris. Though taller than the U.S. Capitol by thirteen feet, the cupola is more slender and appears to float gracefully on the normally cloudless sky. Once inside, you enter the Salon de los Pasos Perdidos (Hall of Lost Steps), a grandiose two-story lobby with an inlaid marble star from which all distances are measured in Cuba. At mile zero (the center of the star) is a replica of a yellowish, twenty-three-carat diamond that once belonged to Czar Nicholas II. One night during the term of President Grau, the original was chiseled out of the floor by a Cuban Pink Panther. A few weeks later, it mysteriously reappeared in Grau's office, no questions asked or answered. The original is now presumably safe in a vault. At the end of the hall is the fifty-six-foot statue *La Republica*, a fierce maiden in a Greek tunic holding a spear and the Cuban coat of arms. Cast in bronze and covered in gold leaf, it is the third largest indoor statue in the world, after the Golden Buddha in Nara, Japan, and the pensive statue of Abraham Lincoln in Washington, D.C. Despite these superlatives, the Capitolio is usually empty save for a stray tourist or two. No longer the seat of government, it now houses the dusty National Library of Science and Technology.

Machado is unfailingly described as a monster, but he was a seductive one. Hailing from Santa Clara, he was originally a butcher and lost two fingers on his left hand to a meat cleaver. During the War of Independence, he attained the rank of brigadier general and thereafter set out to enrich himself, like most of his comrades in arms. After managing a sugar mill, he became vice president of the American-owned Cuban Electric Company, which controlled virtually all public utilities in Havana, and parlayed his wealth into political connections. Photographs of Machado show a dapper, fleshy man with horn-rimmed glasses and bristly white hair. Sharp-witted and amiable, he presented himself as a successful businessman (which he was) and reassured U.S bankers that the status quo would continue. The result was even more credit to prop up Cuba's ailing economy. Chase National Bank loaned $10 million in 1926, $50 million in 1928, and $20 million in 1930.

Flush with cash, Machado embarked on an energetic building program that literally changed the face of Havana. It resulted not just in the lavish new Capitolio but the Carretera Central, a highway that linked one end of Cuba to the other for the first time. It was Machado who hired Forestier, much admired in both Europe and Latin America. The Frenchman began his work by flying over Havana in a plane and determined that the city's monuments and parks needed to be linked by boulevards providing easy access and visual perspective.[3] Bearing this in mind, Forestier enlarged the Prado and planted rows of Spanish laurels between the cast-iron lions. He extended the grounds of the Capitolio with the adjoining Parque de la Fraternidad and landscaped the Avenida de los Presidentes with its statue of Estrada Palma.

But his greatest achievement was the Malecón. The Spaniards never built along the rocky shore west of La Punta, which was often buffeted by fierce winds and high tides. During the occupation, General Wood ordered the construction of a seawall to prevent flooding. It was extended to Belascoain Street in 1919 and farther toward the Vedado in 1921. But it was Forestier who gave the Malecón its present form, modeled on the Costanera in Buenos Aires, another of his projects. Reaching the Almendares River, it was embellished with verdant monuments such as the memorial to the *Maine* and the statue of Máximo Gómez. Porticoed town houses soon lined the waterfront, and Habaneros became accustomed to taking their *paseo* along the Malecón at dusk.

Together with the Capitolio and El Morro, the Malecón is one of Havana's most recognizable landmarks. It spans the city's entire history, from the sixteenth century Spanish battlements of the harbor to the snazzy Hotel Riviera, built on the eve of the Revolution. Like the Plaza de Armas, it is flypaper to fictional characters in Havana. For Hemingway's bootlegger in the 1930s, it was the first thing he saw when approaching Havana by sea. In the 1950s, Greene's ersatz spy dodged the spray that occasionally swept over the seawall. Other writers have described the Malecón as "a brilliantly-lit garland on the water" and "a mosaic of seasons and states of mind." Forestier accurately foresaw that cars would supersede pedestrians, and the Malecón soon became Havana's major thoroughfare, linking the port with the suburbs to the west.

Now there is considerably less traffic. During the Special Period of the 1990s, the streamlined American roadsters were replaced by Chinese-made bicycles with names like "Flying Pigeon." There was once a famous billboard on the Malecón for bathing suits showing an elegant swimmer plunging into the waves. The billboards now bear political slogans rather than advertising, such as one showing a clean-cut revolutionary shouting at a decrepit Uncle Sam: "*¡No le tenemos absolutamente ningun miedo!*" (We are not afraid of you in the least!) Pedestrians have reclaimed the Malecón, and during the day, entire families stroll up and down. After dark, it belongs to lovers.

What fattened the *vacas flacas* of the Cuban Republic was tourism. A steady stream of American tourists had followed the foreign correspondents and carpetbaggers to the Hotel Inglaterra, drawn by Cuba's proximity, lovely scenery, and climate. This stream would increase when travel

to Europe was curtailed in World War I, and become a flood after passage
of the Volstead Act in 1919. Prohibition virtually created the Cuban
tourist industry, adding plentiful rum to the allures of sun and sultry
señoritas. To the dismay of the U.S. Congress, Cuba soon passed a bill allowing casino gambling, and the gold rush was on.

Henry Flagler had completed his monumental railway to Key West
in 1908, providing easy access to Cuba. Tourists could board luxurious
trains like the *Havana Special* at Grand Central Station and connect with
the P&O ferry to arrive in Havana fifty-six hours later. The Ward Line
operated steamships from New York to Havana, and the United Fruit
Company ran ships from Boston and New Orleans. Daily flights between
Key West and Havana began in 1921. Pan American flew seaplanes from
its Miami terminal at Dinner Key, landing directly in Havana Harbor.
The early seaplanes were called "flying submarines" because the passenger cabin was partially submerged until takeoff.[4]

In 1914, there were 33,000 visitors to Cuba. By 1920 this had bal-
looned to 56,000, reaching 90,000 in 1928.[5] Celebrities visiting Havana
during this period included Gary Cooper, Gloria Swanson, Henry Luce
and his bride Clare, New York mayor Jimmy Walker, George Gersh-
win, Tom Mix, Charles Lindbergh, and Babe Ruth. But it was not just
the "jet" set. Havana's proximity and affordability made it possible for
many middle-class Americans to visit as well. At a time when Las Vegas
was a filling station in the desert and Miami was little more than a beach
resort, Havana was welcoming conventioneers like the Shriners and Ro-
tarians. The constant presence of the U.S. Navy meant a randy torrent
of sailors on leave. Havana had something for them as well. The number of prostitutes in the city rose from 4,000 in 1912 to 7,400 in 1931.[6]
When a battleship entered the harbor, it would often be met by boat-
loads of them.

A number of newer hotels had long surpassed the Inglaterra, such as
the Sevilla-Biltmore with its sumptuous tiled lobby and the Hotel Plaza
with a rooftop bar overlooking the Parque Central. The most elegant of
all was the Hotel Nacional, built in 1930. It is still Havana's finest hotel,
and one of the most beautiful in the world. You approach it from O Street
in the Vedado down a long driveway lined with royal palms. Designed by
the New York firm of McKim, Mead & White in the Mediterranean revival style, it resembles the Breakers in Palm Beach, another of their hotels. But the Hotel Nacional is best seen from the water. Its twin,
red-tiled miradors soar regally from a rocky bluff with a waterfall, and its
terraced gardens float above the shore like the deck of a cruise ship. Near

the bar is a massive Krupps cannon, all that remains of the Spanish battery of Santa Clara, still pointing out to sea.

An iron bridge spanning the Almendares River was approved in 1919, and the countryside of Marianao (where Camp Columbia was located) quickly became developed. This became the site of the Gran Casino Nacional and the Oriental Park Racetrack, run by American businessman John Bowman. The nearby Havana Country Club boasted a perfectly manicured eighteen-hole golf course, Cuba's first.

During Prohibition, many saloons moved lock, stock, and barrel to Havana, which had about seven thousand drinking establishments by the 1920s.[7] According to Basil Woon in his rum-soaked 1928 travelogue *When It's Cocktail Time in Cuba*, "Every restaurant and nearly every grocery in Havana is a barroom." These ranged from elegant lounges in hotels like the Sevilla-Biltmore to rowdy saloons like Sloppy Joe's. On Zulueta Street near the Prado, the latter has yet to be renovated, perhaps for fear of a lawsuit from its lucrative namesake in Key West. It was originally known as La Victoria and reportedly renamed by a vengeful journalist when the owner, José López, refused to lend him $50. He wrote an editorial claiming it was filthy, and the notoriety brought in more drinkers.

Nightclubs also proliferated, from the snooty Sans Souci to *fritas* (dives) such as the Zombie Club, not too far from each other in Marianao. Another form of entertainment was provided by *academias de baile* such as the Havana Sport, a rowdy music hall at the corner of Galiano and San José streets where a dance could be had for a *real*.[8]

American tourism peaked in January 1928, when Machado proudly hosted President Calvin Coolidge at the Sixth Annual Pan American Conference in Havana. The Cubans celebrated the visit of the American president with jubilant parades, polo matches, and flying exhibitions put on by Pan American. The crowd at Oriental Park Racetrack was entertained by Will Rogers, who cracked jokes with a beaming Machado. A month later, Charles Lindbergh visited for five days, to even greater hoopla. Before he left on a daring nonstop flight to St. Louis, he took Machado for a quick jaunt over Havana.

## CAPABLANCA AND KID CHOCOLATE

At the time, Habaneros did at least two things better than anyone else.

The first was play chess. One of the most popular openings in the game is named after a fifteenth century Spanish monk named Ruy López,

The original Sloppy Joe's was located on Zulueta Street, near the Prado. (Author's collection)

and chess came to Cuba with the conquistadors. The Havana Chess Club was world-renowned and in the nineteenth century played host to chess-playing luminaries such as Paul Morphy and Captain MacKenzie.

José Raul Capablanca is often regarded as the best player ever. Born in 1888 to a wealthy family in Havana, Capablanca was a prodigy on the order of Mozart. He first learned to play at age four, and within a day, he could beat his father. He became a member of the Havana chess club at age eight, quickly becoming its strongest player. In 1905, Capablanca attended Columbia University and took on all comers at the famed Manhattan Chess Club. He had a special gift for simultaneous play, in which a chess master plays several opponents at once. During a tour of the United States he won an astounding 168 games in ten sessions before finally losing.

Capablanca won a hotly contested tournament in San Sebastian in 1911 in which all the leading European grandmasters played, and from then on he piled one victory atop another. The Cuban played with mathematical precision, and his style was described as "serene" and "lucid." In 1921, he won the world championship in a match against Emmanuel Lasker.

In spite of his fragile physique, Capablanca had a reputation as a lady killer and also served in Cuba's diplomatic corps in czarist Russia and throughout World War I. He later lost his title to Alexander Alekhine, and his play suffered with declining health. Due to Capablanca's legacy (and perhaps the thirty-year Russian presence), Cubans remain formidable chess players.

The other pastime at which Habaneros excelled was boxing. In contrast to chess, the sweet science did not arrive in Cuba until after the War of Independence. Prizefighting was enjoyed by U.S. soldiers during the occupation and quickly caught on. A fight between Jack Johnson and Jess Willard at Oriental Park Racetrack in 1915 attracted an audience of 25,000. Before long, Cuban boxers were appearing on fight cards in the United States.

Eligio Sardiñas, aka Kid Chocolate, was born in the poor neighborhood of El Cerro and reportedly learned to fight while defending his paper route. At the age of eleven, he won a tournament sponsored by the newspaper *La Noche* and remained undefeated as an amateur before turning pro. In 1928, at the age of eighteen, Kid Chocolate (also known as the Cuban Bonbon) went to New York and fought his way from dingy gyms to Madison Square Garden. In 1931, he won his first title with a TKO (technical knockout) over junior lightweight champion Benny Bass. A year later, he won the world featherweight title against Lew Feldman.

Like Capablanca, Kid Chocolate had a natural, fluid style, combining dazzling footwork with two-handed punching skills. He also had a winning personality and was adulated not just in Havana and New York but also Paris, where he fought in 1933. The Afro-Cuban poet Nicolas Guillén even wrote a poem in his honor, praising *el punch de tu sonrisa* (the punch of your smile).[9] Kid Chocolate shared with Capablanca a love for the high life. His winnings were spent largely on fast cars, white linen suits, and alimony. After his retirement in 1938, he lived modestly in Havana on a pension from Batista and later opened a gym.

## EL VEDADO

*. . . a city that is a marketplace of columns, a jungle of columns, an infinity of columns . . .*

—Alejo Carpentier, *City of Columns*

Havana took the onslaught of tourists in stride, and the *norteamericanos* rarely strayed far from the bars of Centro Habana and the nightclubs of Marianao. Due to increased immigration, the city had doubled in size by

1931, and it continued to expand west across the Almendares River and south toward the hills of El Cerro. Like Habana Vieja a century before, Centro Habana was marked by frenetic commercial activity. A shopping district grew along Galiano Street, the location of the chic department store El Encanto. The corner of Galiano and San Rafael became known as the *Esquina del Pecado* (corner of sin). Here every day around five o'-clock, men would line up to watch the shopgirls leave the Woolworths Ten Cent and try their hand at the time-honored Cuban sport of *piropos*.[10] A *piropo* is a spontaneous compliment or comment (generally about anatomy) delivered sotto voce to a woman of scant acquaintance. While such behavior can lead to blows and lawsuits in American cities, in Havana, it remains alive and well. One outrageous but untranslatable *piropo* I heard addressed to a fulsome woman on the Malecón went something like this:

> *Ay, mi negra, usaste toda la libreta en la retaguardia.*
> (You used your entire ration book on your rear end.)

A few blocks north, on the corner of Virtudes and Consulado streets, was the raucous Alhambra Theater. It was the home of the *teatro venacular,* a sort of burlesque show. In between chorus lines of scantily clad dancers and other vaudeville routines, the main event was a comedy act featuring the *Negrito*, an actor in blackface (blacks were not yet allowed to perform on stage) together with the *Gallego*, a parody of a Spaniard in a beret and red sash.[11] *Negrito* often competed with *Gallego* for the affections of a beautiful mulatta, *Doña Fulana*. The wily, duplicitous *Negrito* (played most memorably by the comedian Arquimedes Pous) usually outwitted the skinflint *Gallego*, though the outcome was far from certain. The jokes often lampooned politicians, and rival factions in the audience would try to shout each other down. The Alhambra was torn down in the 1940s, though the *teatro vernacular* continued until the Revolution.

The increasingly proper Cuban middle class abhorred this *chusmeria*.* By the 1930s, it had already migrated to the suburb of El Vedado, a thumbnail-shaped swath of land between Centro Habana and the shore of the Almendares River. In contrast to the rest of Havana, the Vedado was a

---

* *Chusmeria* is a uniquely Cuban form of lower-class vulgarity, exemplified by the Alhambra. But, in fact, the Alhambra's exclusively male audience came from all classes.

carefully planned urban development, one of the first of its kind. *Vedado* means "forbidden" in Spanish, since the fields to the west of the city walls had been the route used by the corsairs in 1555 as well as the redcoats in 1762 to attack Havana, and were left barren for defensive purposes. The military necessity for this killing field had vanished by the nineteenth century, and owners petitioned to subdivide it in 1859. Enlightened zoning laws mandated that the streets be sixteen meters wide and that grassy *parterres* run between the curb and the sidewalk.[12] The effect of an urban garden was further accentuated by houses being set back five meters from the street. The ongoing struggle for independence starting in the 1860s paralyzed development of the Vedado, and only 30 percent of the lots had houses on them by 1894. But that number quickly mushroomed during the American occupation when Centro Habana grew crowded with refugees and the electric trolley on Linea Street provided easy access.

Today this Vedado exists only in yellowing photo albums. The wave of restoration has yet to cross Centro Habana, and there are often huge potholes in the street. Many of the houses have been altered and subdivided by post-Revolution residents and would be unrecognizable to their former owners. Others are in sad disrepair. But to walk down one of the broad avenues like Linea or Paseo is to leaf through a catalog of Cuban architecture. While some remaining houses, like the one-story Spanish villa on Linea and Second Street, were built in the 1880s, most were erected in the 1920s and 1930s. A dizzying variety of architectural styles found expression, from Moorish to Gothic, from Spanish revival to Romanesque, and from French-inspired art deco to art nouveau brought by Catalan architects. There are palaces like that of the Condesa de Revila de Camargo on Seventeenth and E streets, modeled after Versailles, and tiny bungalows in dire need of plaster and paint. There are sleek prairie-style houses and Swiss-style chalets, and true oddities like the house built by one of Machado's ministers on the banks of the Almendares opposite the castle of La Chorrera. It's a gaudy stone fantasy with a faux Japanese water grotto, now a restaurant where *jineteras* (hookers) gather at dusk.

The banyan trees lining the streets offer shade on even the hottest days, but the Vedado is also dotted with parks, usually taking up an entire block. Among the most interesting is the Parque John Lennon, three blocks west of Paseo between Fifteenth and Seventeenth streets. The Beatles have always had a rabid following in Cuba, and on December 8, 2000, the twentieth anniversary of Lennon's death, Castro himself unveiled a life-size statue of the former Beatle sitting on a park bench. By the popular Cuban artist José Villa Soberón, it bears the inscription, "People say I'm a dreamer, but I'm not the only one." Lennon's glasses were stolen twice, and now the statue is illuminated by floodlights and guarded twenty-four hours a day. Nonetheless, it has assumed cult status, and one afternoon I saw flowers, candles, and other offerings around it.

One constant are the porticoes enforced by the original zoning restrictions. Similar to those mandated in public buildings by the Laws of the Indies in Habana Vieja, these porches supported by slender columns act as a buffer between the private home and the public street. The endless rows of Corinthian, Ionic, and Doric columns inspired Carpentier to call Havana "the city of columns." In a celebrated essay by that name, the novelist rhapsodized over "the incredible profusion of columns, in a city that is a marketplace of columns, a jungle of columns, an infinity of columns." For Carpentier, this forest of columns was a prime example of the mestizo baroque that is unique to Cuban architecture.[13]

Nowhere is Havana's eclecticism more evident than in the Colón Cemetery, on the southwestern edge of the Vedado. Habaneros were originally laid to rest within churches, but the threat of epidemic led to a decree that burials should take place outside the city walls. In 1802, the Espada Cemetery was established in San Lazaro, but by midcentury it was desperately crowded, and the poor were often dumped in common graves covered with quicklime. Construction of the Colón Cemetery began in 1871 based on a design by the Spanish architect Calixto de Loira, who soon after expired and was among the first to be buried there. The walled necropolis covers 135 acres and takes the form of a Roman camp, with a numbered grid of streets divided into four symmetrical quarters. The dizzying variety of funerary art has made this a morbid tourist attraction on the order of Pére Lachaise in Paris, and *guias* (guidebooks) are even distributed at the entrance gate. Perhaps the most spectacular is the chapel of Catalina de Lasa, with a glass dome by Lalique and art deco doors of black marble. Many prominent historical figures are buried here, such as Máximo Gómez, and there is a monument to the medical students executed by the Spaniards in 1871.

Tombs often reflect the occupation or tastes of the departed—an architect's final resting place is topped by a pyramid, and a domino player's grave reveals her final move, a *doble tres* (double three.) Needless to say, Capablanca's tomb is topped by a marble chess piece. The Bacardi mausoleum is guarded by cast-iron bats, and an elaborate memorial to fireman features a marble goose. Habaneros still visit the tomb of La

Milagrosa, a young woman who died in childbirth with her daughter in 1901. The baby was placed at her feet, but when the grave was reopened a few years later, the tiny corpse was in her mother's arms, or so the story goes. Expectant mothers ask for her blessing and then leave without turning their backs to the tomb.[14]

## TERTULIAS

If the Jazz Age produced some of Havana's most striking architecture, it was also one of the most artistic and culturally fertile periods in Cuban history.

The avant garde was led by the Grupo Minorista, a loosely knit group of about fifty poets, artists, journalists, lawyers, and other professionals. Beginning around 1923, they began meeting in Saturday afternoon *tertulias* in cafés such as the Acera del Louvre. The uniquely Cuba tradition of the *tertulia* seems oddly quaint today. Inherited from the Spaniards, it was a cordial opportunity for (usually) men to discuss the events of the day, but for the Minoristas it became a lively, no-holds-barred cultural forum. They included painter and cartoonist Eduardo Abela; Ruben Martínez Villena, poet and founder of the Cuban Communist Party; Sorbonne-and Harvard-educated lawyer Jorge Mañach; the first Historiador, Emilio Roig de Leuchsenring; and, of course, Alejo Carpentier, our literary Zelig. The Minoristas were concerned with *cubanidad*, or what it meant to be Cuban. Their ideas were disseminated be several influential magazines, such as *Carteles* (edited by Carpentier) and Roig's *Social*.

It is difficult to pin down the heterogeneous, nondogmatic Minoristas. Roig sparked a reexamination of Cuban history and together with Mañach encouraged a renewed interest in Martí's work. In 1927, the group issued a manifesto of sorts that encouraged the "revision of false and tired values" and "new art in its diverse manifestations." Although the Minoristas were for the most part white, middle-class Habaneros, they did much to promote *afrocubanismo*, which would soon flower in poetry, painting, and music.

Their manifesto also revealed a vague political agenda, calling for the "economic independence of Cuba" and "reform in the public education system." It was also against "Yankee imperialism" and "political dictatorship." This soon brought them into conflict with the increasingly repressive Machado, who jailed Carpentier for a few months in 1927. The group soon dissolved, with many of its members, including Mañach, joining the political opposition and others, such as Carpentier, choosing exile in Paris.

Among the Minoristas were several painters, and today their work is the most sought after Cuban art in the world. They are referred to collectively as the Vanguardia.[15] Nearly all of them studied at the prestigious San Alejandro Academy of Fine Arts, located in the Barrio Chino. The academy was founded in 1818, and its first director was the French neoclassical painter Jean Baptiste Vermay. Vermay painted the three large canvases depicting the founding of Havana in the Templete, where his remains are buried.

One of the earliest members of the Vanguardia was Eduardo Abela. After graduating from San Alejandro in 1921, he traveled to Paris, where he was influenced by the work of Marc Chagall. His inspiration was the Cuban countryside, and in *Guajiros* (1938), he depicts a group of countryfolk in calm, dignified poses, though their roosters suggest they enjoy cockfighting. Abela was also a cartoonist of note, and from 1930 to 1934 he published in the conservative newspaper *Diario de la Marina* a series known as *El Bobo* (the fool). El Bobo is a plump, balding fellow in a straw boater whose seemingly innocuous comments concealed ruthless social commentary. In particular, Abela satirized the Machado regime and remained out of prison with difficulty.

Another alumnus of San Alejandro was Hemingway's friend Antonio Gattorno, who often joined the writer on his fishing boat the *Pilar*. He, too, lived in Paris but returned to Havana to exhibit his work in the May 1927 Exhibition of New Art, which showcased the Vanguardia. *Mujeres Junto al Rio* (1927) shows his use of Gauguin's visual vocabulary, with the voluptuous *guajiras* drying themselves on a riverbank. In 2005, a major retrospective of Gattorno's work was held at the University of Miami.

Best known of all is Wifredo Lam. He studied at San Alejandro from 1918 to 1923 and soon departed for Madrid. He participated in the Spanish Civil War and arrived in Paris in 1938 with a letter of introduction to Pablo Picasso. They grew close, and Lam was profoundly influenced by Picasso's interest in African sculpture. A joint exhibit in 2001 at the Musée Kleber in Paris showed how radically Lam's style had changed. His paintings before that time were mostly still-lifes and prosaic Cuban landscapes, but afterward his mature visual style emerged. Lam returned to Cuba in 1941 and reconnected with his Chinese and African heritage, as seen in *Huracán* (1945). Like many of his counterparts, he spent little time in Cuba and eventually settled down in Paris.

*C*

While the Minoristas held their *tertulias* at the Acera del Louvre and the Vanguardia joined the lost generation in Paris, the rumba was born.

Cuban music is yet another example of transculturation, containing ingredients as diverse as Yoruba drumming rituals and the songs of Spanish student ensembles called *tunas*. What became known as the *son* probably began as street music played in Havana's poor black neighborhoods, such as La Vibora or Jesus del Monte. Before the 1920s, *son* musicians were often persecuted and the police confiscated their bongós and maracas. But the infectious rhythm and the bawdy lyrics caught on. Many of the early *conjuntos* (bands) played in the seamy netherworld of *academias de baile* like the Havana Sport, but by 1926, the Septeto Habanero and others performed at the more upmarket Hotel Plaza.

The legitimization of *son* coincided with the rise of a powerful new medium: radio. The first national radio broadcast in Cuba took place on October 10, 1922, when station PWX transmitted the inaugural speech of President Zayas. Within a few years, radio was ubiquitous in Havana, and transmitters could be found in *bodegas*, barber shops, and cafés, even supplanting the venerable *lectores* in cigar factories. Radio stations multiplied, often with U.S. backing. By 1933, there were sixty-two on the island, surpassing any other country in Latin America. Although radio stations initially played classical music, they soon catered to popular tastes and the *son* was rapidly disseminated to middle-class listeners.

Cuban musicians played in New York, often in Harlem. Since there was no Cuban recording industry, the first *son* recordings were made there, such as a 78-record cut by the Septeto Habanero in 1920. The breakthrough came in 1930, when Antonio Machin sang "El Manisero" at the Palace Theater on Forty-seventh and Broadway.[16] The song was composed by Moises Simons and first recorded by Rita Montaner in 1928. It was inspired the traditional cry of the *pregonero* (street vendor), a familiar figure in Habana Vieja. Each with a distinctive call, *pregoneros* sold everything from buttons to pastries, but most common were peanuts sold in tightly rolled cones of newspaper. "El Manicero" was an instant hit in New York, and Machin went on to record it with RCA Victor. It would become one of the most popular songs of the twentieth century, performed in countless languages and keys. It appeared in the 1931 film *Cuban Love Song* and sold over 1 million copies of sheet music.

The popularity of "El Manisero" launched the rumba craze, not just in the United States but in Europe as well. Strictly speaking, the rumba is not music but rather dance. It was performed by a couple and generally accompanied only by bongós. The lewd, suggestive nature of their movements led it to be banned, like the *son*, but a safer, commercialized version was soon being performed in nightclubs throughout Havana. Dancers René and Estela were among the first *rumberos* to gain international success and performed at the 1933 World's Fair in Chicago. Rumba eventually lost its original meaning and came to stand for Cuban music in general, and specifically the *son*, which remains unpronounceable in English (somewhere between "son" and "song").

*Conjuntos* began appearing regularly in New York, encouraged by the success of Xavier Cugat, a Cuban bandleader who opened at the Waldorf-Astoria in 1932. Musicians followed the Vanguardia to Paris, where Josephine Baker was the toast of the town. There were soon rumba clubs throughout Montmartre. The peanut vendor himself, Moises Simons, performed at a cabaret called Melody's Bar and together with Carpentier organized a concert at the Club du Faubourg.[17]

Rumba lived on in permutations such as mambo (which enjoyed its own heyday in the 1950s) and the omnipresent salsa. But *son* itself staged an unexpected comeback when musician Ry Cooder visited Havana in 1997 and "discovered" it. The result was an album called the *Buena Vista Social Club*, a mega-hit that was the subject of an award-winning movie by German director Wim Wenders. Though the songs (most of them, like "Dos Gardenias," chestnuts from my grandmother's generation) benefited from Cooder's state-of-the-art production facilities, they were hardly sanitized for a mainstream audience. They range from sappy love songs to raunchy tunes full of double entendres. Together with the sexual innuendos are obscure references to Santeria and lyrics from Spanish poet Federico García Lorca, who visited Havana in the 1930s. Many of the musicians, who hadn't performed for years, went on tour and played to packed houses throughout the world, from New York to Amsterdam. One of them, Compay Segundo (the stage name of Francisco Repilado), was virtually unknown outside of Cuba until the *Buena Vista Social Club*. He died in 2003 at the age of ninety-six, presumably a happy man.

## THE MACHADATO

The Machadato* began auspiciously enough. The elections had been reasonably fair, the credit continued to flow from American banks, and Havana was buffed to a shine. Machado enjoyed the high life and could be seen at nightclubs such as the Chateau Madrid, dancing with dazzling showgirls from the Alhambra. But he also had a common touch and a reputation for astuteness, which most Cubans respected more than honesty in a politician. One of his campaign promises had been not to seek a second term. Machado promised national "regeneration," and it appeared that he would deliver.

But there were warning signs early on. Just a few months after the election, a cartoon ran in the newspaper *El Día*, hinting that Machado's daughter was a lesbian. The editor, Armando André, was soon murdered by thugs while leaving his house. As it turned out, Machado took himself very seriously and surrounded himself with sycophants. His supporters gave him fawning titles, such as *El Supremo* and journalists on his payroll outdid themselves in constant praise. Machado and his family also profited handsomely from Havana's building boom. His son-in-law became head of Chase National Bank's main branch in Havana, and the contract to build much of the Carretera Central went to a company that he controlled. It is estimated that Machado's take amounted to $10 million a year, a fifth of Cuba's gross national product.

Machado used this money to suborn the army, which became his power base. After the *fracaso* of 1905, when the revolt of the disgruntled Liberals necessitated U.S. intervention, a standing army of twelve thousand had been established. By Latin American standards, it was a well-drilled professional army with little political involvement. Machado changed this by promoting his people to key positions and expanded the army's reach into civilian matters, such as food distribution. Soon graft was prevalent, and many officers supplemented their pay with a hefty percentage of the take.

These dangerous undercurrents were ignored amid the rising prosperity and President Coolidge's triumphal tour of Havana in January 1928. But by then, Machado had come to regret his promise not to seek a second term. His supporters floated a proposal to change the Cuban constitution

---

* The term *Machadato* refers to the term of President Machado, from 1925 to 1933.

by banning re-election but extending his term by two years. This seemed innocuous, and even his opponents in Congress jumped on the band-wagon because it would extend their terms as well. In April 1928, a Con-stituent Assembly packed with Machado's cronies met to rubber-stamp this proposal. But the genie had been let out of the bottle, and Machado was "persuaded" to accept a second term. Since the term of office had al-ready been extended, it would be for six years. Aided by another law that banned any new political parties, Machado went on to win re-election un-opposed in November, extending his term until 1935.

This political sleight-of-hand became known as *prorogacion* and was too much even for *El Supremo*. By the time of his second inauguration on May 20, 1929, the battle lines were drawn. Much of the resistance came from students, who were among the first to object to Machado's grab for power. In 1908, the University of Havana had been moved from the crumbling Convento de San Domingo to the Vedado. It had a proud tra-dition of independence, and the students had pressed for reforms under President Zayas. At first, the opposition took the form of demonstrations known as *tánganas*. Machado proceeded cautiously, dismissing the stu-dents as *muchachos* (kids). The flashpoint came when on September 1930 a student leader named Rafael Trejo was killed by police during one such *tángana*. The movement now had a martyr, an opposition hardened around a student group known as the Directorio. Machado soon jailed all its leaders and shut down the university, which had the effect of radicaliz-ing the students further.

But the biggest blow to Machado was not the student demonstrations but the crash of the American stock market in 1929. The following year, the U.S. Congress passed the Hawley-Smoot Act, which raised tariffs on Cuban sugar. As in the "dance of the millions," the price of sugar plunged and with it the value of Cuban exports. The effect of this was like a bucket of cold water on the already overheated Cuban economy. Profits dropped, unemployment reached levels unseen since the American occu-pation, and the salaries of public employees were cut. But the depression was worldwide. In the United States there were bread lines and a rash of bank closings. The effect on tourism was immediate. The Pan American seaplanes ran less frequently, and the casinos and flashy new hotels like the Hotel Nacional were ominously empty.

With the *vacas flacas* came increased repression. Shortly after closing the university, Machado suspended constitutional guarantees throughout the island and proclaimed martial law. Newspapers were censored, and soldiers often patrolled the streets. An impressive network of informers spread fear among Habaneros, and suspects were rounded up by Machado's secret police, known as the *expertos*. Others were intimidated by the *porra*, gangsters on Machado's payroll who beat up political opponents and broke up student demonstrations with truncheons made of twisted bull hide.

This dire situation was reflected by Abela's El Bobo in a cartoon which ran on May 1931. El Bobo consoles his young son, who is tired of eating only bananas, by saying: *"Pues no llores, hijito, que ya esta llegando la hora de los mameyes."**

For a time, no one in Havana knew what the letters ABC stood for.

By the end of 1931, there were rumors of a mysterious new organization that took the name of those three letters. Its members were known as *abecedarios* and nothing was known about them except their willingness to use any means necessary to overthrow Machado. They struck first in early 1932. An anonymous phone call directed the police to a house in Flores Street used by the students to hide arms. Finding nothing, a lieutenant picked up the telephone to call the station, which triggered a massive explosion, killing several. Machado retaliated by imprisoning more students in the castle of Atarés. The ABC responded with more bombs and assassinations of policemen and other government officials, and Machado loosed his thugs on suspected members. War was declared, and Havana became a battleground.

The ABC had been founded by two young lawyers in Havana, Joaquin Martínez Sáenz and Carlos Saladrigas, who attracted a diverse group of intellectuals, professionals, and students.[18] Its objective was shared by many other groups, but what distinguished the *abecedarios* were their methods. The ABC openly advocated terrorism, not just as a way of striking at Machado but with the intent of destabilizing Cuba so as to provoke U.S. intervention. The secrecy surrounding them was no accident. Borrowing from Masonic secret societies such as the Illuminati, the ABC was organized in cells. Members knew only the leader of their cell,

---

* "Don't cry, son, it will soon be the time of the mameyes." The mamey, a tropical fruit, refers to the redcoats who stormed Havana. The "time of the mameyes" is a truly desperate hour.

and not those in any other cell. When captured, the *abecedarios* could therefore not betray the leaders of the group.

The founding cell had seven members who were known as A1, A2, A3, and so on. Martínez Sáenz and Saladrigas were one and two, respectively. Each of these seven members then founded another cell, also composed of seven members. This was the B level. For example, members of a cell founded by A1 would be B11, B12, and B13. Each B member would then start a cell of his own. B11's cell would be C111, C112, C113, and so forth. This meticulous hierarchy frustrated Machado's efforts to penetrate the ABC, and made it possible for cells to spread quickly throughout Cuba.

Martínez Sáenz recruited Minorista intellectual Jorge Mañach to help draft the group's manifesto. Given its methods, its ideas were surprisingly moderate. The ABC was committed to fighting for "new men, new ideas" and "political liberty and social justice." Styling itself as neither liberal nor conservative, it advocated reforms such as protection for small farmers, nationalization of monopolies, and special courts to try corrupt public officials. Its manifesto also proposed legislation for the protection of workers, including the right to strike, and suffrage for women.

The group's rivals, such as the Communists, branded it as fascist and racist, and even spread a rumor that ABC stood for Associacion Blanca de Cuba (White Association of Cuba). In fact, the ABC looked for "Cubans with clean hands" and had a surprisingly diverse membership. Its sober ideas drew intellectuals such as Mañach as well as fellow lawyers. If ABC methods were objectionable, many who were disillusioned with Machado flocked to its banner for lack of any alternative.* Many of the foot soldiers were students, and the Directorio established a tenuous alliance with the ABC. Due to their notoriety, the *abecedarios* were soon taking credit for many more attacks than they undertook, but there were never more than about two thousand members.

There were nightly shootings in Havana, often on the street or in public places such as theaters or cafés, and one night there were over one

---

* The ABC flag was a six-pointed Star of David, with the letters intertwined, on a green field. It often bore the words "The ABC is the hope of Cuba." It is unclear what the star alluded to. Perhaps the Maccabees, Jewish insurgents who fought the Romans.

hundred explosions. The ABC scored a victory by gunning down Captain Calvo, the brutal head of the *expertos*. Machado retaliated by increasingly brazen murders by the *porra*. Victims were usually taken to the castle of Atarés, where they were tortured by its vicious commander, Captain Crespo, and often thrown into Havana Harbor weighted down by chains. Another notorious henchman was Chief of Police Ainciart, rumored to be a drug addict and pederast, who conducted his interrogations personally.

The ABC's most spectacular attack was the subject of a little-seen film by John Huston called *We Were Strangers*, starring Jennifer Jones as a beautiful *abecedaria* named China Valdez and Pedro Armendariz as a particularly slimy policeman. In September 1932, Clemente Vásquez Bello, the president of the Cuban Senate and a close friend of Machado's, was shot from a passing car as he left the Havana Yacht Club. As it turned out, the assassination was just a means to an end. The *abecedarios* had tunneled beneath the Colón Cemetery and placed a huge explosive charge beneath the crypt of the Vásquez Bello family. This became known as the *bomba sorbetera*, perhaps because the explosives were placed in tubs of ice cream. Since Machado and his inner circle would attend the funeral, the bomb would be detonated as the coffin was lowered into the grave. This truly fiendish plot, which would have resulted in massive loss of life to innocent bystanders, was thwarted when the widow decided to bury her husband in Santa Clara. The explosives were later discovered by a gardener.

Machado responded with killings such as that witnessed by *New York Times* correspondent Ruby Hart Phillips from her apartment on the Avenida de los Presidentes. Ainciart's favorite means of execution was the *ley de fuga*, an old Spanish custom that allowed the killing of prisoners trying to escape. As Phillips wrote:

> We saw a youth come running. He was alone in the street, his shadow the only other moving thing. He was weaving wildly from side to side, as if he did not know where he was going. Then I saw him halt, raise his arms and wave them wildly . . . as he cried, 'No tire mas, no tire mas' [don't shoot]. Several men posted on the cliff near our house raised their rifles. The first fusillade struck him in the back. He stumbled, falling. The second smashed through his head and shoulders. He fell in front of the huge statue erected to former president José Miguel Gómez.[19]

Afterward, Phillips saw the killers casually strolling down from the cliff, rifles in hand.

Phillips's account in the *New York Times* drew much attention to Machado's excesses. Before long, there were cries for intervention to restore order under the Platt Amendment. In the throes of the Great Depression, the United States was unwilling to dispatch the marines, who had finally left Cuba in 1923. No matter the economic difficulties, Machado continued to make loan payments and maintained the support of the banks. He also had the confidence of the American ambassador, Harry Guggenheim. The two were so close that they were scornfully referred to as Machaheim and Guggenado. But the ABC's tactics worked brilliantly, and the newly elected Franklin D. Roosevelt was eager to see an end to the increasingly messy violence.

The mood in Havana was perfectly captured by El Bobo. In a cartoon that appeared in October 1932, he confronts a white-robed Martí in the afterlife:

"Do you recall, Apostle, how you said our wine was bitter?"
"Yes," replied Martí warily, recalling his famous quote.*
"If only you could taste it now!"

In April 1933, Roosevelt replaced Ambassador Guggenheim with an old classmate from Groton and Harvard named Sumner Welles. The ball was in his court now.

Sumner Welles arrived in Havana on May 8, 1933, amid great fanfare and installed himself in the Hotel Nacional. Tall, patrician, immaculately dressed in a three-piece wool suit despite the withering heat, he was the object of fevered fascination by the Cuban press. The *Havana Post* noted somewhat more cautiously that "the task in Cuba will be one to test the intellectual ability and mettle of the new ambassador."[20] Welles already boasted a distinguished diplomatic career with much experience in Latin America, but his trump card was the ear of his old classmate Roosevelt. His relations with Machado began cordially enough, and the latter grudgingly accepted his offer to mediate an end to the crisis.

---

* This refers to Martí's line that though our wine is bitter, it is our wine.

"If only you could taste it now!" Eduardo Abela's *El Bobo* lampooned the Machadato. This cartoon ran in October 1932 (Author's collection)

The focus of attention shifted away from the Presidential Palace to the U.S. embassy, then located on the Plaza de Armas. From the beginning, Welles acted more like the proconsuls of the occupation than an ambassador, and much of what later happened bears his personal stamp, for better or worse. Calling a truce, leaders of the ABC emerged from the shadows and met with Welles, together with representatives of the government.

Before long, Welles made an appearance in *El Bobo*. The balding diplomat appears to be running a soup kitchen, and responds to the dissatisfied El Bobo:

"You wanted soup, didn't you?"
"Yes, *maestro*, but with something in it!"

By early July, the so-called mediation was well under way, and provoked a split among the opposition. The Directorio refused to participate, as did a faction of the ABC that became known as the ABC Radical. As the violence resumed, Welles cast his lot with the ABC, which damaged his status as honest broker and ultimately led to his *fracaso*. Backed into the corner, Machado played the nationalist card for the first time and complained that the mediation compromised Cuba's sovereignty. This turnabout astounded his opponents, since Machado had always supported U.S. interests large and small. By the end of July, the mediation had floundered.

Welles then began to demand Machado's ouster. But he had already shown his hand, and the Cuban president was starting to dig in. The standoff might have lasted several months more if the bus drivers of Havana hadn't declared a strike on July 25. The cause was an onerous gasoline tax imposed by the mayor, but it quickly subsumed a host of other grievances and spread to the streetcar workers and stevedores. By August 4, a general strike had paralyzed Havana, already reeling from the effects of the depression.

The two adversaries, Welles and Machado, were taken by surprise by this development, and events quickly spiraled out of their control. On August 7, a rumor on the radio that Machado had resigned prompted a huge demonstration in front of the Capitolio. There were songs, speeches and slogans, and the student demonstrators were not intimidated by the *porristas* (thugs, or members of the *porra*) sent to disperse them. Apparently it was the sinister Chief of Police Ainciart who opened fire. The students then rushed the barricades set up around the Capitolio, and the police responded with more gunfire. In all, 22 were killed and 170 wounded.[21]

The massacre of the students at the Capitolio was the straw that broke the camel's back. Machado suspended all constitutional guarantees and declared a state of war, while Welles delivered a final ultimatum for the president to resign. As tension continued to mount, Machado sought reassurance from the military. On the evening of August 11, he went to Camp Columbia to confer with his generals, who withdrew their support. Machado then folded his hand and resigned. Welles himself selected the new president, the aging diplomat Carlos Manuel de Céspedes, whose cabinet would include three *abecedarios*. The next morning, at about nine-thirty, the crowd surrounding the Presidential Palace silently parted as Machado's motorcade left.

The typhoon of violence that then swept over Havana is without parallel, before or after. After Machado fled, the guards abandoned their posts and the crowd stormed the Presidential Palace. According to an eyewitness account, hundreds of people ransacked the palace, throwing the Louis XV furniture out the Tiffany windows and stealing anything of value. Much of the looting was motivated by hunger:

> *There was a live pig in a crate within the palace. Half a dozen people picked up the crate, carried it and the pig to the street, tore the crate apart and divided the pig among themselves then and there.*[22]

Also looted were the nearby offices of the pro-Machado newspaper *El Heraldo de Cuba*. The printing press was smashed to pieces and the newsprint was unrolled in the Parque Central like toilet paper.

In the Plaza de Armas, Welles urged calm from the balcony of the American embassy. Even while the palace was being looted, the mood throughout Havana was one of celebration. The green flag of the ABC was everywhere, draped over balconies and hung from the statue of José

*Abecedarios* attacked the office of Machado's newspaper *El Heraldo de Cuba* on August 12, 1933. (Author's collection)

Martí in the Parque Central. Crowds joyously sang "La Bayamesa," Cuba's national anthem, and cars splashed with green paint roared through Havana, klaxons blaring.

But it soon turned ugly, as the hunt for the Machadistas (Machado's followers) began in earnest. Machado holed up in his farm *La Nenita*, and it is unclear why the *abecedarios* did not follow him there. By early afternoon, he was at Rancho Boyeros airport and secured a plane out just as his pursuers arrived. With him was Captain Crespo, commander of Atarés, who demanded a seat at gunpoint. Machado purportedly left with five revolvers and seven bags of gold for Nassau and a comfortable retirement in Miami. Foreign minister Orestes Ferrara had an equally close call. He and his wife were aboard the Pan American seaplane at the dock when the *abecedarios* arrived and opened fire. The pilot took off without waiting to pick up the luggage or other passengers.

The ABC had detailed lists of Machado's men and systematically tracked them down. Colonel José Antonio Jiménez, the head of the vicious *porra*, was spotted on the corner of Prado and Virtudes. He fired upon the crowd and was wounded by a soldier. The mob then set upon him and literally hacked him to death. This lynching came to be known as an *ajusticiamiento*, an unfortunate terminology implying that justice had been done. His body was dragged through the streets and, according to one account, tied to the hood of a car so he could be displayed throughout Havana, to cheering crowds. A similar fate awaited the louche Ainciart. Disguised in women's clothing, the Chief of Police managed to hide for a couple of days but was discovered heading for the docks. According to some accounts, he committed suicide before the mob reached him, but his body was mutilated, hung from a streetlight, and set afire.

Mansions of prominent Machadistas were looted, as were many government ministries and other buildings, such as the Manzana de Gómez. It has been estimated that one thousand people were killed, though the figure was probably higher. Many used the chaos to settle old scores, and cries of "¡Porrista!" were enough to send many running out of fear. One eyewitness told me, nearly three quarters of a century later, that he recalled seeing severed heads and limbs on the street. The violence was repeated throughout Cuba on a lesser scale, and in Santiago de Cuba, Mayor Arnaz—father of Desi—barely fled with his life. On the ransacked Presidential Palace in Havana, a sign was hung that probably had been taken from one of the nearby houses:

*SE ALQUILA* (to rent)

## ENTER BATISTA

*"Did you see the [revolution] in Cuba?"*
*"From the start."*
*"How was it?"*
*"Beautiful. Then lousy. You couldn't believe how lousy."*

—Ernest Hemingway, *Green Hills of Africa*

For all that, the fall of Machado proved anticlimactic. Welles appeared to have won the duel, and two U.S. battleships, the *Taylor* and the *Claxton*, entered Havana Harbor, though no marines disembarked. As the army gradually gained control of the streets over the next few days, the new government set up shop.

Céspedes's primary qualifications for the presidency were friendship with Welles and his résumé as a distinguished diplomat. The former seems to have tainted him from the beginning, and he never enjoyed public confidence. The ABC made the tactical mistake of joining the government without exercising control. Although A1 himself, Martínez Sáenz, was now the minister of finance, he was perceived as Welles's puppet. The students of the Directorio, who had never trusted the Americans, now withheld their support, together with the ABC Radical and the small but vocal Communist Party. There were rumors of more conspiracies, and Welles soon lost confidence in the patchwork government he had brought together. He tendered his resignation, but Roosevelt insisted he stay on for few more weeks.

The crisis was not long in coming, but from an unexpected direction. On September 4, there was an uprising in Camp Columbia by the enlisted men against their officers, led by three sergeants including one named Fulgencio Batista. The so-called Sergeants' Revolt began as an effort to ameliorate conditions for ordinary soldiers, from better barracks to new boots. Among the rumors were that due to the government's insolvency, salaries for enlisted men would be cut, and a list of grievances was presented to the officers. Had the three sergeants been promptly arrested, the coup would never have taken place. Perhaps wary of being called Machadistas, the officers relented and offered to mediate. Here the sergeants seized their opportunity and appointed noncommissioned officers (NCOs) to take command. The officers withdrew and Camp Columbia was seized bloodlessly. Batista quickly emerged as the leader of the three sergeants. Naming himself chief of staff, he shrewdly contacted NCOs of other military commands throughout Cuba, and the revolt spread.

Word soon spread throughout Havana, and disaffected elements such as the Directorio and other opposition groups gathered at Camp Columbia to show their support. Just one day later, the timorous Céspedes disbanded his cabinet and left the Presidential Palace empty once again. Welles panicked as well, calling for U.S. intervention, and suggested that U.S. citizens gather at the Hotel Nacional. Luckily his boss, Secretary of State Cordell Hull, kept a cool head and advised him to wait for further developments. A five-man Pentarchy (similar to Uruguay's government at the time) was established, but it ended in squabbling, and early on September 10, the students acclaimed one of the Pentarchs, a university professor named Ramón Grau, as president, while the thirty-three-year-old Batista (having promoted himself to colonel) remained firmly in charge of the armed forces.

As would be said of Fidel Castro a generation later, no one could have predicted the rise of Batista. But in many ways, Batista's ascension to power was even more astounding.

Perhaps by design, the details of his early life were always somewhat vague. Both parents were mulattoes, descended from black slaves and the long-vanished Taínos. To his credit, Batista never denied his mixed blood, and it was evident in his reddish brown complexion. There were rumors that he was born outside of Cuba, in the Dominican Republic or Central America, but these were never substantiated. The son of a cane cutter, Batista grew up in the sugar port of Banes in northeastern Cuba, where he attended a Quaker school and cut cane himself. After leaving home, Batista worked as a water boy, a carpenter, and even a barber.[23] At the age of twenty, he joined the army, where he learned shorthand, which was to serve him in good stead. By 1933, he was a sergeant stenographer at La Cabaña and was exposed to the workings of the military hierarchy through transcribing orders. Although charming and energetic, with a keen wit despite his lack of education and rough manners, Batista had risen as far as he could in the army and would not have penetrated the officer class because of his color.

There appears to have been little political involvement on Batista's part before the Machadato, though one biographer suggests that he may have had a connection to the ABC.[24] On August 18, barely a week after Machado's escape, Batista revealed a gift for public speaking at a funeral oration for three soldiers. Amazingly enough, there was as yet no inkling of the Sergeants' Revolt. What transformed it into a revolution? The answer lies with the ambitious young stenographer, in the right place at the right time. Due to his speaking abilities, he quickly assumed a leadership role among the rebellious sergeants. But it was not just luck. Batista had the political genius to see that after the fall of Machado, the army was the only source of power and therefore stability in Cuba, and that the officers had become tainted by their association with the dictator.

Over the next several weeks, Batista proved himself more than a match for the other players on the political stage. The new government headed by Grau quickly assumed its revolutionary mantle, unilaterally abrogating the hated Platt Amendment and instituting a series of progressive measures, such as an eight-hour workday and the first real land reform in Cuba. Welles withheld recognition, perhaps hoping to reinstall Céspedes. The first test for the new order came on October 2. The ousted officers had sought refuge in the Hotel Nacional, and about three hundred of them barricaded themselves in the upper floors. Batista moved decisively, surrounding the hotel and bombarding it with artillery. Many of the officers were excellent marksmen, and the attackers sustained heavy losses, but by late afternoon, the officers surrendered. The soldiers opened fire as the officers left the hotel, killing eleven of them and wounding twenty-two. The survivors were imprisoned in La Cabaña.

Why did the officers trap themselves in the hotel? Perhaps they felt that Batista would not dare move against them, or that the United States would at last intervene, as Welles had demanded. Either way, Batista called their bluff, and thereby cemented his power within the army.

One more rival for power remained—perhaps the most dangerous: the ABC. Its leaders continued to conspire with Welles, but the rank and file remained armed and opposed Grau's government. They were joined by a group of disgruntled ex-sergeants, now lieutenants in the Cuban air force. On November 8, they launched the insurrection by commandeering five aircraft and strafing Camp Columbia. There also appears to have been a split between A1 and A2. While Martínez Sáenz was in Miami, Saladrigas assumed control and gathered two thousand *abecedarios* at the Miramar Yacht Club. They placed themselves under the command of the insurgent soldiers, with the intention of marching on Camp Columbia. But once again, Batista acted swiftly and cut off their advance. The rebels then made the grievous tactical mistake of retreating to the castle of Atarés. The next morning, Batista's men opened fire. The old Spanish walls were no match for modern artillery, and the barrage soon took a heavy toll on the defenders. By that afternoon, the white flag was raised. Once again, Batista gave no quarter. As the *abecedarios* emerged, they were slaughtered by the soldiers, shot against the walls of the fortress.

This marked the end of the ABC. Its leaders went into exile, and it was effectively spent as a political force. Briefly reorganized as an electoral party, it found little support and was dissolved in 1952. Despite his role in the insurrection, Saladrigas went on to serve as foreign minister under Batista; Martínez Sáenz would serve as president of the National Bank and was imprisoned by Castro in La Cabaña. The ABC is derided by historians in Cuba as "adventurers," much the same line their Communist rivals took in 1932, but they were largely responsible for the fall of Machado. Remarkably little has been written about the *abecedarios*, who were once seen as "the hope of Cuba." Unfortunately, they will be remembered for their conspiracies rather than their political ideas, which were remarkably progressive, and their assassinations rather than their courage.

As early as September 5, Batista had called upon Welles, but the ambassador had not been too impressed with the upstart stenographer. Only after the siege of Atarés did Welles realize that Batista could well be the solution to his seemingly intractable problems. Batista candidly asked him for advice, and Welles made it clear that Grau's government would never be recognized by the United States. Batista then drew his own conclusions.

Welles's position was shaky, and Grau threatened to declare him persona non grata. Welles appears to have lost credibility with his superiors as well, for Roosevelt recalled him in mid-November for consultations. It was soon announced that Welles would be replaced by Jefferson Caffery, another veteran diplomat. Caffery quickly announced that "my country's policy toward Cuba will remain the same." This encouraged Batista to finally make his move.

On January 14, 1934, Batista openly shifted his support to Carlos Mendieta, a much more acceptable candidate than Grau to the United States. Facing an ultimatum, Grau quickly resigned, and within the week, the new government received recognition and a salvo from the battleship *Wyoming*. But there was no doubt that the power behind the throne was Batista, who would dominate Cuban politics until 1959.

*El Bobo* would cease publication in 1934, but one of the last cartoons shows El Bobo and his nephew in a movie theater.

"Is another movie coming?" asks the boy.
"I think it's the same one," El Bobo replied.

# CHAPTER 9

# *Hemingway's Ghost*
## *The Hemingway Trail*

*I have often wondered what I should do with the rest of my*
*life and now I know—I shall try and reach Cuba.*

—Ernest Hemingway

*Y*ou can't escape Ernest Hemingway in Havana. Throughout the city, his presence is palpable, and you almost expect him to turn up at the waterfront, fishing pole in hand. Other cities lay claim to him and boast their own respective Hemingway Trails, commemorating where he ate, drank, or laid his head to sleep. Paris has the café where he wrote, the Closerie de Lilas, and Key West puts on Hemingway look-alike contests for his birthday. But neither can hold a candle to Havana, where he lived more than twenty years, longer than anywhere else. This most American of writers was an unabashed Habanero.

In 1932, Hemingway lived in Key West. For $20 a day, he chartered the *Anita*, a low-slung, thirty-four-foot cabin cruiser captained by Joe Russell, who ran a speakeasy called Sloppy Joe's, after the one in Havana. Dubbed "Joe Grunts,"* Russell was a former cigar roller who augmented his income during Prohibition with bootlegging, and was the real-life model for Hemingway's character Harry Morgan. On April 21, they

---

* Hemingway delighted in nicknames. Wife Pauline was "Pilar" or "Poor Old Mama," and he insisted that his friends call him "Papa."

made the fifteen-hour trip across the Florida Straits to Havana, where the marlin were running.

The Hemingway Trail thus begins at the cobblestoned Plaza de San Francisco, across from the dock where the *Anita* moored. Laid out in 1628, Havana's third oldest plaza has been immaculately restored by Eusebio Leal, with a sleek restaurant, a travel agency, and a Benetton boutique. Originally the disembarkation point for the Spanish galleons, it is dominated by the Lonja de Commercio, a six-story office building topped by a bronze statue of Mercury. Erected in 1907, it is now occupied by foreign newspaper bureaus, such as the *Chicago Tribune*. In Hemingway's day, it had a seamier aspect. In *To Have and Have Not*, he notes that "bums [slept] against the walls of the buildings" and one morning "there was only one beggar awake in the square and he was getting a drink out of the fountain." This was the Fountain of the Lions, built in 1836. During the day, the Plaza de San Francisco was a hub for commercial activity, with horse-drawn ice wagons servicing the bars, market stalls, and *pregoneros* hawking their wares in front of the red-tiled customs house.

On the Gulf Stream, the thirty-three-year-old novelist could indulge his lifelong passion for sportfishing. Hemingway's quarry was the legendary black marlin, often weighing over a thousand pounds, with dangerous spears and sickle-shaped tails. In "Marlin Off the Morro," an article Hemingway wrote for the inaugural issue of *Esquire* magazine in 1933, he described them as "traveling along the edge of the dark, swirling current . . . all going in the same direction like cars along a highway." The marlin were lured to the surface with two wooden teasers bobbing in the wake of the *Anita* and hooked using live bait, such as jack crevelles or cero mackerels. The fight to land them could take more than an hour, with the huge fish alternately leaping high above the waves and plunging into the water. If the marlin did not throw off the hook or sever the stout Catalonian line, they were hauled alongside the boat and speared with an iron gaff. Once over the transom, they were clubbed to death.

The vacation was to last only ten days, but Hemingway would not return to Key West until midsummer. By the end of May, he boasted in a letter to John Dos Passos that he had caught nineteen marlin, one of which jumped twenty-three times before being gaffed. This was before the time of catch and release, and the marlin were weighed at the dock beneath La Cabaña and then hacked apart. Although the meat sold for 10 cents a pound, no mean amount in depression-era Havana, Hemingway wrote he was "feeding the waterfront" by giving away his catch.[1]

Hemingway and company on the docks of Havana, ca. 1933. A young man to his left may be Walker Evans. (Ernest Hemingway Collection/John F. Kennedy Presidential Library and Museum, Boston)

At first, Hemingway slept aboard the *Anita*. When his finicky wife Pauline came to visit, he moved into the nearby Hotel Ambos Mundos. Still welcoming tourists, the salmon-colored hotel is reached by following Oficios Street to the Plaza de Armas and turning left into Obispo. Hemingway stayed in room 511, on the northeast corner. His rather spartan lodgings looked out, *to the north, over the old cathedral, the entrance to the harbor, and the sea, and to the east the Casablanca peninsula, the roofs of all the houses in between and the width of the harbor.*

Hemingway added that,

*If you sleep with your feet toward the east . . . the sun, coming up over the Casablanca side and into your open window, will shine on you and wake you no matter where you were the night before.*[2]

Unfortunately, this can't be verified since the room is now a small museum with the requisite Hemingway memorabilia, such as a first edition of *The Old Man and the Sea* and a Royal typewriter. The cost of admission is $2.00, the daily rate in 1932.

The Hemingway Trail then continues up Obispo Street to the Floridita. It dates to 1820, when it was a tavern called *La Piña de Plata* (The Silver Pineapple) by the busy Monserrate gate of the city walls. Supposedly it was the first establishment in Havana to serve iced drinks. During the American occupation, it changed its name to the Florida Bar and was called "El Floridita" by Habaneros. Advertising itself as the "Cradle of the Daiquiri," it catered mostly to Americans. In 1953, *Esquire* named it one of the top bars in the world, alongside the Savoy in London and the Raffles in Singapore.

Hemingway, a creature of habit, always repaired to the Floridita after a day of fishing, still wearing his peculiar uniform of moccasins, khaki shorts held up by a length of rope, and a striped blue shirt, like that of a Basque fisherman, generally stained with fish blood. He was a great favorite of the shoeshine boys on Obispo, who ran before him shouting *"¡El Hemingway!"* (presumably alerting the bartender). His signature cocktail was the *Papa Doble* (also known as the *Hemingway Especial*), a jumbo daiquiri made with grapefruit juice and maraschino liqueur. Hemingway reportedly consumed as many as twelve in one sitting.

Like many bars in Havana at the time, the Floridita was open to the street and secured by metal shutters after closing. Only after 1949, when it lost customers to the air conditioning at the rival Pan American Bar, were the walls built. The thirsty novelist habitually sat in the corner to the left of the entrance. After he won the Nobel Prize in 1954, a small bust was placed on the wall, creating a virtual Hemingway shrine while he was still alive. Then in 2003 a life-size statue was unveiled with much fanfare by José Villa Soberón, also responsible for the statues of John Lennon and the mad *Caballero de Paris*. Hemingway's effigy leans against the bar and appears to be ordering another round.

Sadly, Soberón chose to depict an aging, bearded Hemingway rather than the more vigorous one of the 1930s. By all accounts, the younger version was intensely charismatic and catnip for women. In photographs of the time, he is movie star handsome with a broad smile and a clipped mustache, resembling Clark Gable.* Fueled by the Hemingway mystique, the Floridita is habitually packed with sunburned tourists, many of whom take snapshots of themselves at the bar. Like John Lennon in the Vedado, the bronze novelist has a cult following, and the bartender places a daiquiri before him each day, as an offering of sorts.

Once more with Russell aboard the doughty *Anita*, Hemingway was back in Havana the following year. This was heralded by the *Havana Post* on April 14, 1933, noting that he had returned "in quest of the marlin which will top the record of 1,050 pounds" set by the writer Zane Grey. But Hemingway's carefree mood of the previous trip had darkened. His latest book, *Death in the Afternoon*, had been greeted by such scathing reviews that Hemingway wrote to his editor, Max Perkins, "I am tempted never to publish another damned thing." Havana, too, had changed. The violence of the Machadato was reaching a crescendo, and just after his arrival, the city was rocked by nearly one hundred explosions in a single night.

Hemingway gamely resumed his routine, once more installing himself in the Ambos Mundos for a special monthly rate of $45. Each morning at first light, he boarded the *Anita* after breakfasting on a glass of milk and "a piece of Cuban bread."[3] Weather permitting, they followed the trade wind east, trolling along the coast past Cojimar and as far as Santa Cruz. An icebox ran across the stern of the *Anita*, well stocked with bottles of Hatuey beer. Occasionally they stopped for lunch and a swim in a cove and fished well into the afternoon before heading back toward the

---

* In July 2005, such a statue was erected in front of the Custom House in Key West and is equally popular with tourists.

setting sun. Hemingway meticulously documented his catches in the log book of the *Anita*, now at the Hemingway Collection of the Kennedy Library in Boston. By May 24, he reported hooking twenty-nine marlin with a Hardy Brothers bamboo pole, including a miraculous haul of seven in a single day.[4]

Despite his absorption in fishing, Hemingway closely followed the escalating political crisis. As a newspaperman, he had covered revolutions in Europe and was deeply skeptical of politicians. The vivid first chapter of *To Have and Have Not*, penned in October 1933 while the events were fresh in his mind, depicts the violent struggle between the ABC and Machado.* In the opening scene, Harry Morgan meets with three *abecedarios* at the Perla; they are hoping to buy clandestine passage out of Cuba. Morgan refuses, and as they leave the café he sees

> *a closed car come across the square toward them. The first thing a pane of glass went and the bullet smashed into the row of bottles on the show-case wall to the right. I heard the gun going and, bop, bop, bop, there were bottles smashing all along the wall.*

According to Hemingway's niece Hilary, this was based on an actual attack of the *porra* witnessed by Pauline and her sister Jinny in the Plaza de San Francisco.

Hemingway and "Joe Grunts" Russell ended their fishing trip on July 18 having caught a total of fifty-four marlin. For once, Hemingway was eager to leave, since he was going on a long-awaited African safari funded by Pauline's wealthy uncle. After returning to Key West to pack, he was once more in Havana by August 4, awaiting the Spanish steamer *Reina de la Pacífica*. This visit coincided with the general strike that paralyzed the city, and the Hemingways holed up in the Ambos Mundos. Their ship departed late on August 7, the day of the massacre at the Capitolio that did much to bring down the government. Did Hemingway see the shootings? Though he had a knack for being where the action is, and the Capitolio is quick walk from the docks, he made no mention of it. While at sea, he heard over the ship's wireless that Machado had fallen.

---

* Originally titled *One Trip Across*, it was written as a short story for *Cosmopolitan* Magazine and only later was tacked on to the hodgepodge of the novel, often regarded as Hemingway's worst.

## A PERFECT FACE

More than marlin had kept Hemingway in Havana during those two end-less summers.

Today, Jane Mason might have been a supermodel, or an actress. Hemingway met her aboard the sleek, art deco oceanliner *Ile-de-France* when he returned from France in November 1931. Just twenty-two, Jane was a tall stunner with strawberry blond hair, pale blue eyes, and a creamy complexion. She had been featured in an ad for Pond's Face Cream in *Ladies' Home Journal* for which she received $5,000, though she hardly needed the money. Growing up in swank Tuxedo Park, New York, in 1927 she married Grant Mason, a wealthy graduate of St. Paul's and Yale.[5] They soon moved to Havana, where Grant was the representative of Pan American. The gilded couple lived in a palatial estate on the outskirts of the city in Jaimanitas, near what is now the Hemingway Marina, appropriately enough.

They were introduced by a mutual friend, screenwriter Donald Ogden Stewart. No sparks flew on the cruise, perhaps since Pauline Hemingway was seven months' pregnant, but they saw each other in Havana the next spring. Ironically, it was Pauline who brought them together, since she roundly detested fishing and sought company other than "Joe Grunts." After Pauline returned to Key West, Jane often joined Hemingway aboard the *Anita*, usually without Grant, who traveled extensively.

Jane was not just an expert angler but a crack shot who once bagged a lion on safari. This may have been the basis of their relationship, and Hemingway fondly called her "Daughter." But Jane was not one of the boys. More than a beauty, she was fluent in three languages, dabbled in painting and sculpture, managed an art gallery, and even wrote short stories. Her epitaph, which she herself wrote later in life, was "Talents too many, not enough of any." This hints at the volatile streak in her personality, leading to more than one suicide attempt and extensive psychiatric care. She also scandalized the American colony in Havana with her numerous affairs.

Pauline could hardly compete with Jane and now found the tables turned. In Paris, she had snared Hemingway by befriending his older, less glamorous wife Hadley. Jane's marriage had long soured, and she was bored with her husband. Relegated to the role of a stooge in the Hemingway comedy, he was a successful executive who established most of Pan

American's routes in Latin America. And though Hemingway referred to him as a "rich twerp," he played much the same game with Grant as Jane with his Pauline. The Masons had adopted a three-year-old boy named Tony, and even named Hemingway as godfather.

After Hemingway returned home in 1932, Grant and Jane visited Key West, and the round robin continued that spring. But Jane's condition had worsened, and her behavior grew increasingly erratic. The tipping point came on May 24, when Jane had a car accident with Tony and two of Hemingway's sons in the backseat. They were unhurt, and Jane joined Hemingway fishing for the next three days. Then on the night of May 27, Jane slipped from her second-story window and broke her back.

Here the accounts vary. One Cuban newspaper breathlessly reported that she had been shot by *abecedarios*, but most of Hemingway's biographers regard it as a bungled suicide attempt. Jane was a heavy drinker and she was probably intoxicated, or she may have simply fallen. In any event, she was fitted with a heavy iron brace and Grant sent her to Doctors Hospital in New York aboard the Ward Line boat *Morro Castle*. At Jane's somber going-away party, Hemingway is said to have jokingly told her, "I never had a girl fall for me quite as hard."

Following his safari, Hemingway was drawn irresistibly back to Havana. This time he arrived in a boat of his own, the thirty-eight-foot *Pilar*, which he bought from the Wheeler Shipyard in New York for $7,500 of his advances. It was a larger, more luxurious version of the *Anita*, with additional gas tanks, a lower transom for hauling up marlin, and a second deck chair. He was in Cuba from July through August 1934 and most of October. Jane was back *en plein forme*, and it was here that their affair probably began. Hemingway boasted that Jane climbed through the window of the Ambos Mundos to visit him, though like some of his fishing exploits, that seems doubtful. With or without Grant and Pauline, they had dinner at El Pacifico in Chinatown, shot pigeons at the exclusive Club de Cazadores del Cerro, and danced at nightclubs like the open-air Chateau Madrid in Marianao.

Their affair lasted through 1935, when she accompanied him to the island of Bimini, and into the following year. Perhaps hoping to save her marriage, Pauline ignored the obvious. Yet Jane had no designs on Hemingway, who could hardly provide the lifestyle to which she was accustomed. The break came in 1936, when Jane took up with Dick Cooper, a roguish Englishman who owned a farm in Africa. The circumstances are unclear, but Hemingway was bitter enough to use Jane as the model for that ultimate femme fatale of American letters, Margot Macomber.

There can be no doubt of this, and Hemingway himself admitted it years later. In *The Short Happy Life of Francis Macomber* she is described with

> *a very perfect oval face, so perfect that you expected her to be stupid. But she wasn't stupid . . . no, not stupid.*

A pointed reference is also made to the magazine ad she posed for. The comparison with Grant is less obvious, though Hemingway describes the Macombers' marriage as having

> *a sound basis of union. Margot was too beautiful for Macomber to divorce her and Macomber had too much money for Margot ever to leave him.*

Apparently, Jane was rather tickled by all this.

Hemingway included an even more vicious portrayal of the Masons in the later chapters of *To Have and Have Not.* They appear as Helene and Tommy Bradley, a vacuous, wealthy couple in Key West. Certain passages were cut from the original draft for fear of libel, but in one particularly louche episode, a writer named Richard Gordon loses his erection midstream with Helene when he discovers that Tommy is furtively watching them. One biographer implied that this scene was based on Jane's experience with Hemingway, who suffered from bouts of impotence.[6]

They saw each other for the last time in 1937, though Jane remained close to Pauline and her sister Jinny. The following year, the Masons left Havana and moved to Washington, D.C., where they did divorce, unlike the Macombers. Jane remarried three times, and her last husband was Hemingway's friend Arnold Gingrich, the founder of *Esquire.* She died in 1981.

## A CITIZEN OF HAVANA

Another visitor to Havana in 1933 was the photographer Walker Evans, best known for his portraits of depression-era Americans. In 1933, the twenty-nine-year-old Evans was down and out in New York. Out of the blue, he received an assignment to take pictures for Carleton Beals's book *The Crimes of Cuba*, a strident account of Machado's excesses.

Evans's meager advance covered a two-week stay in Havana, and he arrived in mid-May. Some of the first photos he took depict the celebration of Cuban Independence Day on May 20. Surprisingly festive, they show the crowds milling about the Parque Central and standing beneath the statue of José Martí. Preferring to keep an open mind, Evans had not read Beals's book. But subsequent photographs suggest the rising tide of violence. There are policemen in their dark blue uniforms bordered in black and soldiers in jodhpurs and broad-brimmed hats, toting carbines. Young men in straw boaters, perhaps *abecedarios*, stand on street corners with their hands in their pockets.

One of the most striking pictures is entitled *Havana Citizen*. It shows a tall black in a natty white linen suit, standing by a newsstand with a Coca-Cola sign and magazines including *Bohemia* and *Carteles*. It is possible to pinpoint the day it was taken. A newspaper headline touts *GRAN TRIUNFO DE CHOCOLATE*, which can only be Kid Chocolate's victory over Louis Saerens on May 28 in London. The man's expression is ominous, and he could well be a member of the *porra*, one of Machado's thugs Yet he is oddly seductive, with the barest trace of a smile.

Evans's eye was also drawn to the economic crisis. His most striking shots are of beggars on the street and sooty dockworkers dressed in rags. One called *Havana: Country Family* shows a decrepit family of *guajiros* staring grimly at the camera. Though Evans had been to Havana only once before, he evinces a keen eye for detail. One series of shots shows piles of fruit in the marketplace, while another shows the lottery tickets used for *El Chino de la Charada*.

It is uncertain how Evans came to meet Hemingway. Whatever the circumstances, in the log book of the *Anita* Hemingway notes that he is having, "Dinner with Walker Evans." It probably took place at the Floridita. In a later interview, Evans recalled: "I had a wonderful time with Hemingway. Drinking every night. He was at loose ends . . . and he needed a drinking companion, and I filled that role for two weeks."[7] These drinking bouts took place just after Jane's apparent suicide, so Hemingway was in need of consolation.

No doubt Hemingway took on his accustomed role of tour guide and showed Evans around. One photograph shows a poster for the movie version of *Farewell to Arms*, then showing in Havana. Did Evans go fishing aboard the *Anita*? There is a famous snapshot (not taken by Evans) of a crowd at the pier gathered around Hemingway and an enormous marlin. The pale young man to Hemingway's left is probably Evans. Evans also took numerous pictures of the waterfront and the live fish cars beneath La Cabaña. Indeed, many of Evans's photographs could serve as illustrations for scenes in *To Have and Have Not*. There are *pregoneros* such as those in the Plaza de San Francisco and bums sleeping on the sidewalk. I suspect that lurking in the background, or just behind Evans's shoulder, is the grinning writer.

Evans also had an influence on Hemingway. He collected a number of archival shots from newspapers showing atrocities committed by the *expertos*, and a picture of Chief of Police Ainciart. The most chilling shows a young man whose throat has been cut. A sign on him reads:

*El ABC dara esta muerte a todos los lenguilargos.*
[The ABC will give this death to those who talk.]

The dead man was Manuel Cepero, one of Machado's stool pigeons, apparently killed in retaliation by the ABC. In Harry Morgan's encounter with the *abecedarios*, they ask him if he is a *lengua larga* (literally, a long tongue.) Morgan retorts, "I'm sure you've cut plenty people's throats."[8]

Evans soon ran out of money, and Hemingway loaned him $25 so he could prolong his stay until mid-June. Since Beals's book was slanted against Machado, Evans was afraid that his photographs would be confiscated. He therefore made forty-six prints and entrusted them to Hemingway for safekeeping aboard the *Anita*. Evans returned to New York without incident, and the prints were forgotten until 2002, when they were found in the storeroom of Sloppy Joe's. They were shown in a critically applauded exhibit called *Havana 1933* in Key West's Custom House, together with other items, such as Hemingway's baby booties and a bloodied uniform from World War I, from which he could presumably be cloned. These haunting black-and-white images, together with the taut prose of *To Have and Have Not*, comprise an indelible portrait of Havana during the troubled years of the Machadato.

## A GOOD PLACE TO WRITE

The most evocative stop on the Hemingway Trail is the writer's former home in San Francisco de Paula, a village just south of Havana. Known as Finca Vigía, it is a breezy, hilltop villa with spectacular views of the city on one side and the ocean on the other. It was built in 1887 on the site of an old Spanish watchtower and originally owned by a Frenchman named Joseph D'Orn Duchamp. How Hemingway came to live there has much to do with his wives.

Already on the ropes, his marriage to Pauline hit the mat when another fierce blonde walked into Sloppy Joe's in December 1936. She was Martha Gellhorn, a novelist in her own right. It was a *coup de foudre*. Unlike Jane Mason, she was unattached, and she and Hemingway soon rendezvoused for a steak dinner in Miami. A few weeks later, Hemingway left for Madrid to cover the Spanish Civil War, and Martha followed him there. They kept their liaison secret until their hotel was bombed and they had to flee their bedroom in the middle of the night. Then rumors spread among the foreign correspondents and soon reached Key West.

But the break with Pauline (who was devoutly Catholic and divorced him reluctantly) would not come until April 1939, when Hemingway left for Havana. Martha joined him at the Ambos Mundos but soon began looking for a house and found the Finca in the classified ads. At first, Hemingway was nonplussed. It was dilapidated and in need of paint and new plumbing. But Martha was enchanted with the view and the grove of mango trees surrounding the house, with eighteen varieties of the fruit. She rented it for $100 a month and set to work with a small army of carpenters to make it livable. When he next saw it, Hemingway was enchanted and settled in to complete the novel he had begun about his experiences in Spain. *For Whom the Bell Tolls* proved to be a critical hit as well as a best seller, and it rejuvenated his sagging literary reputation. In December 1940, he bought the Finca for $18,500 from the sale of the movie rights. His friend Gary Cooper, who had also starred in *A Farewell to Arms*, was to play the lead.

If Martha gets credit for discovering the Finca, her tenure was brief. Their marriage ended in acrimony, and the true chatelaine of the Finca was Mary Welsh, Hemingway's fourth and final wife.* Nicknamed "Pickle," she added amenities such as a refrigerator and a hot water heater, and livened the garden with flowers. But her greatest contribution was the four-story tower she had built between the villa and the pool. It was to house Hemingway's growing tribe of six-toed cats, and the top

---

* They were married in 1946.

floor had a terrace overlooking Havana. This was to be Hemingway's writing studio, though he preferred to work in his bedroom.

The Finca has been a museum since 1964. Visitors can wander through the gardens of the twenty-acre estate, bright with jacaranda blossoms, and peer through the windows at the interior. Journalists are sometimes permitted to enter, and I was given a delightful hour to poke around beneath the stern eyes of the curators.

There is a ninety-year-old ceiba tree by the entrance, entwined with lush orchids. As you pass beneath its branches, it is as if time has stood still. The house has been artfully maintained just as it was when Hemingway left Cuba for the last time in 1960. There is a half-empty bottle of Cinzano on the lowboy and a Cole Porter record on the vintage hi-fi. Yellowed copies of hunting magazines such as *Sports Afield* are in the magazine rack, and Hemingway's worn slippers lie expectantly on the floor. Strewn on the bed are letters that arrived after his death, and on the nightstand are his spectacles. The dining table is set as though company were expected. The gray and white china is engraved with the odd coat of arms Hemingway designed himself, consisting of three hills (representing Paris) above an arrowhead (representing the Ojibway Indians he encountered as a boy in Michigan) and two horizontal lines (captain's stripes, which he earned in World War II.)

As can be expected, the décor is decidedly masculine. A menagerie of stuffed trophies hangs on the walls: the heads of kudus, gazelles, and even a water buffalo that he killed on safari. Graham Greene visited during the 1960s and wondered how anyone could write surrounded by so many dead animals. Beneath one of the heads is the weapon that felled it, Hemingway's trusty Mannlicher carbine. The African theme is continued with a collection of tribal masks, knives, and a Masai beaded headdress. There are also bullfight posters from Spain and a ceramic plate with a bull's head, a Picasso original that Hemingway bought in Paris in 1957.

Mary's taste coexists uneasily. The armchairs are bordered with chintz, and there is a kitschy reproduction of Goya's *La Infanta*. Throughout the living room are knickknacks she brought back from their travels: lamps made from candlesticks of Sheffield silver, a Venetian platter, and a Danish crystal bowl. There are also oddities that could be found in a suburban garage sale, such as a Mexican ashtray, a piece of driftwood, and a Russian *matryoshka* doll, which was a gift from Anastas Mikoyan when he visited Hemingway in 1960, together with a model of Sputnik.

Virtually every wall contains shelves housing Hemingway's library of nearly nine thousand books. He read omnivorously, and there are books of every description, from novels to travelogues, from history tomes to detective stories, arranged in no particular order. Many of them have Hemingway's handwritten notes in the margins, which Cuban researchers have been assiduously cataloging for years.

Most interesting of all is where Hemingway wrote. A few steps from his bed, atop a battered white bookcase, is the famous Royal typewriter. Due to back trouble, he worked standing up, and the typewriter rests on a wooden cigar box to reach the level of his chest. Beside it are two sharpened pencils and the clipboard he used to write dialogue. There is also a chunk of copper that he used as a paperweight. Enjoying the cool of the morning, he was up at dawn and often pecked at the keys until noon, standing barefoot on a frayed animal skin. In a 1954 interview for *Paris Review*, he told George Plimpton that the Finca was "a good place to write."

Hemingway's creative regimen was often interrupted by the arrival of guests. After the war, the Finca became a waystation for the likes of producer Howard Hawks, bullfighter Antonio Ordoñez, and movie star Ava Gardner, who reportedly swam naked in the pool. Jean-Paul Sartre, whom Hemingway had met during the liberation of Paris, arrived in August 1949. I can't imagine the conversation between the bantam philosopher and the bearish author, but apparently it was quite banal and they discussed royalty payments. Hemingway loved company, and Mary was an adroit hostess. The cocktail of choice was no longer the daiquiri but the martini. He called them "Montgomeries," since they were made at the ratio of fifteen to one (Gordon's gin to vermouth), the numerical superiority the British general claimed he needed for victory.

In December 1950, Hemingway began writing a new book about an old Cuban fisherman. The seed for the novel had been planted many years earlier. In "On the Blue Water," published in *Esquire* in April 1936, he recounts a story he had heard about a fisherman in Cabañas who had hooked a giant marlin that pulled him far out to sea. After he caught it, the sharks moved in:

> *[T]he old man had fought them out alone in the Gulf Stream in a skiff . . . until he was exhausted and the sharks had eaten all they could hold. He was crying in*

*the boat when the fishermen picked him up, half crazy from his loss, and the*
*sharks were still circling the boat.*

Hemingway changed the setting to Cojimar, the fishing village near the
Finca where the *Pilar* was moored, and the words flowed easily. By February 1951, he was done.

*The Old Man and the Sea* is an undoubted classic and perhaps his best
known work. It first saw the light of day in the September 1, 1952, issue
of *Life* Magazine, which sold 5.3 million copies. Scribner's hurriedly went
to press and sales surpassed any of Hemingway's previous books. This
time critics were effusive with their praise. William Faulkner, who had
sniped at his earlier work, commented that Hemingway had "found
God." Even the snide Vladimir Nabokov, who once said that Hemingway
wrote for children, declared it "superb." It won Hemingway the Pulitzer
Prize in 1952 and the Nobel Prize in 1954. He accepted the latter "in the
name of the Cuban people" and donated the medal to the shrine of the
*Virgen de la Caridad del Cobre** near Santiago de Cuba, where I saw it during a visit in 2001.

Cojimar is thus the last stop on the Hemingway Trail. It was here
that the British landed in 1762, and afterward the Spaniards built a small
fort called El Torreon to guard the bay. In 1962, one year after Hemingway's death, the local fishermen each donated a brass fitting from their
boats to cast a bust of the author that was placed beneath a rotunda near
the Torreon. Called the Monumento Ernest Hemingway, it's a dubious
likeness that some have said resembles Lenin. More atmospheric is the
nearby restaurant La Terraza. Hemingway often enjoyed the paella there
and mentioned it in the novel.

Until his death in 2002 at the age of 104, Cojimar's most famous resident was Gregorio Fuentes, the skipper of the *Pilar.* Hemingway hired
him in 1938, and he remained at the writer's side for the next two
decades. It is often said that Gregorio Fuentes was the inspiration for the
old fisherman, and he was granted a pension by Castro and allowed to eat
free at La Terraza. A cigar in his mouth, he gleefully held court to visiting
tourists, who were charged $50 for a fifteen-minute conversation.

As for the *Pilar,* it was placed in drydock in the tennis court of the
Finca.

---

* The patron saint of Cuba, also venerated by devotees of Santeria as Ochún, the *orisha* of love.

## ADIÓS, PAPA

*It happened by chance that after three days, I caught a huge marlin, which gave me first place.*

—Fidel Castro

During his last decade, Hemingway was decidedly apolitical, concerned more with reviews than revolution. But without a doubt he despised Batista, referring to him as an *hijo de puta* (son of a whore). He would have heard about Castro from reporter Herbert Matthews, whom he met in Spain. In February 1957, Matthews trekked up the Sierra Maestra to interview the bearded young revolutionary, and his articles in the *New York Times* created a sensation. Directly after the interview, Matthews stopped by the Finca. Though sympathetic, Hemingway lent only moral support to the cause. A tall tale of Gregorio Fuentes was that Hemingway ran arms for Castro in the *Pilar*, but this seems unlikely.

The writer's one brush with Batista occurred in August 1958. Rebel sympathizers in San Francisco de Paula had been rounded up by the secret police and shot. Perhaps suspecting the American writer of complicity, soldiers made a routine search of his house, and one of them killed his dog Machakos with a rifle butt. This incident may have prompted Hemingway to leave Cuba in October and begin searching for a house in Ketchum, Idaho.

During his final years, Hemingway had an alarming variety of physical ailments. The injuries he suffered from a plane crash in Africa in 1954 continued to plague him, and he suffered from high blood pressure, failing eyesight, and skin disease. His drinking was finally taking its toll, and according to biographer Jeffrey Meyers, he had become an alcoholic. But he continued to write, working on a nostalgic memoir of his Paris years that would be published after his death as *A Moveable Feast*.

Hemingway returned to Havana after the triumph of the Revolution but soon set out for the bullfights in Spain. He then came back amid much hoopla in November 1959. By then, many in the United States had begun to have doubts about Castro. To the assembled crowd at the airport, Hemingway declared:

*I am happy to be here again, because I consider myself one more Cuban. I don't believe any of the information about Cuba being published in the foreign press. My sympathies are with the Cuban government and all our difficulties.*

When he was presented with a Cuban flag, he kissed the hem. A reporter asked him to do it again for the cameras, but Hemingway shot back: "I said I was a Cuban, not an actor."[9]

Despite this, Hemingway maintained his distance from the new government. He met Castro only once, at the annual fishing tournament he had helped organize in 1950. In May 1960, Castro turned up on the last day of the competition aboard the yacht *Cristal*, together with Che Guevara.[10] Guevara was uninterested in fishing and went belowdecks with a copy of Stendhal's *Le Rouge et Noir*, but Castro supposedly landed a huge marlin and won first place. Hemingway presented him with the trophy, and the photograph by Alberto Korda of the two clenching hands with frozen grins is today one of the most widely disseminated in Cuba. Castro seems bashful, obviously in awe of the writer.

"I would have liked so much to have had the time to talk with him," Castro said many years later.[11] According to Gabriel García Márquez, Castro is intimately familiar with Hemingway's work and often takes his novels with him on trips. Castro himself has declared that *For Whom the Bell Tolls* helped him plan his guerrilla strategy in the Sierra Maestra.

Hemingway left Havana for the last time in July 1960. Following his sixty-first birthday, he suffered what was probably a nervous breakdown and was hospitalized. After receiving electroshock treatment, he spent a grim Christmas in Ketchum and complained of memory loss, a common side effect. His first suicide attempt was on April 21, 1961, when Mary found him clutching a shotgun. This was only days after the failed Bay of Pigs invasion of Cuba, and Hemingway must have realized that he would never be able to return. Like many Cuban exiles, he had seriously misjudged the political situation, and worried whether the Finca would be safe. He was given more shock treatments, and friends and relatives who saw him during the last weeks of his life saw a frail, broken old man. On the morning of July 2, while his wife slept, Hemingway found the keys to the locked storage room where the guns were kept and shot himself as his father had before him.

The fate of the Finca would be determined a few months later. Mary was able to return to Havana in August 1961 only through the intercession of Hemingway's friend Bill Walton, who knew President Kennedy. She briskly set about disposing of their belongings and lit a bonfire on the tennis court to burn old periodicals and possibly some intimate correspondence. Castro made an appearance, and Mary gave him a personal tour of the Finca. According to writer Norberto Fuentes, he was particularly interested in the firearms and the hunting trophies. What transpired between Mary and Castro is uncertain, but she diplomatically donated the Finca to the Cuban people. The *Pilar* had been bequeathed to Gregorio Fuentes, who made a similar donation. In return, Mary was permitted to leave with Hemingway's art collection, which included the priceless *Farm*, by Joan Miró,* the manuscripts she had collected from a safety deposit box at the National Bank of Cuba, and a few other personal effects. They were all loaded onto a shrimp boat heading for Tampa.

Perhaps because of the Kennedy connection, Mary donated what items were salvaged to the Kennedy Library in Boston, an invaluable resource for researchers and Hemingway nuts alike. But most of Hemingway's papers still remain at the Finca. He was an inveterate pack rat, keeping not just letters but also receipts, ticket stubs, and scraps. In the basement are stored more than two thousand letters and other documents, three thousand photographs, an early draft of *For Whom the Bell Tolls*, the log books of the *Pilar*, and much more.

But even this treasure trove of Hemingway incunabula has fallen victim to the Cold War. U.S. researchers were denied access for many years, until Jenny Phillips, granddaughter of Hemingway's editor Max Perkins, enlisted Massachusetts congressman Jim McGovern, an advocate of normalizing relations with Cuba. The result was a 2002 agreement allowing U.S. conservators to work with their Cuban colleagues to catalog and preserve the Finca papers and scan documents for the Kennedy Library's digital collection. At the ceremony marking this groundbreaking agreement, McGovern noted that Hemingway could help bring Cuba and the United States closer together: "He was an American through and through, but he also loved this country and the Cuban people loved him back."[12]

Yet like much of Havana, the Finca is crumbling, a victim of hurricanes and humidity. According to one estimate, repairs will cost $3 million, and the cash-strapped Cuban government has allocated only $340,000. Phillips' group, the Hemingway Preservation Foundation, was

---

* Hemingway had given it to his first wife, Hadley, but later kept it. Strangely, Mary left the ceramic bullfighting plate, a Picasso original.

denied a license from the U.S. Treasury to help fund restoration efforts, even though the U.S. National Trust for Historic Preservation has listed the Finca as one of its "most endangered places." It was temporarily closed in late 2005 for renovation. When someday Americans return to Cuba in force, it may well be the country's biggest tourist attraction.

Ironically, the Hemingway legend has grown in inverse proportion to his literary reputation. His work fell decidedly out of fashion in the 1980s, when he took a beating from feminist professors on American campuses who berated him for being a "sexist pig." Most critics now rank him beneath his erstwhile friend and eternal rival F. Scott Fitzgerald, and fellow Nobel laureate V.S. Naipaul declared that no one reads Hemingway unless he has to.

Yet Hemingway has become a shrewdly managed international brand on the order of Walt Disney. His name has been licensed to everything from computers (an ad for Apple), to clothes (a Gap ad for khakis), to cigars (which he didn't smoke), to a shotgun (believe it or not!). There is an safari-themed Hemingway line of furniture, a Hemingway Montblanc pen, and many, many Papa t-shirts. In Oslo, Norway, where he never went, I found a bar named Hemingway's, replete with a stuffed marlin on the wall, bullfighting memorabilia, and Viking-size daiquiris. I have seen similar establishments in Tokyo, Buenos Aires, and Sydney. It is difficult to understand this fascination among people who have never read him and probably never will. Is it nostalgia? A reaction to political correctness?

A Google search on the internet turns up more than 9 million entries on Hemingway. Few writers have been written about as effusively, spawned as much controversy, and inspired such devotion or derision. Hemingway has even appeared as a fictional character in several novels— some good, some bad. One has only to visit Key West during the raucous Hemingway Days festival each July to see hundreds of bearded, middle-age men vying to be "Papa of the Year," a surreal spectacle that must have the real one turning rumbas in his grave.

The latest wave of biographies, such as those by Kenneth Lynn and Jeffrey Myers, have savaged his personal life, detailing not just physical and psychological afflictions but his numerous fistfights (my favorite is with a loutish Wallace Stevens in 1936); his quarrels with friends, such as

John Dos Passos and Archibald MacLeish; and his neglect of spouses and offspring. Perhaps the most bizarre theory to surface is his alleged homosexuality. Hemingway was resolutely heterosexual, and there is no evidence to the contrary.

Despite all this, he appears to be making a comeback. At a recent conference of the Hemingway Society, many of the scholarly papers presented were by women, acknowledging his ability to create strong female characters—such as Margot Macomber (aka Jane Mason). And it is easy to dismiss Hemingway as a brawling, drunken blowhard until you realize that he held his own with the likes of James Joyce, Gertrude Stein (until their feud), and Edmund Wilson. Quite possibly, he was the most influential novelist of the twentieth century. A whole generation of postwar writers, from James Jones to Norman Mailer, struggled desperately either to write like Hemingway or not to write like Hemingway, and many still do. In the backpacks of American college students in Europe you still see dog-eared copies of *A Moveable Feast*, inspiring novels yet to be written.

And you will always find him in Havana. According to an old Spanish *dicho* (proverb), one's spirit returns to where one was happiest in life. Little wonder that Hemingway's ghost occasionally strolls up Obispo Street, dressed in moccasins, khaki shorts, and a striped Basque fisherman's shirt, on his way to the Floridita.

# CHAPTER 10

## Havana Nights

### Welcome to the Tropicana

*The defining feature of a Cuban is a person who will do just about anything to get a minute of pleasure.*

—Ofelia Fox, *Tropicana Nights*

Described as a *must* in guidebooks, the Tropicana invariably disappoints. Still, Havana's most famous nightclub of the 1950s tries hard to recapture its lost glory. Open to the sky, the stage appears to float in a prehistoric jungle of oversize ferns. Coffee-colored girls dressed in spangles (and not much else) slink down the branches toward the audience or else shimmy down creeping vines. The retro orchestra kicks in with a mambo, and the warm breeze carries the perfume of expensive cigar smoke. Waitresses even more stunning than the dancers bring another round of mojitos, and you wonder just how you got to heaven.

But the spell is broken when you notice that the carpet is threadbare, the girls' smiles are a bit tired, and the crowd is of the packaged-tour variety, sunburned Germans in loud shirts. There are no Cubans except the much younger companions of the tourists, and they trade knowing looks with the waitresses. Occasionally one of them yawns.

You can't help but wonder what the Tropicana was like fifty years ago, when tuxedoed guests were entertained by Nat King Cole and Carmen Miranda, and the floor show by the celebrated choreographer Rodney was *Diosas de Carne* (Goddesses of Flesh), in which the guitar-shaped dancers dressed like Greek goddesses. High rollers were flown in on a nightly chartered flight from Miami called the "Tropicana Special" and won or lost fortunes at the roulette tables. At the time, the nightclub combined the glamour of Monte Carlo and the spectacle of Hollywood.

The Tropicana was the setting of Guillermo Cabrera Infante's novel *Tres Tristes Tigres** in which the master of ceremonies announces:

> *Showtime! . . .the most fabulous nightclub in the world . . . presents its latest show . . . where performers of Continental fame will take you all to the wonderful world of supernatural beauty of the Tropics. . . .*

On such nights, there was electricity in the air, and the Tropicana had an undeniable sizzle. What was it like?

In her book *Tropicana Nights*, Rosa Lowinger recounts in loving detail how the Tropicana first opened its doors in 1939. Its location was an estate in Marianao called the Villa Mina, built by the former president of the Havana Yacht Club. Located next to the Colegio Belén, the Jesuit school favored by Cuba's elite (Castro, the son of a wealthy landowner, enrolled in 1941), it had six acres of lush gardens. According to one theory, the name *Tropicana* comes from "tropical" and "Mina." But the war brought tourism to a halt, and gambling was banned by President Grau, who took office in 1944.

By then the Tropicana had been acquired by Martín Fox, a burly, rough-hewn gambler from Ciego de Avila.[1] Known as the Guajiro, he made his fortune running illegal but lucrative *bolita* games and used his mob connections to keep the police at bay. When the casinos were reopened in 1949 under President Prío, the Guajiro added roulette, baccarat, and blackjack to his repertoire. The Tropicana soon became Havana's glitziest cabaret. The allure was not just gambling but musical acts like Rita Montaner and Xavier Cugat. Inclement weather often closed it down, so the Guajiro commissioned architect Max Borges Jr. to

---

* Titled after a children's tongue-twister, it's usually translated as "Three Trapped Tigers." Published in Spain and promptly banned in Cuba, it won the Prix du Meilleur Livre Etranger in Paris in 1971.

build an indoor stage. The result was known as Arcos de Cristal (Arches of Crystal), a tour de force of soaring concrete arches and glass sheets, like a vast modernist seashell. At the entrance was a fountain ringed by eight marble nymphs that had once graced the Casino Nacional.

One of Rodney's most famous efforts was called *Omelen-ko*, in which a white woman wanders into a Santeria ritual and is possessed. According to Lowinger, Rodney's shows were razzle-dazzle productions that cost an unprecedented $12,000 a night. They featured Cuban music, African drums, elaborate costumes, and, above all, gorgeous dancers. In 1954, NBC broadcast live from the stage for its show *Wide, Wide World.*

The guests at the Tropicana included Marlon Brando, Elizabeth Taylor, Rocky Marciano, David O. Selznick, and Joan Crawford with her husband, Alfred Steele, the president of Pepsi-Cola. Hemingway came once or twice, according to Fox's widow, Ofelia. Headliners were not just Cuban stars such as Celia Cruz and Benny Moré but Josephine Baker, Liberace, and Yma Sumac.

The Tropicana was also a favorite of Graham Greene, who knew Cuba well. In *Our Man in Havana*, British vacuum cleaner salesman *cum* spy Wormold celebrates his daughter Milly's birthday there. As he describes it,

> *Chorus girls paraded twenty feet up among the great palm trees, while pink and mauve searchlights swept the floor. . . . Then the piano was wheeled away into the undergrowth, and the dancers stepped down like awkward birds from among the branches.*

Greene adds that it "was not a night [Wormold] was ever likely to forget."

## THE WOUNDED STORK

A few days before the Arcos de Cristal were completed, Cuban democracy died with hardly a whimper, much less a bang.

Nearly twenty years had passed since Batista seized power in the Sergeants' Revolt of 1933. Consolidating his hold on the army and growing hugely wealthy, he ruled through several so-called puppet presidents. Grau and other disaffected leaders formed the Auténtico Party, forgoing armed revolt for peaceful opposition. Batista then did something unexpected. Opening up the political process, he called for a constitutional convention. The result was Cuba's Constitution of 1940, a remarkably progressive document in which workers were guaranteed minimum wages and paid vacations. Supported by a broad coalition, including the Communists, Batista was elected president, beating out Grau in a reasonably fair vote. Contrary to expectations, after one term he stepped down and Grau won the next election.

But the former doctor, now nearing sixty, had changed. The aging revolutionaries who had supported him were more interested in sharing the spoils, and Grau proved to be as venal as Machado. Corruption took the usual form of bogus government jobs and sales of lottery tickets, but Grau further refined the Cuban art of graft, and many government contracts went directly through his sister-in-law, Paulina. Hugh Thomas calls his administration an "orgy of theft" and comments that Grau "did more than any single man to kill the hope of democratic practice in Cuba."[2]

One phenomenon that emerged during his term is known as *gangsterismo*. Many of the action groups of 1933 had degenerated into armed gangs. Among them were Rolando Masferrer, who had fought in Spain and now maintained a private army known called *Los Tigres*, who went about in white baseball caps. Another was Jesús González Cartas, known as *El Extraño* (the strange one) who received visitors on a throne, surrounded by flags. These picturesque hoods found refuge at the University of Havana, which had been granted autonomy by the new constitution and was off-limits to the police. Grau not only condoned their excesses but recruited them to attack the Communists, whom he bitterly opposed.

Grau was succeeded in 1948 by Carlos Prío, another revolutionary gone soft. Known for being *simpatico* (pleasant), Prío enjoyed the good life at his estate of La Chata. Just outside Havana, it had a swimming pool with a dramatic waterfall and its own barbershop, where Prío enjoyed getting a shave with his cronies each morning. He did little to stem the growing violence in the streets and continued the easygoing corruption of his mentor Grau.

Meanwhile, Batista had retired in baronial splendor to Daytona Beach, Florida. The next election was to be held in May 1952. The Auténtico candidate was Carlos Hevia, who served as secretary of state under Prío. He was opposed by Roberto Agramonte of the Ortodoxo Party, an offshoot of the Autenticos led by the volatile Eddy Chibás. When Chibás committed suicide during his weekly radio show (not on the air, as is often thought, since the microphone had been turned off), the less charismatic Agramonte became the candidate. As the election neared, Batista threw his hat in the ring.

Could he have been elected? Batista later claimed that he acted because he learned that Prío was to seize power after the defeat of his party. This is unlikely if only because the Autenticos were far ahead in the polls. The Ortodoxos never recovered after the strange death of Chibás, and Batista was far behind. The latter's coup d'etat was wholly unexpected and masterfully planned. At midnight on March 9, two months before the election, three Buicks left his farm Kuquine for Camp Columbia. Batista went directly to the officer on duty, who immediately handed over command. His coconspirators quickly rounded up any officers loyal to Prío, took command of La Cabaña, and seized the telephone exchange. By 3:00 AM, the island was Batista's once again.[3]

When Prío learned of it, there was little he could do. Assembling his ministers at the Presidential Palace, he debated his limited options. A detachment of soldiers appeared, claiming to support the government. In reality, they had been sent by Batista and planned to arrest Prío. The

Fulgencio Batista ended Cuban democracy in 1952. (Author's collection)

president saw through this obvious subterfuge, and the lieutenant in charge was shot dead. These were the only shots fired in anger that day. Batista then surrounded the palace with tanks, hoping to force a surrender, but soon withdrew. A delegation of students arrived and pledged their support to Prío, who promised to send arms to the university, where they were building barricades. But Prío never acted. Instead, he fled by car to Matanzas, where the garrison was still loyal. When he learned that it had gone over to the rebels, Prío returned to Havana and sought refuge in the Mexican embassy. Cuba's last elected president left the country a few days later with a safe conduct pass from Batista.

There was little opposition. Batista was at least a familiar face, and the Auténticos were thoroughly discredited. The students staged a demonstration in which a copy of the constitution was symbolically interred beneath a bust of José Martí in the Vedado, but Batista's police acted with restraint. By March 27, the U.S. had rubber-stamped the new regime. According to one diplomat, recognition would have been withheld if Prío had resisted, but these were crocodile tears. The following week, a beaming Batista appeared on the cover of *Time* magazine, above the caption: "Cuba's Batista: he got past Democracy's sentries."

The favorable publicity deeply angered many Cubans, who still remembered how Sumner Welles had propped up Batista in 1933. It is curious how the events of 1952 paralleled the Machadato. Most of the players were the same, only twenty years older. In both cases, some argued, the United States had betrayed the democratic principles it was supposed to stand for. This hypocrisy fueled the anti-Americanism that was to explode after 1959. Newly elected president Dwight D. Eisenhower named a good friend of Batista's as ambassador, and the cozy relationship between the Presidential Palace and the U.S. embassy was reestablished.

Declaring himself provisional president, Batista suspended the constitution he had helped draft in 1940. He had intervened, he claimed, in order to save the island from chaos and end the corruption of the Auténticos. Batista effectively quashed *gangsterismo*, and many of the gunmen, including Masferrer, threw in their lot with him. Others left for Miami to begin plotting. A new constitutional code was enacted, and Batista ran without opposition in a phony election held in 1954. In his speeches, he compared Cuba to a wounded *grulla* (stork) that he had found and lovingly nursed back to health. Though this homely metaphor was mocked incessantly in the press, a stork standing on one leg became Batista's talisman and his campaign slogan was *"¡Viva la Grulla!"*

## HAVANA BABYLON

*Lucy, you got some 'splaining to do.*

—Ricky Ricardo

The image of Havana in the 1950s as a sleazy, Mafia-infested cesspool of vice is so pervasive that it has entered popular culture. After the Revolution, it was gleefully embellished by leftist historians, and Hollywood followed suit in films such as Francis Ford Coppolla's *Godfather II*. A usually perspicacious historian described Havana as:

> *a place of license and loose morality, of prostitutes, pimps, and pornography, of bars and brothels, casinos and cabarets, gambling and drugs, gangsters, mobsters and racketeers, politicians on the take and policemen on the make. Daily life had developed into a relentless degradation.*[4]

This point of view has turned Havana into a gross caricature. Was it really as bad as all that?

Surprisingly, Grau's ban on gambling during the postwar years shut down the Cuban tourist industry, and Americans flocked to Mexico. For example, in 1951, Cuba took in $50 million of the $19 billion that Americans spent on travel. Mexico's share was $300 million. Cuba also faced stiff competition from Puerto Rico and Haiti. From 1949 to 1954, its share of the Caribbean market declined from 43 percent to 31 percent.[5] But just as Prohibition had spurred tourism a generation earlier, the straitlaced morals of the 1950s made Havana ideal for a dirty weekend. In the Broadway musical *Guys and Dolls*, Sky Masterson takes the prim, puritanical Sister Sarah Brown to Havana in the hopes of seducing her. Most Americans' view of Cuba was shaped by *I Love Lucy*, a television phenomenon that began in 1951 and soon reached 50 million viewers weekly. The character of Ricky Ricardo was played by Desi Arnaz, Jr., who often lapsed into rapid-fire Spanish to Lucy's bewilderment. In contrast to the couple's humdrum existence, Havana seemed sexy and exhilarating.

The casinos of the 1920s, such as the elegant Jockey Club and the sedate Casino Nacional, were a far cry from the brassy Tropicana. Big-time gambling came to Havana by way of Miami. Meyer Lansky, once a bootlegger and associate of Bugsy Siegel, ran a lucrative gambling business in south Florida throughout the 1940s. Just as *I Love Lucy* hit the airwaves, Senator Estes Kefauver's televised hearings cast the national spotlight on mob-related activities. The public outcry soon shut Lansky down, and he served a two-month jail term.

American organized crime had yet to establish a beachhead in Cuba. Al Capone tried to establish a pool room in Marianao during the 1920s but had been chased out by the *expertos*. Even by Chicago standards, Havana was a tough town. But Batista had seen Lansky's operation firsthand in Daytona Beach. When he returned to power, he put the resilient mobster on the payroll. Lansky's first proposal was to revamp the Hotel Nacional, a bit long in the tooth, and build a Las Vegas-style casino called the Parisien. Run by Wilbur Clark, Lansky's front man in Las Vegas, it opened in 1955. But Havana sorely lacked hotel rooms, and incentives were offered to investors. If $1 million were spent on a hotel, then a casino could be added. Licenses cost $25,000, plus a monthly fee of $2,000 and a percentage of the receipts.[6] Batista also received a generous kickback on such fees, reportedly collected by his wife.

Lansky himself took advantage of this by building the Hotel Riviera. Another modernist masterpiece, it has a soaring, Y-shaped tower balanced elegantly on the Malecón, facing the water. In *Tres Tristes Tigres*, Guillermo Cabrera Infante describes it as "a square soap dish with an oval bar of soap on one side." and the round, windowless Gold Leaf Casino as the "veined egg of a roc." When it opened in December 1957, Ginger Rogers sang in the Copa Room. Lansky's $14 million investment began to pay off immediately. By March 1958, the Riviera had already grossed $4 million.[7]

Not surprisingly, Havana's casinos were professionally run. Lansky had a reputation for efficient, honest management, essential to attracting tourists. Croupiers and floor managers attended a special school and were rigorously trained. After an incident at the Sans Souci casino where a visiting American lawyer lost several thousand dollars to a scam called "razzle-dazzle," several arrests were made. Batista's inspectors regularly shut down crooked games and banned cardsharps and hustlers from the tables.

Another new casino was at the $5 million, 250-room Hotel Capri. Run by Tampa crime boss Santo Trafficante Jr., it featured movie tough guy George Raft as host. Also opening in 1958 was the $25 million Havana Hilton. It was funded by the pension fund of the restaurant workers' union, but the vast casino was also run by the mob. These hotels burnished Havana's tourist infrastructure, and the room capacity doubled between 1955 and 1958. One visitor was Senator John F. Kennedy, who arrived in December 1957 for a three-day stay. Without a doubt, he visited the Tropicana. Trafficante once claimed he supplied him with three hookers at the Comodoro and watched from behind a two-way mirror but failed to film it.

Like Machado, Batista went on a building spree, financed by $350 million in bonds. This was spent on roads, bridges, port facilities, and sewage lines throughout the island. In Havana, the airport at Rancho Boyeros was expanded and a long-awaited tunnel was completed beneath the harbor in 1958 by a French concern. It linked the Malecón directly to the Via Blanca, the highway leading to Matanzas and the beaches of Varadero.

Batista's most visible contribution to the city was the vast, trapezoidal Plaza Civica. Just south of the Vedado, it is dominated by the stark obelisk commemorating José Martí. Renamed the Plaza de la Revolución, it is the scene of the May Day festivities in which Castro addresses the crowd. Behind the monument to Martí, Batista erected the Palacio de Justicia, another example of the fascist-inspired architecture he was enamored of. It is now the Palacio de la Revolución, the seat of the Cuban government. Across the plaza is the Ministerio del Interior, known as MININT, charged with national security. Built in 1953, its facade features a bronze likeness of Che Guevara and the words *Hasta la Victoria Siempre* (Until Victory Forever).

At the time of the Revolution, Havana was a city with a population approaching 1.5 million. The center of gravity had continued to shift west from Habana Vieja. The old colonial core retained a bohemian aspect, with bars like the Bodeguita del Medio, yet this coexisted with the financial district. A number of banks were located on Obispo and O'Reilly streets, such as the American-owned Havana Trust and the Bank of Nova Scotia. Centro Habana was still the shopping district, and the Esquina del Pecado (home of the *piropo*) at the corner of Galiano and San Rafael was crowded as ever. But the action was now at La Rampa. Actually Twenty-third Street in the Vedado, it rises steeply from the Malecón up to L Street and the Habana Libre. La Rampa grew rapidly in the 1950s and was the site of many of the new nightclubs and restaurants. At intervals on the sidewalk are gorgeous, multicolored tiles by Wifredo Lam, Rene Portocarrero, and other artists. They complement the strikingly blue ceramic mural by Amelia Peláez on the hotel itself. Even today, La Rampa retains its buzz, with the offices of several international airlines and an exhibition hall called the Pabellón Cuba with a statue of Sancho Panza, used for international trade shows.

Nearby is another landmark from the period, the thirty-five-story Focsa building. Occupying an entire city block, this monstrous apartment complex was the largest structure of reinforced concrete at the time and had its own power plant, beauty salon, and several restaurants. During the 1960s, it became known as the *Edificio Coño*, after the expression used by many *guajiros* in Havana to describe its size.* Most of its wealthy inhabitants had fled and the Focsa housed Soviet personnel. For a time, many of its 375 apartments remained empty, but it's been lavishly restored and the rooftop restaurant offers an unrivaled view of the city.

This building boom, increased revenue from tourism, and a total U.S. investment of $1 billion accounted for Cuba's relative prosperity. During the 1950s, the average per capita income was as high as $550.[8] In Latin America, this was surpassed only by Venezuela, and Cuba was fourth in the consumption of meat, third in number of telephones, and first in the number of television sets.

Cuba's burgeoning middle class rode the economic tide. Leaving their parents' homes in the Vedado, many younger families lived in new suburbs, such as El Country and Siboney. This insulated them from the tourist trade, since the *norteamericanos* tended to stay at the hotels in Centro Habana and drink in places like Sloppy Joe's. The vaunted brothels were limited to seedy neighborhoods, such as Pila Street near the fortress of Atarés, the back alleys of Chinatown, and the red light district known as the Barrio Colón. Indeed, middle-class Habaneros inhabited another Havana altogether, rarely seen by tourists. They rightfully regarded their city as one of the greatest in the world, and would have been baffled and offended by its portrayal in *Godfather II.*

Social life centered around private clubs such as the Havana Yacht Club, founded in 1886. It refused to accept Batista, unlike the Biltmore Country Club, which received a marina in exchange. Together with the Miramar Yacht Club, the Vedado Tennis Club, and the Casino Español, they comprised the "Big Five." There was a busy round of dances, sporting events, and extravagant *quinceañeras*, (coming-out parties for a girl's fifteenth birthday).

---

* *Coño*, nominally the word for female genitalia, is a common exclamation in Havana. Lacking a pejorative connotation, and generally indicates surprise or amazement. In Spain and other Latin American countries, the meaning is quite different, similar to the nasty, English-language equivalent.

My parents' generation, coming of age in the 1950s, was character-
ized by long engagements and seemingly puritanical mores. Proper
young ladies could not go out unaccompanied, and first dates were inevitably with a chaperone, often a maiden aunt. Increasing numbers of
young men (and women) studied in the United States and found employment with American companies in Cuba. Just as Americans crossed over
from Key West, many Cubans escaped the sticky weather by summering
in Asheville, North Carolina, or sending their children to Camp Acadia
in upstate New York. It was a world away from the milieu of flashy gam-
blers and mobsters at the Hotel Rivera. Ricky Ricardo would not have
been admitted to the Havana Yacht Club, nor would Sky Masterson.

Yet it was a shaky prosperity, and the economy was overwhelmingly
dominated by sugar, as it had been since the early 1800s. The industry occupied a fourth of the arable land and a third of the workforce during harvesttime. By 1958, sugar was 30 percent of Cuba's gross national product
and 85 percent of its exports.[9] In 1956, tourists spent $30 million in
Cuba, but that sum was only 10 percent of that year's sugar crop. This
made Cuba increasingly vulnerable to price shifts in the world market
and ever more dependent on the United States, which bought nearly the
entire harvest at a subsidized price and owned 40 percent of the *centrales*.
Despite the boom, there was hefty unemployment, estimated at 17 percent in 1957 with another 13 percent classed as underemployed.[10]

Batista had indeed brought back the *vacas gordas*, but they would be
short-lived.

## THE ATTACK ON THE PALACE

To reach the University of Havana, you follow L Street three blocks
south from La Rampa until you come to San Lazaro. There, to your
right, is the *escalinata*. The eighty-eight-step stone staircase telescopes up
to the elegant, neo-classical rectory, with four Corinthian columns.
Nearly at the top is the Alma Mater, a bronze statue cast by Czechoslova-
kian artist Mario Korbel in 1919. Dressed in a Roman tunic, she wel-
comes students with outstretched arms, seated atop a marble pedestal.

The university had been founded in 1728, and its majestic campus
was inspired by Columbia University in New York. Behind the rectory is
the shady Plaza Ignacio Agramonte, and porticoed buildings such as the
Aula Magna, where Father Varela's ashes are kept. The tranquil colonnades belie the fact that the university was traditionally a hornet's nest of

political conspiracies. The *escalinata* was the site of the demonstrations, known as *tanganas*, during the Machadato and the refuge of gangsters during the Grau years. Its autonomy had been codified in the Constitution of 1940, and in theory, police were barred from the "sacred hill." The nearly eighteen thousand students, in thirteen faculties, were governed by the Federation of University Students (FEU). During the 1950s, the students would once again lead the fight against Batista.

It is here that Castro enters our story. After graduating from Belén, he had enrolled as a law student in 1945, more interested in politics than in attending classes. Castro dreamed of being elected president of the FEU but met with little success. He then attached himself to the Ortodoxo Party, hoping to ride the coattails of Eddy Chibás. Briefly practicing law but finding few clients, he attempted to run for congress in the aborted election of 1952. Batista's coup ended Castro's efforts to win elective office, and before long he was conspiring to storm the Moncada police barracks in Santiago de Cuba. The attack took place on July 26, 1953. Castro and 160 followers, lightly armed with pistols and .22 caliber rifles, were easily repulsed by the garrison. About half of the insurgents were captured, and many were brutally murdered. Castro himself was arrested a few days later and escaped death only through the intercession of the archbishop. He was later sentenced to a fifteen-year prison term in the Isle of Pines.

The attack on Moncada had little impact on Cuban politics other than bringing Castro into the public eye. After winning the election of 1954 and all his talk of the wounded stork, Batista could at least claim to rule constitutionally, and the influx of tourists had won him the support of the business community. He was so confident as to grant a general amnesty to political prisoners, freeing Castro and his coconspirators, who were languishing in the Isle of Pines. Castro soon left for Mexico to launch his invasion the following year, but the students in Havana had plans of their own.

The FEU was headed by José Antonio Echevarría, an architecture student from Cardenas. Affectionately called *Manzanita*,* Echevarría was a Catholic intellectual with a gift for oratory. In November 1955, he organized a rally on the *escalinata* to commemorate the death of the medical

---

* *Manzana* means "apple." Echevarría received this nickname because of his rosy cheeks.

students shot by the Spaniards in 1871. Batista's enforcers, known as *esbir-ros*, moved in, hospitalizing several students. Echevarría himself was severely beaten. The FEU called for a student strike, and riots spread throughout the island, met with ever more brutality by Batista secret police, the dreaded SIM.

This convinced Echevarría that there could be no political solution to the crisis. He started a new organization, the Directorio Revolucionario, modeled after the action groups of the Machado years. After 1956, with the failure of the civic dialogue in which Batista tried to negotiate a compromise with the opposition, the violence would continue to escalate on both sides. Borrowing the tactics of the ABC, the Directorio Revolucionario planned to assassinate Minister of the Interior Santiago Rey at the Montmartre nightclub. Rey did not turn up, but the students instead saw Colonel Manuel Blanco Rico, the chief of SIM. He was killed and several of his party wounded, and the students sought refuge in the Haitian embassy. Violating the right of asylum, the police raided the embassy, killing ten students in a blazing gun battle.

By then, Castro was preparing to embark from Mexico with eighty-two men aboard the yacht *Granma*, named for the original owner's grandmother. After a hellish crossing in which most of the revolutionaries became violently seasick, the *Granma* reached the eastern shore of Cuba on December 2. Che Guevara later remarked that it wasn't a landing but rather a shipwreck. The worst was yet to come, since they had been spotted and were ambushed after coming ashore. Most were either killed or captured, and the bedraggled survivors, with only a few rifles between them, escaped to the mountains to regroup. For several weeks, it was assumed that Castro was dead. This was disproved only when Hemingway's pal Herbert Matthews interviewed him in the Sierra Maestra. According to legend, Castro had the same men march back and forth to convince Matthews that he had a much larger force. At the time, he had just eighteen men. The ruse worked, and the starstruck portrait of Castro in the *New York Times* as an idealistic young revolutionary was in stark contrast to Batista and made him more of a hero in America than in Cuba.

Already wary of Castro, the students decided to strike again. Echevarría met with members of the Auténtico Party to plan a blow against Batista himself. The audacious assassination attempt took place on March 13, 1957. Today the Presidential Palace is the Museo de la Revolución, and it is easy to follow the route taken by the attackers. The first wave consisted of about fifty men who approached the palace at 3:20 PM in two cars and a red truck marked "Fast Delivery," which is displayed outside the palace near the *Granma* itself.

Firing submachine guns, the students quickly overwhelmed the guards and rushed into the palace. Batista's soldiers mounted a defense from the third floor, firing into the open courtyard and killing many of the attackers. The police quickly surrounded the palace and prevented a second wave of twenty-six men who had been delayed by traffic from attacking. A few of the students shot their way up to the living quarters on the second floor and entered Batista's office. They found an unfinished cup of coffee beside the bust of Abraham Lincoln that he kept on his desk, indicating that he had been there only a few moments before. When he heard the first shots, Batista had taken his private elevator to the third floor, where his bodyguards were. While most of the attackers were killed, fifteen managed to escape by fleeing into the chaotic streets.[11] The attack had failed.

Echevarría had gone with another group to the CMQ Building in the Vedado to take over Radio Reloj, a popular station that broadcast the news with the time, each minute. As the attack on the palace began, he broadcast a message that started "People of Cuba! The revolution has begun!" But his voice was too loud and the microphone automatically shut off. After shooting up the studio, Echevarría and his men returned to their headquarters at the university. On the way, they encountered a police car, and Echevarría (who was driving) pulled over and began firing. He was killed instantly.

What if Batista had lingered over his coffee? Apparently he had been warned and placed his bodyguards on alert, though the students nearly caught him. Perhaps if the first wave had been able to enter without firing shots and alerting the soldiers, and the second wave had arrived in time, the outcome would have been different. But the Directorio Revolucionario had no plans for a general uprising and no political agenda other than getting rid of Batista. Even had the dictator been killed, the political consequences were unclear.

Perhaps the greatest tragedy was Echevarría's death at age twenty-four. Better known than Castro at the time, he was a brave and charismatic leader whose integrity was admired even by his opponents. His absence left the students rudderless, and the initiative passed to Castro's isolated band in the mountains and his 26th of July Movement, named after the date of the attack on Moncada.

## NEW YEAR'S EVE

The last night of 1958 was like any other at the Tropicana. Its owner, Martin Fox, and the nightclub's four hundred employees kept the guests happy, the rum flowing, and the roulette wheels turning. It was a clear, breezy evening, and at eleven-thirty the show began beneath the stars. It was *Rumbo al Waldorf*, a Rodney extravaganza in which the stage itself was a Cubana Airways plane, and the chorus line emerged carrying suitcases. At midnight, champagne corks flew, kisses were exchanged, and twelve doves were released to celebrate the New Year.[12]

The struggle against Batista had reached even the Tropicana. Two years before, just as Castro and his men were reaching the Sierra Maestra, a bomb exploded at the bar. Several guests suffered cuts and bruises, but a seventeen-year-old girl lost her arm. With his customary generosity, Fox paid her hospital bills, even though his wife, Ofelia, suspected it was she who had planted the bomb.

It was a peculiar war. At first, Batista refused to take the insurgence seriously. Castro had survived, but remained isolated in the far-off Sierrra Maestra with only a handful of men. Then in May 1957, Castro made his move, attacking the small army outpost of El Uvero. The rebels overran the barracks and then quickly withdrew. Although it burnished the legend spread by Matthews, it was hardly a crushing defeat for Batista's army of forty thousand. This cat-and-mouse game would continue for another year, with inconclusive, small-scale attacks.

Most of the fighting was in Havana, with the surviving remnants of the Directorio now allied with the 26th of July Movement and waging a fierce, running battle with Batista's forces. The university had been closed since November 1956, yet the demonstrations on the *escalinata* continued. The pedestal of the Alma Mater provided a podium for many passionate speeches. The students then marched down the stairs, arms linked, singing the Cuban national anthem and shouting *"¡Abajo Batista!"* The police awaited them on San Lazaro Street, assaulting them first with water cannons, then truncheons, then bullets.

In an eerie replay of 1933, the brutality of Batista's response dissipated his support and alienated his greatest friend, the United States. The pliant Ambassador Gardner had been replaced by Earl Smith, a tough-minded investment banker, and an arms embargo was imposed. This was primarily a symbolic gesture, since Batista continued to buy weapons elsewhere, even from Britain, but it sent a clear message. The students' weapons were assassinations, bombings, and kidnappings. Batista replied with arrests, tortures, and killings. Writer Pablo Medina recalls going to an artificial lake called El Laguito in the neighborhood of El Country. This was the dumping ground for Batista's victims, and human remains were often found along the shore.[13]

Batista did not make a serious attempt to dislodge Castro until May 1958. Since the attack on the Presidential Palace, he spent most of his time at his farm Kuquine, surrounded by barbed wire and armed guards. Strangely detached, Batista wasted hours playing canasta or watching American horror movies.[14] His lack of combat experience was also telling. The commanders in the field had suggested airlifting troops to the mountains and forcing the guerrillas down to the sea, but Batista insisted on an assault from below. By then, Castro controlled much of the Sierra Maestra, though he only had about three hundred men. Batista attacked with two battalions, coming from the north and south. For a while, the pincer movement was effective, and Castro's men held only a four-square mile area. But the 11th Battalion, led by one of Batista's most able commanders, Colonel Sánchez Mosquera, was surrounded in a narrow valley and took heavy losses. This setback thoroughly demoralized Batista's high command, and the army withdrew. From then on, Castro operated with impunity and seized the initiative.

By mid-1958, the struggle was dampening the overheated Cuban economy. High-profile attacks like those at the Montmartre and the Tropicana had stemmed the flow of tourists. One rebel group hijacked a plane from Miami to Varadero, which crashed into the Bay of Nipe. For the first time, Batista must have faced the possibility of defeat. Other reporters had followed Matthews to the mountains, and Castro demonstrated his mastery of the media. In Havana, he was heard regularly on the clandestine *Radio Rebelde* and his picture frequently appeared in magazines like *Bohemia*.

In August, Castro dispatched Guevara and another lieutenant, Camilo Cienfuegos, west with 230 men. Repeating the tactics of Máximo Gómez, Guevara was to take Santa Clara, while Cienfuegos attacked Pinar del Río. Guevara's campaign was the only significant engagement of the insurrection. In late December, he reached Santa Clara in two columns, having bribed his way past several army outposts. The defense of the city depended on a slow-moving heavily armored train, a dubious tactic against a guerrilla force. Guevara's men pulled out the tracks with tractors and derailed the train. The 350 men inside (more than Guevara's entire force) haplessly surrendered.

Yet the Cuban army was still intact and controlled all of western Cuba, which Cienfuegos had failed to penetrate. Batista was no coward. During his presidency, he had once faced down a potential coup by driving to Camp Columbia wearing a leather jacket, which became a political symbol, along with the stork. It was assumed that when the going got tough, Batista would *ponerse la chaqueta* (put on the jacket) and directly confront the rebels. He never did, perhaps because his soldiers refused to fight. Established by the U.S. occupiers, the Cuban armed forces had been decimated by the Sergeants' Revolt, which eliminated the officer class. By 1958, it was led by corrupt, lazy cronies more interested in graft than counterinsurgency.

It nonetheless came as a great surprise to most Cubans when during the early hours of January 1, 1959, just as the champagne was flowing at the Tropicana, Batista boarded a plane and left the island to Castro.

Posterity has not been kind to Fulgencio Batista. Universally despised, this descendant of the Taínos is still blamed for many of Cuba's woes. Yet Batista's twenty-five-year hold over the island could not have been possible without the support of the United States. To paraphrase Franklin Delano Roosevelt, he was "our son of a bitch." For much of this time he was a proxy for American interests, and he might have remained in power had not Eisenhower abandoned him at the eleventh hour. Batista was no more corrupt than Grau, less hypocritical than Prío, and not as violent as Machado. In many ways, he is a more sympathetic figure than any of these three.

Had he remained playing canasta in Daytona Beach with Meyer Lansky, he would have been remembered as one of Cuba's greatest leaders, the man who brought the wounded stork of democracy back to health. If so, the Cuban Republic might have endured (however tenuously), Castro might have been elected rather than taking up arms, and much else would have been different. These parallel possibilities, like the reflections in the Hall of Mirrors in the Presidential Palace, still haunt many dreams in Miami.

Batista escaped to the Dominican Republic. Unlike Machado, he had no need to take bags of gold. His personal fortune, approximately $300 million,* was mostly invested abroad. He was denied asylum in the United States and found refuge in another lovely island, Madeira. For a time, he stayed in the elegant Reid's Palace Hotel, where I found his photograph still displayed discreetly. Batista later moved to Spain, where he died in 1973.

Currently he resides in the dustbin of history with fellow dictators Somoza and Trujillo, and is not likely to make a comeback. But in the looking-glass world of Florida politics, who can tell? President George W. Bush's point man on Cuban policy is the formidable Congressman Lincoln Diaz-Balart, the son of a prominent Batistiano as well as Castro's nephew by marriage. And in 2002, Raoul Cantero, Batista's Harvard-educated grandson, was named to the Florida Supreme Court by the president's brother, Governor Jeb Bush.

---

* As conservatively estimated by Hugh Thomas, in 1958 dollars. There is no way of knowing the real figure; today it would probably approach $1 billion. Batista had his hand in the Cuban till since 1933, and his cut of casino revenues during the late 1950s was enormous.

# CHAPTER ELEVEN

## *Che's Revolution*
### *New Year's Day*

*The world changed while I slept, and much to my surprise, no one had consulted me.*

—Carlos Eire, *Waiting for Snow in Havana*

*W*ord of Batista's flight spread quickly. According to *Bohemia*, the three planes carrying him and his inner circle (his family had left the week before) left the airfield at Camp Columbia around 2:00 AM.[1] *New York Times* reporter Ruby Hart Phillips recalls that the New Year's Eve party at the Hotel Riviera was muted. One guest at her table had seen a telltale sign: cars loaded with baggage heading for the airport. The noise of planes taking off at such an hour must also have raised suspicions. Ofelia Fox relates that at the Tropicana, a call came in to a Batistiano slumped over the roulette table. Upon hearing the news, the Guajiro's partner Alberto Ardura, a Batista family friend, swiftly made plans to leave the island. On the radio, the song *"Mama, son de la loma"* (Mama, they're from the mountains) could be heard. It was played often on the clandestine Radio Rebelde, and had been banned from the airwaves.

Most Habaneros were in bed. "The world changed while I slept," wrote Carlos Eire in his National Book Award-winning memoir, *Waiting for Snow in Havana*. But in the morning, there was an eerie silence, as if Havana were catching its breath. Then at around ten o'clock, there was a roar, and the streets began to fill with raucous crowds. Many carried the red-and-black banner of the 26th of July Movement and sang the Cuban national anthem, while others simply wanted to be outside and greet the new year.

Those who remembered the Machadato, a quarter century before, were full of foreboding when joy turned to violence. "It was like sitting through a bad movie a second time," recalled Phillips.[2] The mobs began with the parking meters in Centro Habana, knocking them off the metal poles with baseball bats. This seems odd, but the concession belonged to a relative of Batista's. To this day, parking meters have yet to reappear in Havana. Telephone booths were also destroyed, as well as Shell Oil service stations, other symbols of corruption. The mobs then moved on to the casinos, invading the plush salons and overturning roulette tables. All of Havana's thirteen casinos were sacked except for the Capri, where George Raft held off the mob by snarling "You're not coming in my casino!" in his best tough-guy voice. This seems apocryphal, though one eyewitness swore to it and the incident has entered the folklore of that memorable day.

The attack on the casinos was not just a political gesture, since the looters were after the night's receipts. They smashed plate-glass windows of jewelry stores along the Prado, and the emptied the contents. Along Galiano Street, the window displays of the department stores such as El Encanto were ransacked. But Phillips recalls that before long, a truck with a loud-speaker drove around the Parque Central announcing: "Get off the street or be killed." Young men and women wearing 26th of July Movement armbands, emerging from the shadows after two years of urban warfare, began to patrol the streets and restore order. Some had entered into police stations unarmed and announced they were taking over, sending the rank-and-file policemen home.

As a result, only a handful of houses were vandalized. Most of the Batistianos had fled or gone into hiding, and there were no scenes such as the gruesome lynchings of Machadistas on the Prado. There were sporadic firefights with the remnants of the SIM and a group of Masferrer's *Tigres* who holed up in the Manzana de Gómez. The gangster was a particularly hated figure, and the offices of his newspaper *El Tiempo* was attacked. Masferrer himself fled in a yacht for Miami. But order was soon established by the self-appointed militias, and the Boy Scouts volunteered to direct traffic.

The flights continued out of Havana until the airport was closed at noon. Many American tourists found themselves stranded and gathered with their suitcases on the lawn of the Hotel Nacional. Wayne Smith,

Havana's casinos were looted by mobs on January 1, 1959. (Author's collection)

then a young consular officer at the U.S. embassy, organized convoys to take them to the Key West ferry. One irate tourist declared that he had important business in New York the next day. Revolution or no revolution, he was going home.[3]

The first *barbudos** arrived that afternoon. They were members of the so-called Second Front of the Escambray, led by Eloy Gutiérrez Menoyo, whose brother Carlos had been killed during the attack on the palace. The Second Front was a small group that had coexisted uneasily with Guevara's troops in the Escambray Mountains but had not participated in the battle for Santa Clara. Nonetheless, they looked the part, with beards and olive-green fatigues, and were greeted rapturously by Habaneros, who kissed their hands and gave them religious medals and rosaries.

Other guerrilla fighters soon trickled in. Over the next few days, the city would swell with these unkempt, bearded men who were greeted as the saviors of the island. Those who were from Havana simply returned to their homes, to their parents and sweethearts. But most were *guajiros* from the countryside who had never seen a big city before. By all accounts, they were gracious and polite, and received the adulation humbly. Still clutching their rifles, many camped out in the lobbies of the hotels along the Malecón, a picturesque contrast to the fleeing tourists. Several hundred slept in the ballroom of the new Havana Hilton. Carlos Eire recalls that he and other young boys asked them for bullets as souvenirs.[4]

Castro himself was equally surprised by Batista's abrupt departure. Already convinced that victory was in his grasp, he thought Batista would hold out for a few months more. The rebel forces had been advancing toward Santiago de Cuba, and Castro spent the night at a sugar mill near Palma Soriano. Nearby was Errol Flynn, apparently filming a movie.[5] According to one biographer, Castro awoke on the wrong side of the hammock. Hearing celebratory gunfire, he complained that his men were wasting ammunition. Castro was told the news as he tucked into a plate of *arroz con pollo* for breakfast.

"Where did you hear that?" was his immediate reaction.[6]

---

* Literally, "bearded ones," as the shaggy revolutionaries were called.

Putting down his fork, Castro swung into action. Batista had handed over power to a junta led by General Eulogio Cantillo, and Castro feared that victory would be snatched away from him. He read a statement on shortwave radio and for the first time it was broadcast nationally. Denouncing the junta and likening it to a coup d'état, he proclaimed a general strike. Then he ordered Camilo Cienfuegos and Che Guevara to occupy Havana.

One puzzling announcement made by Castro was that Santiago de Cuba was once again, after four hundred years, the capital of Cuba. This move was impractical if only because of the sheer size of the government. Nothing ever came of this, and the idea was soon dropped. It has been interpreted as showing Castro's disdain for Havana, but more likely it was an attempt to undercut the junta.

The next day, Castro entered Santiago de Cuba and symbolically took possession of the Moncada barracks, which he had attacked unsuccessfully in 1953. That night, surrounded by a jubilant crowd, Castro gave the first of many, many speeches. He named Manuel Urrutia, a judge known for integrity and not much else, as the new president of Cuba. He himself would remain in command of the rebel army. Castro invoked the Apostle, José Martí, and recalled how American troops had marched into the city in 1898 and "made themselves masters of our country." This time, it would be different:

> *The Revolution begins now. . . . [It] will not be made in two days, but now I am sure that we are making the Revolution, and that for the first time Cuba will be free and people will have what they deserve. . . . The Revolution was won by the people![7]*

Yet despite Castro's defiant tone, that night he had dinner with the U.S. consul, who had aided the movement.

At 3:00 AM on January 2, Cienfuegos arrived at Camp Columbia with a handful of men. By then, the junta had already collapsed. Cantillo ceded power to Colonel Ramon Barquin, who had conspired against Batista and been imprisoned in the Isle of Pines. Barquin was flown into Havana, and the U.S. ambassador urged him to form a government. But Barquin happily turned over the keys of Havana to Cienfuegos. Carlos Franqui, who served as Castro's media advisor and ran Radio Rebelde, arrived a few days later and was amazed to see the troops at Camp Columbia, long a symbol of oppression, timidly saluting their former enemies, the *barbudos*. Later that day, Guevara occupied the fortress of La Cabaña. Guevara was one of Castro's closest confidants, second only to his brother Raul. But Castro shrewdly made the popular Cienfuegos the standard-bearer, since there were already suspicions that Guevara was a communist.

Castro then began a slow, triumphal march across the island toward Havana. Why did he not go immediately? From the start, Castro showed himself to be a master of political theater. Despite the publicity he had received, he was still an unknown quantity. The five-day, six-hundred mile procession was widely televised and gave most Cubans the first glimpse of their new leader. It was an image that would become familiar to the world: A vigorous, bearded young Castro (only thirty-two at the time) in a rumpled green uniform, smoking a cigar, with a medal of the *Virgen de la Caridad del Cobre* around his neck and a rifle with a telescopic sight slung over his shoulder. He rode in a open jeep or atop a tank, surrounded by his fighters and an ever-growing mass of well-wishers. He halted constantly, whether to embrace a friend or simply to work the crowd. But it was not just for show. At each town, he named a member of the 26th of July Movement as mayor, establishing his authority where fighting had not taken place.

For many, he was "almost Christlike," and they hoped to kiss his hand or simply touch him. The comparison was heightened by a special issue of *Bohemia* that soon appeared, with a circulation of 1 million. It showed a messianic Castro gazing into the distance, surrounded by what looked like a halo. He stopped at Cardenas to lay a wreath on the tomb of José Antonio Echevarría, although the two had been rivals and Castro had done nothing to support the fatal attack on the palace.

In the meantime, Urrutia had formed a well-regarded, moderate cabinet, which did much to dispel American anxiety. Indeed, the United States recognized the new government on January 7—recognition that has never been formally withdrawn. But the Presidential Palace had been occupied by students from the Directorio Revoluciónario, and for a time it appeared they would have to be dislodged by force. Though they remained armed, the students allowed Urrutia to take possession of the palace after tense negotiations, and he reached Havana on January 5 and formally set up the new government.

Castro (already he was referred to simply as Fidel) finally reached the outskirts of Havana on January 8. There he was greeted by his ten-year-old son, Fidelito. With typical Cuban *moneria*,* he had been dressed in a miniature guerrilla uniform. Castro arrived on the Via Blanca Highway from Matanzas and passed by the fortress of Atarés. Two warships in the harbor fired a salute, but Castro stopped first at the *Granma*, which had been freshly painted and moored at the Avenida del Puerto. Then he paid his respects to Urrutia, nominally his boss. Perhaps tired, he spoke only briefly to the crowd those gathered before the Presidential Palace. When he finished, they blocked his path, but Castro asked them to make way, noting that the world would see how disciplined Cubans were. Franqui, an eyewitness, recalls that the crowd parted miraculously, like the Red Sea before Moses, and Castro declared, "The people are my bodyguard."[8]

That night, he gave his first major address in Havana. The heavily fortified gates of Camp Columbia were thrown open and, for the first time, ordinary Cubans entered. Castro spoke from the same reviewing stand used by the former president, surrounded by Urrutia and his cabinet, with Cienfuegos to his left. It was his first speech to be televised, but Castro spoke informally and without notes. He began by applauding the victory of the rebel army and stressing the need for unity. Every so often he would stop to ask "How am I doing, Camilo?"

"Fine, Fidel," replied the grinning Cienfuegos, coining a popular slogan.[9]

Then Castro quickly solved a problem that had remained unresolved. Though they had ceded the palace, the students of the Directorio Revoluciónario still occupied the University of Havana and smaller groups, such as the Second Front of the Escambray (which had taken over a school in the Vedado), remained armed.

"Arms, for what?" Castro asked rhetorically. "To fight against whom? Against the Revolution?"

"No!" the crowd chanted.

That very night, the Directorio began to turn over its weapons, leaving the 26th of July Movement in control of the streets.

As Castro spoke, someone loosed a pair of white doves, and one alighted on his shoulder. As seen by an awestruck television audience, it was a brilliant and priceless political prop. Not just the Christian dove of peace, it was also the dove of Santeria, which stood for eternal life. Even

---

* *Moneria* comes from *mono*, or monkey. It might be translated as "cute" but describes a peculiar brand of Cuban kitsch.

the staid *Diario de la Marina* called it an "act of Providence." But how on earth did the dove happen to land on his shoulder?*

Castro has yet to reveal all his secrets.

## HABANA LIBRE

*I'll tell the future for you: someday there will be only
one pair of whiskers around here—yours.*

—Carlos Franqui to Fidel Castro

Castro and his ebullient entourage established themselves in the Havana Hilton, later renamed the Habana Libre. There was nowhere else to go. Camp Columbia (now Camp Liberty) was a symbol of the *ancien regime*, and President Urrutia occupied the Presidential Palace. Castro himself took a $100-a-day suite on the twenty-third floor, previously reserved for high rollers. The gleaming, air-conditioned lobby of the vast hotel, open less than a year, became the nerve center of the Revolution. It provided keen contrasts: armed *barbudos* cheek-to-jowl with carefully coiffed ministers, anxious businessmen together with bewildered tourists, inquisitive journalists alongside even more inquisitive spies.

After January 5, a working government was in place, headed by Urrutia. This left Castro ostensibly free of responsibility, and he attended none of the cabinet meetings where Urrutia tried to impose order on revolutionary chaos. But there was no question where power lay. The disparate characters in the lobby all wanted a moment of Castro's time, but could scarcely keep up with him. Castro was a whirlwind of activity, giving twelve major speeches in the first month and holding five press conferences, where he enjoyed jousting with reporters. He generally ignored appointments, or else was hours late. Castro had no office, and many decisions were made in his bedroom, where he greeted government officials wearing striped pajamas. He generally ate at the coffee shop in the lobby, or else at Hemingway's favorite Chinese restaurant, El Pacifico. Castro worked at all hours, and if it was too late, he raided the hotel's kitchen.

Despite being the eye of the hurricane, he occasionally disappeared, and one day when Fidelito was injured in a car accident, he could not be

---

* According to one skeptical eyewitness, the dove had been carefully trained. Force-fed marbles, it was too heavy to fly away.

located for several hours. Castro could often be found playing basketball with his bodyguards or watching target practice with Guevara at La Cabaña. If not at the Habana Libre, he was at the apartment on Eleventh Street in the Vedado of his adoring secretary, Celia Sánchez, or else a house in Cojimar lent by a wealthy friend. In addition, he often went fishing in the Cienega de Zapata, a wild, swampy area to the south of Havana. He had a small aluminum-frame house erected at the Laguna de Tesoro, which became his secret hideaway. His familiarity with that area would later prove fatal to the CIA-trained invaders at the Bay of Pigs.

Castro carried no money, and practical details were taken care of by Celia, who tightly controlled access to him. It was she who paid the hotel and restaurant bills, from money they had collected from landowners in the Sierra Maestra. Castro often seemed to tire of the incessant demands made on him in Havana, and once wistfully declared, "I miss my mountains."

At the end of January, Castro flew to Venezuela, his first trip abroad since the victory. He was greeted as a Bolivarian hero but returned to face a crisis. The puritanical Urrutia hated gambling, and his first measure was to shut down the casinos and brothels. This ignited a public firestorm, and protesting croupiers, bartenders, and prostitutes joined the motley crowd in the lobby of the Habana Libre. Castro relented, citing the jobs that would be lost.

Equally important was the fact that the casinos were needed to fill Cuba's coffers. At the time of Batista's flight, the island was nearly bankrupt, with a debt of $1.2 billion, a budget deficit of $800 million, and cash reserves of less than $1 million. American visitors were projected to spend $6 billion per year by 1964, and Castro made a concerted effort to lure them back. In October, he hosted the annual meeting of the American Society of Travel Agents (ASTA), telling the cheering delegates, "Just tell us what you want, and we will give it to you."[10]

Castro's decision to reopen the casinos sank Urrutia's government. The prime minister, a prominent lawyer named José Miró Cardona, resigned in protest. Castro replaced him and from then on made all government decisions. The lame-duck president was reduced to signing government decrees and rarely spoke at cabinet meetings.

Perhaps the first shadows to darken the euphoria of the Revolution were the executions of Batistianos accused of war crimes, which began almost immediately. As his brother proceeded east, Raul Castro had been left in charge of Santiago, and seventy prisoners were summarily machine-gunned and dumped into a trench. In Havana, by January 20, drumhead tribunals had sentenced over two hundred men to death. Most of these were army officers or SIM agents, and many freely admitted their guilt. But evidence was rarely presented in favor of the defendants, and the judges were often the *barbudos* themselves. Within a few months, several hundred would meet the firing squad. Since the birth of the Cuban Republic in 1902, only six men had been executed by order of a court, and the Constitution of 1940 prohibited capital punishment. But without question the public demanded a bloodletting.

The most egregious example of the lust for revenge was the trial of Jesus Sosa Blanco, which took place in the Sports Palace in late January. The notorious commander of the garrison at Holguin undoubtedly got what he deserved. But his trial, which was carried live on television and radio, was pointedly compared to a Roman circus. Vendors sold ice cream and peanuts, and spectators hooted, stomped, and clapped their hands. The evidence against Sosa Blanco was hearsay, and he was not allowed to call witnesses. Like the other Batistianos, he was shot by a firing squad.

These spectacles, rather than the threat of communist subversion, raised the only complaints Castro heard when he visited the United States in April. The rollicking, two-week trip began in Washington, D.C., where he had been invited to speak at the National Press Club. Eisenhower was on a golfing trip, so Castro met alone with Vice-President Nixon for over two hours. Apparently they did little more than establish their mutual dislike. Nixon told Eisenhower that Castro was "incredibly naive," while Castro found Nixon to be a "lightweight." Castro also found time for sightseeing, visiting the Lincoln Monument and George Washington's home in Mount Vernon.

From there, Castro and his traveling party of seventy went to New York, where he met with Jackie Robinson and Henry Luce, and Boston, where he spoke to students at Harvard. He had hired the public relations firm of Bernard Relling to manage the trip, and they found him to be a quick study. Castro captivated crowds wherever he went, speaking fluent if charmingly accented English, and behaved like a more traditional politician: shaking hands, posing for pictures, and kissing babies.

The inevitable showdown with Urrutia occurred after Castro's return to Havana. Castro waited until the city had been flooded by *guajiros* to celebrate the 26th of July. Speaking on television, he stunned the nation by resigning his post, citing his disagreements with Urrutia. He accused the former judge of obstructing the Revolution by failing to sign decrees and noted that he had bought an expensive house. More serious was the fact that Urrutia had implied Castro was a communist, which he said "bordered on treason."

The impact of the speech was immediate. Angry crowds took to the streets, demanding Urrutia's resignation and shouting "*¡Viva Fidel!*" Urrutia had been listening to the speech on television in the Presidential Palace and saw which way the wind was blowing. Putting on a *guayabera*, he slipped out the back door and sought asylum in the Venezuelan embassy.

The next day, Castro spoke for over four hours at the Plaza de la Revolución. Looking over the assembled crowd of half a million, he reluctantly agreed to stay on. There was no need for elections, he declared, because the will of the people was supreme. He concluded: "This is real democracy."

By the end of 1959, Havana had changed irrevocably.

One victim was Santa Claus. By the 1930s, he had gained ascendancy over the Three Kings in the hearts of Cuban children. Now he was replaced by "Don Feliciano," a vague figure wearing the typical straw hat of the *guajiro*. Christmas trees were also discouraged. One unconvincing Christmas carol trotted out by the propagandists was "Jingle bells, jingle bells, always with Fidel . . ."

Castro's efforts to court tourists continued at a New Year's Eve gala at the Habana Libre. Attempting to lure African American visitors, he invited the aging boxer Joe Louis. The Oriental Park Racetrack reopened with a splash, and many hotels offered discounts. Despite this, they remained empty, and receipts fell to 20 percent of what they had been in 1958. The chant "*¡Cuba si! ¡Yanqui no!*" was first heard at a May Day rally in 1960, and the rising tide of anti-Americanism frightened away the tourists. At first, Meyer Lansky had been eager to work with the new government. Yet even after the casinos reopened, they lost their luster and the Riviera was forced to close. In the end, Lansky lost $4 million. So ended the mob's brief and ultimately unprofitable stay in Cuba.

Many of the *barbudos* had shaved, though others still made their presence felt. Some had moved into the homes vacated by fleeing Batistianos and now lived the good life. For several months, they were able to ride buses for free. According to one joke, a clean-shaven man entered a bus without paying and was confronted by the driver, who said, "You're not a *barbudo!*" "I'm secret service," replied the man, to the applause of the other passengers.[11]

If the beards were disappearing, they were replaced as a symbol of the Revolution by the light blue uniforms of the militias. Originally volunteers, they were eventually integrated into the new army, and would be sent into combat against the counter-revolutionaries soon to take up arms against Castro in the Escambray Mountains. Before long, the militias were a constant presence on the streets of Havana.

Another new institution were the Committees for the Defense of the Revolution (CDR). At a speech on September 1960, Castro proposed the formation of these neighborhood watches ostensibly to prevent sabotage. Today, there are 15,000 CDRs in Havana and 100,000 throughout Cuba. Often they are little more than sinecures for local busybodies, yet they report directly to the Cuban intelligence service, known as the G–2, on the comings and goings of neighbors. The CDRs perform useful tasks such as caring for children and organizing blood drives, yet they are a potent weapon against political dissidents and helped foster a climate of fear that continues to this day. Although they have dimmed somewhat in importance, they remain active and still provide an effective spy network on each block.

Also new to Havana were the Russians. The courtship between Cuba and the Soviet Union began with the visit of Foreign Minister Anastas Mikoyan to Havana in February 1960 to inaugurate the trade show at the Museo de Bellas Artes. It was an elaborate exhibit showcasing Soviet industry, with farm machinery and satellites such as Sputnik. It lasted three weeks and was seen by over 1 million Cubans. The encounter led not only to the establishment of diplomatic relations but a lucrative trade agreement in which the Soviet Union agreed to barter 1 million tons of sugar for each of the next four years in exchange for petroleum, wheat, iron, and other raw materials. It also agreed to provide technical assistance, and from that point on the Russians were frequent visitors to Havana.

The Habaneros were singularly unimpressed. Many of the Russian "advisors" acted and dressed like coarse peasants, the women wearing the headscarves known as babushkas and the men ill-fitting suits. Though Cuba was supposedly the underdeveloped country, the Russians gawked like *guajiros* at the window displays in the department stores, the flashy cars, the modern appliances. They kept to themselves, lived in heavily guarded enclaves, and their pasty white skin quickly sunburned. They were soon tagged *bolos*, since their figures resembled bowling pins. Perhaps the most common complaint was their smell. The Russians did not use deodorant, which offended the finicky Cubans, many of whom bathed several times a day to stave off the tropical heat. But one legacy of this period is the number of Cubans of a certain age named Vladimir or Natasha.

Along with Santa Claus, another casualty of the Revolution was Cuba's vigorous independent media. The first warning sign had come early on. Castro proved notoriously thin-skinned and had little tolerance for jokes at his expense. During the first weeks of the Revolution, the humorous magazine *Zig-Zag* had run a cartoon lampooning the sycophants around him. Castro demanded an apology and threatened to close it down.* By 1960, the battle lines were drawn. Castro struck first by ordering that stories critical of the government should run a brief disclaimer at the end, known as a *coletilla*. Through the unions, Castro controlled the printers, and the newspapers were forced to accept this editorial infringement. In January, the union refused to typeset an editorial in *Avance*, whereupon the newspaper was "intervened." The following month, the editor of *El Pais* resigned after failing to run a *coletilla*. *Diario de la Marina* closed down in May, and *Prensa Libre* soon followed.

The most important television network in Havana was CMQ, owned by Abel and Goar Mestre. They also owned Radio Reloj, the radio station seized by José Antonio Echevarría in 1957, during the attack on the Presidential Palace. CMQ had been critical of the government, and the bank accounts of all four hundred employees were frozen. Abel Mestre then went on the air himself during the program *Ante la Prensa*, denounced Castro, and went into exile. CMQ was soon taken over as well.[12]

More ironic was the fate of *Bohemia*, Cuba's largest magazine, which had been a strong supporter of Castro from the start. The editor, Miguel Angel Quevedo, ran a series of articles criticizing the growing Russian influence. He then left Cuba, claiming that the Revolution had been betrayed. Exiled in Caracas, Quevedo would commit suicide in 1969.

---

* Another bête noir of Castro's was the satirical cartoonist Antonio Prohias, who appeared in *El Mundo*. Threatened with the firing squad, he fled and later created the popular *Spy vs. Spy* series for *Mad* magazine.

Alarmed by these changes, the Cuban middle class chose exile. By the end of 1960, over 100,000 had already left, mostly to the United States. An increasing number of houses were vacated in Havana, occupied by the servants of the owners or else poorer families from the countryside. Many of the exiles belonged to the managerial class, and the resulting "brain drain" created innumerable difficulties in expropriated businesses, leading to much waste and inefficiency. Castro referred contemptuously to the exiles as *gusanos* (worms), borrowing Martí's term for collaborators with the Spanish.

Relations with the United States were by then irreparably poisoned. Throughout the first year of the Revolution, the two countries resembled dance partners determined to step on each other's feet. The new ambassador was Philip Bonsal, an accomplished diplomat with much experience in Latin America. Castro refused to meet with him for many months, and he was recalled in January 1960. The Cubans made an overture in February that was in turn refused by the United States. Castro's shift to the left and his growing relationship with the Soviet Union doomed any chance of a rapprochement . The, grim two-step continued until June, when Esso, Texaco, and Shell refused to refine Soviet petroleum and were promptly nationalized. Eisenhower then cut the sugar quota, Cuba's economic lifeline, and Castro retaliated by expropriating all remaining U.S. businesses.

The music stopped when on October 19, 1960 the United States imposed the trade embargo that has outlasted several wars, presidents, and the Soviet Union itself.

## CHE

*Shoot, coward, you are only going to kill a man.*

—Last words of Che Guevara

The image of Ernesto "Che" Guevara on the MININT building in the Plaza de la Revolución comes from a snapshot by the Cuban photographer Alberto Díaz Gutiérrez.* Taken on March 5, 1960, during the funeral procession for those killed in the explosion of the freighter *La Coubre* in Havana Harbor, it shows the Argentine wearing his trademark

---

* Better known as "Korda."

beret and gazing off into the distance, a fierce, compassionate look in his dark eyes. If the look is familiar, it's because you recognize it from posters hung in college dormitories around the world.

For Guevara, the passage from man to myth was remarkably swift. After his death in 1967, he became not just a revolutionary martyr but a hippie icon, which the authoritarian, ascetic Guevara would have found puzzling. *Time* named him one of the "One Hundred Most Important People of the Century," citing that "he remains the potent symbol of rebellion and the alluring zeal of revolution." Posthumously, he eclipsed Castro, who did not make the list. The only other Latin American chosen was Brazilian soccer god Pelé.

The image of Castro as a young revolutionary has been diluted not just by the passage of time but by successive iterations. We've known Castro in his stout forties, mature fifties, waning sixties, feisty seventies, and now his uncertain eighties. In contrast, Korda's photograph of Guevara in his beret has remained pristine and unalloyed. It has little political relevance today, but it's used to sell t-shirts, coffee mugs, and baseball caps. The Web site Chestore.com, which claims to satisfy "all your revolutionary needs," lists among its top sellers "an authentic Che beret" and a Zippo lighter, purportedly similar to the one he used in the Sierra Maestra to light his pipe.

Guevara's apotheosis was complete with *Motorcycle Diaries*, a movie that received a standing ovation at the Sundance Film Festival in 2004. It's a romantic, idealized version of a motorcycle trip Guevara took in his youth through South America. Portrayed by the Mexican heartthrob Gael García Bernal, young Ernesto appears as a carefree, somewhat callow medical student whose social consciousness is awakened during the journey. It ends with Guevara swimming across a river at a leper colony in the Peruvian jungle, presumably to start a revolution of his own.

In fact, he would have to wait only a few more years. Guevara returned home to Argentina in 1952 to finish his degree. But rather than practice medicine, he hit the road once again, going from Bolivia to Ecuador to Guatemala. It was here that he witnessed the CIA-sponsored ouster of Jacobo Arbenz's leftist government in 1954. This hardened Guevara's inchoate political views, and when he fled to Mexico, he looked up a young Cuban he had met named Ñico López, who had taken part in the attack on Moncada. From him, Guevara received a primer on Cuba as well as a famous nickname. *Che* is a Guarani word used often in Argentina, meaning something to the effect of "hey, you."

Apparently Guevara addressed everyone this way, and so López called him Che. It stuck.

López also introduced him to the Castro brothers after they had been freed from prison and arrived in Mexico. Guevara met Fidel in July 1955 at the home of María Antonia González, a Cuban woman married to a Mexican wrestler.[13] They had dinner in a nearby restaurant and, after a conversation lasting several hours, Castro invited him to join the movement. Guevara had more of an ideological affinity with Raul (who was already a member of the Communist Party) but was impressed with Fidel's audacity. He agreed instantly.

Though Guevara had no military experience, he showed a talent for violence when the guerrillas-to-be underwent training at a farm near Mexico City. He was thus chosen to accompany them when the *Granma* sailed the following year, ostensibly as the expedition's doctor. His friend López was killed soon after the disastrous landfall, but Guevara managed to rendezvous with the other survivors in the mountains. He received a vicious tongue-lashing from Castro for losing his rifle but soon distinguished himself in the first skirmishes against Batista's troops.

Of all the *barbudos*, Guevara was perhaps the most gifted military leader. Always in the thick of the fighting, he was famous for physical bravery, undergoing any hardship suffered by his men despite his frail physique and frequent asthma attacks. In contrast, Castro had to fend off accusations of cowardice for abandoning his men at Moncada. Guevara also inspired fanatic loyalty. His lightning strike against Santa Clara in December 1958 effectively divided the island in two and may have convinced Batista to throw in the towel. By then, Guevara was a full-fledged member of the revolutionary pantheon that included not just the Castros but Camilo Cienfuegos.

From the old Spanish commander's office at La Cabaña, Guevara must have looked with satisfaction across the harbor to Havana. A law was passed for his benefit in February 1959, making him a Cuban citizen by birth—a distinction also given to Máximo Gómez. But at the time, he was experiencing acute domestic difficulties. Guevara had long been separated from his wife, Hilda Gadea, with whom he had a daughter. In the Sierra Maestra, he had met Aleida March, a member of the 26th of July Movement, and the two hoped to marry. But then Hilda showed up in Havana, hoping for a reconciliation. This was complicated by the arrival of Guevara's family from Argentina, including his stern and still disapproving father. Not until May did Hilda grant him a divorce, and he quickly married Aleida.

It would appear that Guevara did little more than mug for the cameras. At the museum in La Cabaña, we see photographs of Guevara happily posing with Castro, playing chess, and grinning with a cigar in his mouth. But during the early months of 1959, Guevara was in charge of the military tribunals, styling himself the "Supreme Prosecutor." Guevara had the final say in all cases and personally reviewed the evidence. The trials began at nine o'clock each night and were over by three o'clock that morning.[14] Prisoners in La Cabaña were kept in the *galeras*, tunnel-like enclosures 120 feet long that run from the courtyard of the fortress to the moat, and secured with heavy iron bars at each end. After each trial, condemned men would be taken to the *capillas* (chapels), small punishment cells to await death. Due to the volume of cases, often executions were performed almost immediately; on some nights there were as many as a dozen. The other prisoners could hear the condemned men walking down the stone steps to where the executions took place. The victims were tied to a wooden pole known simply as the *palo* (stick). Then came the orders of the firing squad: "*¡Preparen! ¡Apunten! ¡Fuego!*"

One peculiarity of the Cuban firing squads was that all eight soldiers fired live ammunition. It is a military tradition for at least one round to be blank, so that it can never be ascertained who killed and who did not. The executions were supervised by an American named Herman Marks. This sinister figure was a Korean War veteran reputed to have a criminal record, including a rape charge. He had joined the insurgents in May 1958 as a weapons instructor. According to John Martíno in *I Was Castro's Prisoner*, Marks was a sadist who often taunted condemned men and took particular pleasure in administering the coup de grace, a shot to the head.[15] Graham Greene encountered him at the Floridita while he was filming *Our Man in Havana*, and Marks invited him to witness the firing squad.[16] Apparently, Greene demurred. Martíno notes that Marks was later caught stealing from the prison and left Cuba in a small boat. In the United States, he was later arrested, and his end is unclear.

Mock executions were also staged to break prisoners, particularly counter-revolutionaries. As meticulously described by sociologist Juan Clark in *Cuba: Mito y Realidad*, victims were led before the firing squad, and the execution was "carried out" with blanks.[17] The prisoners sometimes fainted, and were then taken back to the *capillas*. In some cases, mock executions were carried out more than once. The element of psychological torture lay in the uncertainty, since men occasionally were shot the second or third time. This practice was apparently begun in the Sierra Maestra as a punishment, due to the need to save bullets.

Those who were not shot generally received twenty- to thirty- year prison sentences in deplorable conditions at the infamous Presidio Modelo on the Isle of Pines. This was the grim fate of political prisoners such as Jorge Valls and Huber Matos, and it continues today with dissidents. Even a half century later, this remains the darkest stain on the frayed tablecloth of the Revolution.

Today La Cabaña remains a brooding, sinister place despite attempts to prettify it for tourists. Many of the *galeras* have been whitewashed for use as conference centers, and there is even a restaurant called La Divina Pastora, which overlooks the harbor. But at the entrance to the fortress, just beyond the drawbridge, are steep stone steps like those used by the prisoners. They take you down into the moat, once filled with water but now covered by grass. Before long, you come to the killing field. The location of the *palo*, where the condemned men were shot, is marked by a low cast-iron fence and a massive bronze plaque on the wall depicting an angel hovering over a firing squad.

Guevara was unrepentant about his role in these executions and wrote to a friend that they were "a necessity for the people of Cuba."[18] But Castro may have placed him in that role for another reason. Biographer Jon Lee Anderson quotes Guevara's own account in his diary of an incident that took place in February 1957. The rebels had been betrayed by a *guajiro* named Eutimio Guerra, and when the treachery was discovered, it was Guevara who executed him, pulling the trigger himself. This cold-blooded side to his nature is hardly guessed at by those wearing Che tank tops.

Most Cubans enthusiastically supported the executions, and Castro's speeches were often interrupted by cries of "*¡Paredon!*" (To the firing squad!) But American outrage at the summary trials may have prompted Castro to send Guevara abroad for an extended goodwill tour to Africa and Asia. After his return, Guevara would received a new assignment, as president of Cuba's National Bank. Guevara himself liked to tell the oft-repeated joke about how he was picked. At a cabinet meeting, Castro announced that he was looking for a good *economista*. Guevara raised his hand and got the job. Later Castro expressed his surprise that he was an economist. "*¿Economista?*" said Guevara. "I thought you said *communista*."[19] The financial community didn't find it amusing, and Guevara further rankled them by ostentatiously signing Cuba's new banknotes as "Che."

More impressed with him was Jean-Paul Sartre, who visited Havana for several weeks in February 1960 with Simone de Beauvoir. Sartre was enchanted by the "honeymoon of the Revolution" and lauded the "direct contact between leaders and people." The French philosopher spent many hours talking with Guevara and described him as "the most complete human being of our age."[20]

Far from over, the story of the Revolution has been told and retold many times, from various points of view. It is not my purpose here to detail its byzantine metamorphoses, amazing survival, and always imminent demise—an entire continent's worth of intrigue for a small island—for there is little evidence of it in Havana. Due to the precarious economic situation he inherited and exacerbated, Castro could not undertake a public works program like his predecessors Batista and Machado, and Tacón before them. Even the landmarks most associated with Castro, such as the Plaza de la Revolución, were built before he came down from the Sierra Maestra. Today Havana's skyline is virtually unchanged from 1959, although a bit worse for wear.

Nor are there any monuments to the *Maximo Lider* save for a plaque at the corner of Twenty-third Avenue and Twelfth Street in the Vedado. It was here, on April 16, 1961, that Castro gave a barn-burning funeral oration for those killed in the air raid that started the Bay of Pigs invasion and proclaimed the socialist character of the Revolution. The plaque shows Castro with his arm extended, a favorite speechifying pose, surrounded by soldiers, one holding an AK–47. The plaque repeats his words:

> *Ésta es la Revolución socialista y democratica de los humildes con los humildes y para los humildes. . . .*

> [This is the socialist and democratic Revolution of the humble, with the humble and for the humble. . . .]

It is a deliberate echo of José Martí, who could hardly have imagined the fate of his beloved island.

The revolutionary roller coaster continued on through the truly sobering Missile Crisis of October 1962, when Soviet submarines armed with nuclear-tipped torpedoes nearly fired on American warships; farcical attempts on the part of the CIA to kill Castro, such as poisoning his cigars or putting cyanide in the milk shakes he enjoyed at the Habana Libre; Kennedy's assassination in November 1963, spawning a myriad Cuban conspiracy theories; and the rest of the turbulent decade. But Guevara's departure for Bolivia in November 1966 on his quixotic and ultimately suicidal quest to spread revolution marks a turning point.

The true nature of the break between Guevara and Castro remains a much-debated mystery. Though it has been suggested that Castro "encouraged" him to leave the island, it had always been Guevara's dream to spread revolution throughout the world, particularly in his native Argentina. The fundamental disagreement between them now seems trivial: Guevara believed that only "moral incentives" could motivate the New Man,* while Castro took a more practical view of human nature. Yet this theoretical hair-splitting hints at a deeper chasm. In contrast to Castro, Guevara deeply mistrusted the Soviets and had suggested an alliance with their bitter rivals, the Chinese. And after the Revolution had triumphed, there was little left for him to do in Cuba, which increasingly was being run by the petty, ideologically rigid bureaucrats he despised.

Guevara died on October 9, 1967, hunted down by Bolivian commandos and a Cuban American CIA operative named Felix Rodríguez. Rodríguez had hoped to take Guevara to the United States for questioning, but the order to kill him came directly from the Bolivian president. Rodríguez, among the last to see Guevara alive, wrote: "His moment of truth had come, and he was conducting himself like a man. He was facing his death with courage and grace."[21]

Rodríguez, too, had read Hemingway. Less than a year later, Castro stunned the world with his endorsement of the Soviet Union's brutal repression of dissidents in Prague. This deeply soured European intellectuals such as Sartre and signaled the end of what has been called *l'illusion lyrique*—the early, idealistic phase of the Revolution. Throughout the 1970s and 1980s, Castro unhesitatingly followed the Kremlin's lead, even

---

* Presumably a byproduct of the Revolution. The phrase is taken from Guevara's comment that "To build communism it is necessary . . . to build a New Man."

supporting the invasion of Afghanistan. Until the collapse of the Soviet Union, Cuba would remain smothered in the Russian bearhug.

Guevara's remains were believed lost but in 1997 were found in a mass grave at an abandoned airstrip in Bolivia. They were returned not to Argentina but Cuba. The man known to the world as Che received a hero's burial in Santa Clara, the site of his greatest victory.

# CHAPTER 12

# *Adiós, Havana*

## *Rain*

*O*n my last trip to Havana, it rained incessantly.

Rain has many guises in Havana. It can be fierce, with sudden squalls that blot out the sky and threaten to flush the city out into the Gulf Stream. The rain pummels the red-tiled rooftops of Habana Vieja and often floods the narrow, cobblestoned streets. Sponging up the dirt and filth of the day before, it becomes a muddy brown torrent that drains off into the bay. Habaneros go about their business, staying beneath the porticoes built just for such weather. You could traverse the entire length of the Prado without getting wet if not for the gaps between street corners.

Yet unlike much of the Caribbean, where a shower is followed by antiseptic sunlight, here the rain lingers beneath a curdled sky. After a storm in Havana, it continues to fall in glutinous raindrops that splatter on the sidewalk. Eventually, it dwindles into a warm, sticky fug. Even under the porticoes, the soupy air gets under your skin, soaking your clothes, and you can see why little boys take to the streets barefoot, in their underwear. The manic blues and greens of the postcards are now melancholy shades of gray, from the dull patina of the sea to the damp soot of the old stone walls.

I arrived on May 20, 2006, the anniversary of the founding of the Cuban Republic in 1902. In Miami, it is celebrated with parades, street fairs, and even a festival held in a convention center called Cuba Nostalgia, in which you can buy memorabilia such as a Havana phone book from 1959. In Havana, there was no mention of it, though *Granma* ran an

article about the death of José Martí at Dos Ríos, which took place on
May 19.

Ignoring the rain, the booksellers were out in force at the Plaza de
Armas, their wares protected by plastic sheets. Occasionally, a damp
tourist stopped on the well-trod path between the Plaza de la Catedral
and the castle of the Real Fuerza to buy a book. But the *candonga* (market)
on the Avenida del Puerto was nearly empty, the merchants standing dis-
mally by their wares. Just behind them, the water in the harbor was un-
naturally still, with a metallic sheen. There were no boats in the channel,
not even the skiffs of the fisherman who often cast nets for bait in front of
El Morro, though the beacon of the lighthouse continued to sweep the
bleak horizon.

I found that Havana had changed little since my previous visit, the year before. Though it was low season, there were plenty of tourists. One morning
at the Palacio O'Farrill, a boutique hotel on Cuba Street, I saw a French
group setting out to brave the elements. The Palacio is the exquisitely restored early nineteenth century mansion of Don José Ricardo O'Farrill,
whose fortune came from the slave trade. The spacious courtyard where
carriages once entered was now the breakfast room, and the tourists finished their *café con leche* and picked up their guidebooks. They were ready
for action, wearing cargo shorts and rugged high-tech sandals. Last year it
was the jungles of Angkor Wat, and now the puddles of Habana Vieja.

According to *Granma*, Cuba had a banner year for tourism in 2005,
with over 2.3 million visitors, a growth of 13.2 percent. In 2006, the figure was expected to reach 2,500,000.[1] It is often pointed out that the island attracts mostly packaged tours, like the hardy Frenchmen, and few
upscale tourists. But moored off the Plaza de San Francisco was a gleaming white ocean liner, the *Holiday Dream* of the Spanish line Pullmantur.
The U.S. trade embargo effectively prohibits cruise ships that stop in
U.S. ports from docking in Havana, and so the *Holiday Dream* must have
come directly from Cadiz or Barcelona. Ships such as the old Ward Line
and P&O steamers once docked there, as did the ferries from Key West.
Visitors were once greeted by rumba bands and hostesses passing out
daiquiris. . Boys dived into the brackish water to retrieve money tossed
overboard, popping up with the coins in their teeth. There was no such
fanfare now, and the *Holiday Dream* left quietly the next day.

There were more cars on the street, a product of Castro's growing partnership with Venezuelan president Hugo Chávez. It is speculated that Venezuela barters petroleum to Cuba in exchange for medical services, and Cuba then resells the petroleum abroad, providing much-needed foreign exchange. In addition, Cuba has been aggressively drilling for oil in the Gulf of Mexico. Recently, a 5,166 meter directional well was drilled by Sherrit, the Canadian oil company, near Varadero. Costing $6.5 million, the well was expected to produce over 200 tons of crude oil per day.[2]

Traffic jams are still a rarity in Havana, but automobiles are taking back the city from pedestrians and bicycles. Most famous are the classic American cars from the 1950s, sleek-finned DeSotos and Cadillacs. Known as *almendrones*,* they are often immaculately maintained, though without spare parts the engines are kept running through what can only be described as Cuban ingenuity. Russian-made Ladas are ubiquitous, serving as police cars with flashing blue lights, though you see an increasing number of Nissans and Toyotas. Officials usually get around in chauffeured Mercedes-Benz sedans or even Land Rovers. Despite this, public transport is still a daunting challenge in Havana. Tourists can readily find taxis, including the smart, open-air "cocotaxis," but Habaneros must make do with interminable lines at bus stops and the uncertain *camellos* (camels), huge trailers drawn by trucks. Hitchhiking is common, as are bicycle-drawn rickshaws. According to the *Miami Herald*, the government hopes to alleviate this through the recent purchase of eight thousand Chinese-made buses.

Any visitor must navigate Cuba's tortuous currency restrictions. In 1993, the U.S. dollar became legal tender and was accepted at all restaurants, stores, and hotels. This created a parallel economy of dollar-only establishments as well as a thriving black market. There was also a dramatic surge in remittances sent by Cuban exiles to their families, as much as $800 million per year, roughly the value of Cuba's exports. This changed abruptly in November 2004, when the dollar (as well as other foreign currencies) was banned once again. Tourists must now exchange their money for the Cuban convertible currency known as CUCs (pronounced "kooks"), or *chavitos*. Although *chavitos* supposedly have parity with dollars, there is a surcharge of 20 percent, so that for one dollar you

---

* From the word *almendra*, meaning "almond." The rounded shape of the passenger section recalls the nut.

receive eighty cents of *chavitos*. Cubans receive wages in pesos, which can be exchanged for chavitos at the rate of twenty-four to one. The average Cuban monthly salary is just under 300 pesos. In rough arithmetic, divided by twenty-four, this equals the much-touted figure that the average Cuban earns twelve dollars a month.

What will this buy in Havana? Despite the embargo, virtually any American product is available in *chavitos*, from Coca-Cola to Nike sneakers. Since prices are roughly comparable, a running shoe or dinner for two at the Floridita can cost an entire year's salary for the average Habanero. Throughout Havana are American-style supermarkets, formerly dollar-only and now accepting *chavitos*. They rival those found in the United States, with gleaming produce, choice cuts of meat, and a wide selection of wines. Since filling a shopping cart would bankrupt most Cubans, these stores are for diplomats, foreign residents, or those with relatives abroad. Others rely on the monthly ration book, known as the *libreta*, which supplies limited quantities of staples such as rice, sugar, and cooking oil. Fresh produce can be obtained in *mercados agro-pecuarios*, cooperative markets that accept not *chavitos* but pesos. The *mercados* have a good selection of fruits such as pineapples, bananas, mangoes, and papayas, and vegetables such as onions, malangas, tomatoes, and peppers. But if not prohibitive, like the *chavito* stores, they are nonetheless expensive. For example, at a *mercado* just a block from the Plaza Vieja, I found prices such as 10 pesos for a pound of tomatoes, 3 pesos for a pound of yucca, and 2 pesos for a pound of garlic. Meat was substantially more expensive, 25 pesos for a pound of pork tenderloin. What most Americans would consider a single square meal (meat, starch, two veggies) would cost a sizable chunk of a typical Cuban's monthly salary.

It is easy to distort these figures. As is often parroted from the left, no one dies of starvation. The government provides a balanced if unappetizing meal, generally lunch, at school or the workplace. There has been an increase in fast-food restaurants accepting pesos, such as the DiMar seafood chain. Perhaps because of the dire economics, Habaneros have an ingrained talent to *resolver*. Literally this translates to solving a problem, but it implies much more. It is a talent for surviving against the odds, making do with little or nothing, and surmounting unbelievable difficulties through pluck and persistence.

Here's how it works: A cousin from Las Villas can obtain a leg of pork, but he needs aspirin for his mother. You don't have any, but you can get a spare light bulb from your cousin, who works in a hotel. Your friend's sister is a nurse, and it just so happens her light went out. Aspirins and light bulbs change hands, and that night you serve *lechon asado* (roast pork). Though a single meal might bust the family budget, Habaneros provide copious feasts for guests in their homes. Somehow they *resolver*.

One antidote to these difficulties is the Cuban sense of humor, unique in many ways. Laughter is a constant accompaniment on the streets of Havana—you hear it around the corner, behind closed doors, and a few steps ahead of you. Cuban jokes lack the scatological tinge of their Mexican counterparts or the often vicious puns of Peru. Usually they concern politics. The targets are pompous policemen, overzealous bureaucrats, and nosy members of the CDRs (the neighborhood watch committees).

An essential ingredient in Cuban humor is *choteo*. This untranslatable word refers to a joke in which nothing is taken seriously, much less oneself. Cubans are nothing if not irreverent, and to *chotear* is to mock. But *choteo* also refers to a situation which would be extremely painful if one didn't laugh at it. The *choteo* is thus a response to that other Cuban idiosyncrasy, the *fracaso*, a bitter failure. One joke recently making the rounds in Havana is that, while in most countries, where there is life there is hope, in Cuba so long as there is life there is no hope. Get it?

Despite the laughter, hope is a rare commodity in Havana. While crude barometers such as the number of cars on the street show that the economy is growing and the quality of life improving, I found the billboards increasingly ominous. Bereft of paid advertising, Havana's billboards carry propaganda. Some are well-worn quotes from José Martí, such as *Sera immortal el que lo merece* (He who deserves it will be immortal) or slogans such as *Revolución es construir* (Revolution is to build) or *En cada barrio revolucion* (Revolution in each neighborhood). If these are good clean fun, some recent billboards compare President George W. Bush to Hitler and warn that *El Plan Bush* will take away benefits such as healthcare and education. One billboard near the U.S. Interests Section savagely caricatures Secretary of State Condoleeza Rice. Another shows Bush arm in arm with Luis Posada Carilles (the alleged anti-Castro bomber currently in the United States) under the American president's own words: "Whoever gives refuge to terrorists is a terrorist."

Curiously, there has been an increase of photographs of Castro himself. In the past, Castro's image appeared rarely in Havana—at least, compared to icons such as Che Guevara and Camilo Cienfuegos. Without exception, the scruffy yet charismatic Castro of 1959 was pictured. Now, I found a billboard of a better groomed, grandfatherly Castro, beneath the reassuring caption *Vamos bien* (We're doing well).

This coincided with *Forbes* magazine naming Castro the seventh-richest leader in the world, with up to $900 million in assets. This ranked him above Queen Elizabeth of England ($500 million) and just below Prince Albert of Monaco ($1 billion), though not even close to King Abdullah of Saudi Arabia ($21 billion). Castro responded by staging a four-hour *mesa redonda* (round table) on Cuban television. Surrounded by obsequious officials, including Minister of Culture Abel Prieto and the Historiador himself, Eusebio Leal, a feisty Castro challenged the world to produce a smoking gun. Holding up a copy of the magazine, he demanded: "What do I want money for if I'm going to turn eighty? What do I want money for now if I never wanted it before?" Amid thunderous applause, with a perfectly straight face, Castro then offered to resign if even a "single dollar" was found.[3]

It was a master class in *choteo*.

## BASEBALL DIPLOMACY

Just a few weeks before, Cuba had come close to winning the first-ever World Baseball Classic, held in San Diego.

But the Cubans nearly didn't get the chance to play. In 2006, relations between the U.S. and Cuba reached an all-time low, recalling the icy trenches of the Cold War. It should have come as no surprise when the State Department denied the Cuban team a visa. A spokesman cited security concerns, since Cuba was suspected of sending MININT agents along with the team, perhaps to keep players from defecting. And since U.S. law prohibited doing business with Cuba, the Treasury Department's Office of Foreign Asset Control denied the license submitted by Major League Baseball (MLB).

It appeared that Cuba would sit the Classic out. Castro's nephew and arch-enemy Congressman Lincoln Diaz-Balart gleefully floated the idea of forming a team of Cuban exiles to play. Then all hell broke loose. The International Baseball Federation withheld its imprimatur, Venezuela threatened to boycott the games, and even Puerto Rico pulled out as a first-round host. MLB commissioner Bud Selig personally lobbied Bush, who once owned the Texas Rangers baseball team. Lambasted by world opinion, the United States finally relented. A last-minute compromise was suggested in which Cuba would donate its proceeds to the victims of

Hurricane Katrina. No money would change hands in violation of the embargo. Surprisingly, Cuba agreed and the visa was quickly granted.

Cuba's team included ace pitcher Danny Betancourt and slugger Yulieski Gouriell, either of whom would shine in most MLB rosters. Rather than a spy, Castro sent his son Antonio.* An orthopedic surgeon, he was the team doctor, bandaging sore ankles in the dugout. This surrealistic detail was endlessly discussed on Miami radio stations, and Antonio reportedly called his father during the games to tell him the score. There was one question on the minds of sports fans and diplomats the world over: Would Cuba beat the United States?

For all the hullabaloo, we never found out. The tepid U.S. team sputtered, losing to Canada and beating Japan only after a disputed call. Barely making the cut, it lost by a run to Korea in the semifinals, but could still advance if it beat Mexico. Meanwhile, Cuba was not in top form either, losing to Venezuela. But it managed to beat Puerto Rico in perhaps the best game of the series, in which manager Herminio Velez was ejected after saying something to the umpire through an interpreter. When the underdog Mexico put the Americans out of their misery (cheered on by what amounted to a hometown crowd in San Diego) Japan was catapulted into the championship game against Cuba. It appeared as if Castro would dance a victory jig, and thousands watched the game in the Parque Central, where a giant television screen was erected at José Martí's elbow. But the stoic, methodical Japanese trounced the Cubans 10 to 6.

Nonetheless, it was a moral victory. As often happens, Cuba looked good, and the United States looked bad. No one defected, and Cubans lined the Malecón to welcome the team home. A jovial Castro declared that so many people watched the game that "our electrical grid was at risk of collapsing."[4]

Baseball is as Cuban as apple empanadas.

America's favorite pastime reached the island as early as 1864. A young man named Nemesio Guilló, a student at Springhill College in

---

* Castro has five sons with his wife of forty years, Dalia Soto del Valle. In addition to Antonio, there are Alexis, Alexander, Alejandro, and Angel.

Mobile, Alabama, returned home to Havana with a bat and ball.[5] Before long, he was playing with his friends in the Vedado. In 1868, the Habana Base Ball Club was founded, and it beat the crew of an American schooner. Because of its American origins, the game was viewed as a threat by the Spaniards, who banned it in 1869, at the start of the Ten Year War. But this order was quickly rescinded, and another club was started in Matanzas. One of the first recorded games there was with Havana in 1874 at the Palmar del Junco stadium, which still stands. Havana won 51 to 7 in seven innings, when the game was thankfully called because of darkness. Teams sprang up throughout the island, and four years later the first Cuban baseball league was founded.

*Beisbol* fever gripped Havana. A game in 1886 attracted six thousand spectators. Middle-class amateurs like Guilló were replaced by professionals, and the game's popularity in sugar mills meant that soon many blacks were playing. Whereas bullfighting was Spanish, baseball was American, and came to stand for progress, modernity, and independence.* Many baseball players fought for the *mambises*, and Emilio Sabourin, player-manager of the Havana club, was arrested by the Spaniards and died in a North African prison.

In 1886, the Philadelphia Athletics took on a Cuban team in an exhibition game, and by 1890, the New York Giants played winter ball in Havana. Major league teams were soon barnstorming the island, but Cuban players also headed north. Rafael Almeida was signed by the Cincinnati Reds in 1911, and others soon followed. Perhaps the greatest was Adolfo Luque, who pitched for the Reds as well as the Boston Braves and the New York Giants. In 1933, the forty-two-year-old Luque struck out Joe Kuhel in the tenth inning to clinch New York's victory over the Washington Senators in the World Series.

Stung by this defeat, the Senators sent Joe Cambria to Havana the following year. Known as Papa Joe, Cambria was a Runyonesque figure who scouted ballgames wearing a white linen suit and a Panama hat and smoking a huge cigar. Over the next twenty-five years he would sign over four hundred Cuban players, including such legends as "Tarzan" Estalella and Roberto Ortiz. It is an often-repeated fabrication that Cambria offered Castro a contract to play for the Senators. In fact, Castro's game was basketball.

---

* Indeed, just as the Spanish authorities felt threatened by baseball, the American occupiers prohibited bullfighting in 1899, and the sport never made a comeback.

The charismatic *barbudo* Camilo Cienfuegos donned a baseball uniform in 1959. (Author's collection)

In 1946, Cambria founded the Havana Cubans, a class B team that played in Gran Stadium, a state-of-the-art stadium seating 35,000. He later sold the team to visionary promoter Robert Maduro. In 1954, the latter renamed it the Havana Sugar Kings, stepping up to triple A. Maduro's goal was to bring a major league team to Havana, and he might well have succeeded if not for the Revolution.

At first, Castro enthusiastically promoted baseball. He and other *commandantes*, such as Camilo Cienfuegos, hammed it up in uniforms with players, and Castro even pitched two innings at an exhibition game. But following the nationalization of U.S. businesses in 1960, the franchise was transferred to Jersey City, New Jersey.

Even then, baseball was inseparable from politics.

Hopes that Cuba's participation in the World Baseball Classic, like Ping Pong matches with China in the 1970s, would lead to better relations were soon dashed. Even as the players laced their cleats, the U.S.

Interests Section in Havana unveiled a five-foot-high electronic message board on the fifth floor. In red neon letters, it streamed news headlines in Spanish, together with quotations from Abraham Lincoln (still venerated in Cuba because of his fight against slavery) and the Universal Declaration of Human Rights.

If provocative, it had little impact. According to one Habanero, the words could hardly be made out. News from American radio stations (including Radio Martí) is often heard in Havana. Many Habaneros receive U.S. Spanish-language broadcasts via pirated cable and are great fans of telenovelas and programs like *Sabado Gigante* on the Los Angeles-based Univision network.

Castro denounced the message board as yet another Yankee provocation and organized a massive rally at the U.S. Interests Section. In record time, 138 flagpoles were erected on a marble reviewing stand, each flying a black banner with a white star. According to the plaque at the base, each flag stands for a year in Cuba's struggle for independence, starting in 1868. The effect is at once somber and startling. Seen from a distance, or as you drive up the Malecón, the flags effectively blot out the message board. But they also draw your eye toward it. Through the black flags, you can still see a glowing letter or two, and you can't help but wonder what they spell out.

"It's all political theater," said an old classmate of mine, now a correspondent in Havana for an American newspaper.

## ON THE MALECÓN

The rain continued, and I remained in the hotel. My room looked out over Chacon Street, and from my balcony I could see an old black woman sitting in her kitchen, watching me watch her. Through the drumbeat of the rain, I heard tinny music from a radio, a dog barking, and two boys splashing about on the wet cobblestones below.

No one, it seemed, was around. My friend the novelist hadn't answered my last e-mail and a painter that I once interviewed had just left for Barcelona, uncertain if he would ever return. That night, another friend was to meet me at the Floridita, but he must have missed his bus and after an hour I went on to dinner alone. The next morning the rain let up and I walked up and down Obispo like the *Andarin Carvajal*, the madman that my grandmother remembered. But when the skies opened up with renewed vigor, I ducked inside a courtyard lined with dusty, cracked Moorish tiles. The building seemed abandoned. Precarious scaffolds propped up the staircase, and I could smell the uncollected garbage, but voices floated down from the second floor. The editor of a magazine agreed to join me for lunch, but she was in a bad mood and kept looking at her watch. She didn't want to talk about what she called "the situation." Nor had she heard any more jokes about Castro for me to write down in my notebook.

ſ

While Castro's photograph is popping up unexpectedly in Havana, his name is hardly mentioned. At the time of the triumph of the Revolution, he was simply Fidel, a mark of his intimate bond with the Cuban people. This ended during the difficult decade of the 1990s, when honorifics like *comandante en jefe* (commander in chief) became common. Later, this morphed into vague words like *el tío* (the uncle), *el tipo* (the guy), or even *el abuelo* (the grandfather). Now, even this is too explicit, and he is referred to only in pantomime. The most common gesture is to scratch your chin, tracing an invisible beard, or to tap your shoulder with two fingers, marking epaulettes. This phenomenon might be explained through fear of police spies, but Habaneros are quite outspoken and have no problem saying everything is a *fracaso* (failure). Rather, it is a form of denial, as if saying his name is to admit complicity.*

If "the situation" remained unspoken, Havana kept its grip on American popular culture. During my trip, a movie by actor Andy Garcia called *The Lost City* opened in Miami. Boasting a screenplay by Guillermo Cabrera Infante, it was filmed in Santo Domingo (the usual location for movies of Havana) and depicted the waning days of Batista's regime. A big-budget biopic of Che Guevara starring Benicio del Toro was in the works, as was an HBO production about Hemingway in Cuba, starring James Gandolfini of *The Sopranos*.

Havana remains a politically correct setting for novels. Perhaps the most celebrated Cuban writer today is Pedro Juan Gutiérrez, a sort of

---

* On August 13, 2006, Castro spent his eightieth birthday recuperating from intestinal surgery. He had not appeared in public for several days, and there were rumors of his death. Havana was eerily calm, while people literally danced in the streets of Miami. But before long, photos of Castro appeared in *Granma*. He was gaunt but very much alive.

tropical Henry Miller. His *Dirty Havana Trilogy* paints an unsparingly bleak portrait of the city. It is a Havana of raunchy liaisons, rotgut liquor, and seedy apartments. A typical review lauded it as "bursting with vivid images of exhilaration, depravity, desire, and isolation."[6] This appears to be the prevalent literary vision of Havana, reflected in the fiction of Zoe Valdés and other contemporary novelists.

Havana is also a popular destination for travel writers. Like much else about Cuba, their accounts often reflect opposing political positions. But whether from the left or right, they bring to mind young Winston Churchill, who in 1895 felt as if he were sailing with Long John Silver to Havana. Havana has become a literary fourth world where hipsters go in search of the bizarre and picturesque. Generally, they find it.

Tom Miller edited an interesting anthology of such travelers' tales, which includes writers such as Dave Eggers, Pico Iyer, and Bob Schacochis.[7] For example, Eggers goes seeking "what makes Cuba Cuba." Driving through the island in a rented Subaru, he meets "typical Cubans" by picking up hitchhikers, encountering a basketball player, a magician, and the son of a *balsero*. Iyer describes Cuba as "the ultimate getaway." His descriptions of the city verge on the fantastic, as if he were a character in one of his own novels. Havana is as "flawless as a postcard," with the "ramshackle glamor of an abandoned stage set." Shacochis seeks to exorcise Hemingway's ghost by going marlin fishing. Afterward, he wanders Havana's "strange and marvelous streets," and describes the city as "flaunting the edges of self-destruction, semiferal but with a hip intensity, sidling up to disaster but then fluttering away."

Yet Havana has always been a palimpsest on which travelers write their own hopes and dreams. From Christopher Columbus searching for a New World to Che Guevara seeking the New Man, visitors have seen only what they wanted to see. Whether viewed through the rose-tinted lenses of exile or distorted by the funhouse mirrors of politics, the real Havana remains veiled.

On the day I was to leave Havana, the rain exhausted itself and a tentative light began to shine through the clouds. There were patches of blue in the whitish sky, like brushstrokes on canvas. A weak sun emerged and began to burn off the hazy mist that hung over the harbor.

Before long, the city itself began to wake. A bus rumbled down the Avenida del Puerto, followed by a red Chevrolet older than I was. Habaneros began crossing the Plaza de Armas to go to work, turning left at Mercaderes toward the Plaza de San Francisco or else up Obispo toward the Parque Central. Then came the schoolchildren, the girls in neatly pressed maroon skirts, white blouses, and matching scarves, the boys carrying backpacks like those my son takes to class.

The same breeze that had once filled the sails of Spanish galleons was blowing out to sea. From the harbor, I could hear the putt-putt-putt of the ferry making the first run of the day to Regla. As the sky cleared, a fisherman in a tiny boat began rowing towards La Cabaña. He anchored beneath the craggy walls of the fortress and tossed out a net for *machuelos*, silvery baitfish the size of one's palm. Others fished from the embankment, casting lines that barely made a ripple on the glassy water.

My flight would not leave for several hours, so I walked toward the Malecón. A few kids in bathing suits pranced atop the seawall, playing hooky after the endless days of rain. One appeared ready to dive into the ocean, while another scrambled about the rocks below, pointing at a frigate bird skimming over the waves. The last of the clouds had vanished, and the breeze freshened as the sun rose high above the lighthouse of El Morro. It turned the water from metallic gray to bright jade, and the dazzling light made the whitecaps sparkle.

I followed the curve of the Malecón west, heading toward the Vedado. Across from the Hotel Nacional were several more Habaneros, young and old, men and women. Unlike the bathers, they seemed indifferent to the glorious sunshine. Like me, they were killing time, waiting for the next chapter to be written. Some watched the cars go by, drumming their fingers on the briny, weathered stone. Others sat with their backs to the city, facing north, as if trying to discern a boat on the horizon.

# Notes

## PREFACE

1. Tom Miller, *Trading with the Enemy* (Atheneum, 1992), p. 3.
2. Quoted in Louis A. Pérez, Jr., *On Becoming Cuban* (University of North Carolina Press, 1999), p. 188.
3. Quoted in Tom Miller, ed., *Cuba* (Traveler's Tales, 2004), p. 8.
4. José Martí, *Selected Writings* (Penguin Books, 2002), p. 74.
5. Basil Woon, *When it's Cocktail Time in Cuba* (Liveright, 1928), p. 51.
6. Irving Berlin, "I'll See You in Cuba," Irving Berlin, Inc., New York, 1920.
7. Pérez, *On Becoming Cuban*, p. 189.
8. Miller, ed., *Cuba*, p. 150.

## CHAPTER 1

1. Samuel Eliot Morison, *Admiral of the Ocean Sea* (Little, Brown, 1942), p. 227. Other claimants to this honor have included Grand Turk and Cat Island, but according to Morison, only Watlings Island fits the course laid down in Columbus's log book. It was known as Guanahani, and renamed San Salvador. For a more critical view, see Kirkpatrick Sale, *The Conquest of Paradise* (Penguin Books, 1991), p. 92.
2. Irving Rouse, *The Tainos* (Yale University Press, 1992), p. 69.
3. Alejo Carpentier, *The Harp and the Shadow* (Mercury House, 1990), p. 158.
4. Irene A. Wright, *The Early History of Cuba* (Macmillan, 1916), p. 8. See also Jaime Suchliki, Cuba: *From Columbus to Castro and Beyond* (Brassey's, 1997), p. 28.
5. See Bartolomé de las Casas, *The Devastation of the Indies* (Johns Hopkins University Press, 1992), pp. 43–47. A good description of the rebellion is found in Philip S. Foner, *A History of Cuba*, vol. 1 (International Publishers, 1962), p. 20.
6. Foner, *A History of Cuba*, p. 25.
7. De las Casas, *The Devastation of the Indies*, pp. 45–46.
8. Quoted in Sale, *The Conquest of Paradise*, p. 140.
9. For a general discussion see Hugh Thomas, *Cuba, or The Pursuit of Freedom* (Da Capo Press, 1998), p. 1525. Establishing the pre-Columbian population of Cuba is little more than guesswork. Thomas argues it was as low as 16,000; according to Kirkpatrick Sale, the entire Taino population in the

Caribbean numbered 8 million (!). Irving Rouse puts the figure at 600,000 in Cuba.

10. Richard Gott, Cuba: *A New History* (Yale University Press, 2004), p. 22. See also Rouse, *The Tainos*, p. 161.
11. Bernal Díaz, *The Conquest of New Spain* (Penguin Books, 1965), p. 44.
12. Joseph L. Scarpaci, Roberto Segre, and Mario Coyula, *Havana: Two Faces of the Antillean Metropolis* (University of North Carolina Press, 2002), p. 13.
13. Ibid., p. 15.
14. Juliet Barclay, *Havana: Portrait of a City* (Cassell, 1995), p. 23.


CHAPTER 2

1. Bob Sheets and Jack Williams, *Hurricane Watch* (Vintage Books, 2001), p. 6.
2. Samuel Eliot Morison, *Admiral of the Ocean Sea* (Little, Brown, 1942), p. 590.
3. Louis A. Pérez Jr., *Winds of Change* (University of North Carolina Press, 2001), p. 30.
4. William H. MacLeish, *The Gulf Stream* (Houghton Mifflin, 1989), p. 16.
5. Robert H. Fuson, *Juan Ponce de Leon* (McDonald & Woodward, 2000), p. 106. See also Hugh Thomas, *Rivers of Gold* (Random House, 2003), p. 282.
6. Bernal Díaz, *The Conquest of New Spain* (Penguin Books, 1965), p. 47.
7. Ibid., p. 55.
8. Henry Kamen, *Empire: How Spain Became a World Power*, 1492–1763 (HarperCollins, 2003), p. 88.
9. David Cordingly, *Under the Black Flag* (Harcourt Brace, 1995), p. 35.
10. A detailed look at the Spanish treasure fleet and the daily life of sailors at the time can be found in Pablo E. Perez-Mallaine, *Spain's Men of the Sea* (Johns Hopkins University Press, 1998), p. 9.
11. David Ewing Duncan, *Hernando de Soto* (Crown, 1996), p. 243. It was a massive expedition that literally squeezed Cuba dry. Provisions included 3,000 loads of cassava, 2,500 shoulders of bacon, and 3,800 bushels of corn. Soto had a personal retinue of nearly 100 bodyguards, pages, and clerks.
12. Ibid., p. 241. Isabel later testified that the fortune in dispute amounted to 200,000 ducados, a substantial figure.
13. Cordingly, *Under the Black Flag*, p. 36.
14. German Arciniegas, *Caribbean: Sea of the New World* (Markus Wiener, 2003), p. 119. To the Spaniards, Verrazano was known as Juan Florentin or simply the Frenchman. Before his demise, he imparted his navigational lore to his brother Hieronymus, who in 1529 compiled one of the most complete world maps of the time.
15. See Saturnino Ullivari, *Piratas y Corsarios en Cuba* (Editorial Renacimiento, 2004), p. 49. Other accounts of the attack can be found in Cordingly, *Under the Black Flag*, p. 37, and Nigel Cawthorne, *A History of Pirates* (Chartwell, 2005), p. 34.
16. Joaquín E. Weiss, *La Arquitectura Colonial Cubana* (Editorial Letras Cubanas, 2002), p. 42.
17. Ullivari, *Piratas y Corsarios en Cuba*, p. 65. Juan Francisco de la Roque was also known as Roberto Baal.
18. Ibid., p. 85.
19. Ibid., p. 48.

## CHAPTER 3

1. María Luisa Lobo Montalvo, *Havana: History and Architecture of a Romantic City* (Monacelli Press, 2000), p. 64. See also Joaquín E. Weiss, *La Arquitectura Colonial Cubana* (Editorial Letras Cubanas, 2002), p. 65.
2. Joseph L. Scarpaci, Roberto Segre, and Mario Coyula, *Havana: Two Faces of the Antillean Metropolis* (University of North Carolina Press, 2002), p. 326.
3. Ibid., pp. 83, 374. Strongly influenced by Le Corbusier, Sert first visited Havana in 1939 and had a profound influence on a generation of Cuban architects. His master plan envisioned substantial population growth—a Havana of 4 million inhabitants, nearly double what it is today.
4. Richard Gott, *Cuba: A New History* (Yale University Press, 2004), p. 288.
5. Scarpaci et al., *Havana*, p. 332.
6. Tracey Eaton, "Property Bonanza Awaits Investors in Post-Castro Era," *CubaNews* (April 2005). According to Joseph Scarpaci, more than half the water entering Havana leaks from faulty water mains.
7. Nancy San Martín, "High Winds, Old Age Threaten Buildings throughout Havana," *Miami Herald*, September 19, 2004.
8. Eaton, "Property Bonanza Awaits Investors in Post-Castro Era."
9. Luisita López Torregrossa, "Waiting for Havana," *New York Times*, November 27, 2005.
10. Juliet Barclay, *Havana: Portrait of a City* (Cassell, 1995), p. 59.
11. Joaquín E. Weiss, *La Arquitectura Colonial Cubana* (Editorial Letras Cubanas, 2002), p. 59.
12. Ibid., p. 76.
13. Scarpaci et al., *Havana*, p. 28.
14. Hugh Thomas, *Cuba, or The Pursuit of Freedom* (Da Capo Press, 1998), p. 1.
15. Ibid., p. 7.
16. José Lezama Lima, *Paradiso* (Dalkey Archive Press, 2000), p. 233.

## CHAPTER 4

1. James Suckling, "The Partagás Family," *Cigar Aficionado* (Winter 1995).
2. Richard Carleton Hacker, *The Ultimate Cigar Book* (Autumngold, 2003), p. 48. See also William P. Mara, *Cubans* (Lyons Press, 2002), for an introduction to the world of cigars.
3. Quoted in Fernando Ortiz, *Cuban Counterpoint* (Duke University Press, 1995), p. 40.
4. Ibid., p. 90.
5. Suckling, "The Partagás Family."
6. Quoted in Ortiz, *Cuban Counterpoint*, pp. 109–110.
7. Ibid., p. 182. See also Hugh Thomas, *Cuba, or The Pursuit of Freedom* (Da Capo Press, 1998), p. 23.
8. Iain Gately, *Tobacco* (Grove Press, 2001), pp. 57–58.
9. Marvin Shanken, "A Conversation with Fidel," *Cigar Aficionado* (Summer 1994). Shanken holds his own in this fascinating encounter and even puts the Maximo Lider on the spot with a few tough questions about the embargo and human rights. Castro was pleased to learn that President Clinton liked

cigars (pre-Monica Lewinsky) and joked that he might even have one with him in the White House.

10. Mara, *Cubans*, p. 28. Kennedy might have acquired his taste for H. Upmanns during a three-day visit to Havana in December 1957.

11. Guillermo Cabrera Infante, *Holy Smoke* (Faber & Faber, 1985), p. 31. Written in English, the late Cuban novelist's paean to puffing is a treasury of tobacco trivia.

12. Rudyard Kipling, *Departmental Ditties*, 1890. Quoted in ibid., p. 283.

13. Quoted in Gately, *Tobacco*, p. 48.

14. H. Paul Jeffers and Kevin Gordon, *The Good Cigar* (Lyons Press, 2002), p. 15.

15. Narciso Menocal, *The Tobacco Industry in Cuba and Florida* (Cuban National Heritage, 1995), p. 4.

16. Peter Macinnis, *Bittersweet* (Allen & Unwin, 2002), p. xviii.

17. Henry Hobhouse, *Seeds of Change* (Harper & Row, 1986), p. 55.

18. Thomas, *Cuba*, p. 61.

19. Ibid., p. 27.

20. Ibid., p. 80.

21. Quoted in ibid., p. 169. The source of the figures is Ramon de la Sagra's *Historia*, published in 1831. This was nearly 25 percent of Cuba's total population of 272,000.

22. Ibid.

23. Richard Gott, *Cuba: A New History* (Yale University Press, 2004), p. 45.

24. Thomas, *Cuba*, p. 129.

25. Charles A. Coulombe, *Rum* (Citadel Press, 2004), p. 19.

26. Ibid., p. 34.

27. Ian Williams, "The Secret History of Rum," posted on the Web site of *The Nation* on November 22, 2005.

28. Ibid.

29. Ortiz, *Cuban Counterpoint*, p. 3.

30. Thomas, *Cuba*, pp. 36, 171.

31. Ibid., p. 36.

32. Hobhouse, *Seeds of Change*, p. 78.

33. Andres Oppenheimer, *Castro's Final Hour* (Simon & Schuster, 1992), p. 349.

34. See Raúl Canizares, *Cuban Santeria* (Destiny Books, 1999), p. 5.

## CHAPTER 5

1. Quoted in Claudia Lightfoot, *Havana* (Interlink Books, 2002), p. 34. See also Otto Olivera, *Viajeros en Cuba* (Ediciones Universal, 1998), p. 109. This intrepid Yankee preacher spent several months in Cuba to cure a pulmonary infection.

2. See Jorge J. Beato, ed., *Cuba en 1830* (Ediciones Universal, 1973). See also Olivera, *Viajeros en Cuba*, p. 121. A diplomat, Ney visited Cuba in February 1830.

3. See Condesa de Merlin, *Viaje a la Habana* (Editorial de Arte y Literatura), 1974. Born María de la Merced in Havana, she married the French general Antoine Merlin and lived most of her life in Paris.

4. Ibid., p. 112.

5. Joseph L. Scarpaci, Roberto Segre, and Mario Coyula, *Havana: Two Faces of the Antillean Metropolis* (University of North Carolina Press, 2002), p. 32.
6. Philip S. Foner, *A History of Cuba*, vol. 1 (International Publishers, 1962), p. 91.
7. Maturin Ballou in 1854, quoted in Juliet Barclay, *Havana: Portrait of a City* (Cassell, 1995), p. 173.
8. Joseph and Helen M. McCadden, *Felix Varela* (Romallo Bros. Printing, 1969), p. 59. See also Juan M. Navia, *An Apostle for the Immigrants* (Factor Press, 2002).
9. Tim Padgett, "Cuba's Catholic Dissident: The Saga of Oswaldo Payá," *America*, October 20, 2003.
10. Tristan Schweiger, "The Making of a Saint," *Florida Times-Union*, June 10, 2003.
11. Quoted in Roberto Méndez, *José María Heredia: La Utopía Restituida* (Editorial Oriente, 2003), p. 22.

## CHAPTER 6

1. Oscar Montero, *José Martí* (Palgrave, 2004), p. 59.
2. Martí's doomed relationship with María Granados was the subject of a novel by Francisco Goldman, *The Divine Husband* (Atlantic Monthly Press, 2004).
3. José Martí, *Selected Writings* (Penguin Books, 2002), p. 32.
4. Hugh Thomas, *Cuba, or The Pursuit of Freedom* (Da Capo Press, 1998), p. 245.
5. Richard Gott, *Cuba: A New History* (Yale University Press, 2004), p. 80.
6. Ibid., p. 75.
7. Martí, *Selected Writings*, p. 73. Martí's diaries contain some of his most personal writing, often in the form of aphorisms. In 1881 he wrote, "To live in exile—to sculpt clouds." Another revealing line: "Nothing so terrifies a great soul as the little things."
8. See the introduction by Phillip S. Foner in José Martí, *Our America* (Monthly Review Press, 1977), pp. 15–16.
9. Montero, *José Martí*, p. 23.
10. See Martí, *Selected Writings*, p. 79. This potboiler ran serially from May to September 1885 in a bimonthly New York magazine called *El Latino Americano*. Martí did not care much for novels, complaining that they consisted of "dialogues that have never been heard between persons who have never lived."
11. Martí, *Selected Writings*, p. 272. The celebrated lyrics come from the first lines of *Versos Sencillos*, published in 1891. There is no mention of the fetching girl from Guantanamo, however.
12. Martí, *Our America*, p. 19.
13. Martí, *Selected Writings*, p. 353.
14. Martí, *Our America*, p. 56.
15. Martí, *Selected Writings*, p. 390.
16. Lillian Guerra, *The Myth of José Martí* (University of North Carolina Press, 2005), p. 117.
17. Martí, *Selected Writings*, p. 347. This famously apocalyptic line comes from an unfinished letter to his friend Manuel Mercado written at Dos Ríos on May 18, 1895, two days before his death.

18. José Martí, *Thoughts/Pensamientos* (Las Americas Publishing Co., 1985), pp. 43, 57. This is a bilingual compilation of Martí's often contradictory statements by scholar Carlos Ripoll.

## CHAPTER 7

1. María Luisa Lobo Montalvo, *Havana: History and Architecture of a Romantic City* (Monacelli Press, 2000), p. 166.
2. Quoted in ibid.
3. G. J. A. O'Toole, *The Spanish War* (W.W. Norton, 1984), p. 52.
4. Quoted in ibid., p. 53.
5. Richard Gott, *Cuba: A New History* (Yale University Press, 2004), p. 94. Weyler had experimented with these camps in the Ten Year War and now established them throughout the island. The first was built in Pinar del Río in October 1896. Apparently Weyler did little to stop the starvation that ensued. As cruel as it was, this strategy is credited by historians with turning the tide of the war. See Jaime Suchliki, *Cuba: From Columbus to Castro and Beyond* (Brassey's, 1997), p. 79.
6. O'Toole, *The Spanish War*, p. 82.
7. Ibid., pp. 28–29.
8. Ibid., p. 22.
9. Ibid., p. 34.
10. Quoted in Hugh Thomas, *Cuba, or The Pursuit of Freedom* (Da Capo Press, 1998), p. 101, n. 35. See also Philip S. Foner, *A History of Cuba*, Vol. 1 (International Publishers, 1962), pp. 124–125. For all his vaunted idealism, Jefferson was "no friend of Cuban independence." He considered Cuba vital for defending the United States from naval attack and even entertained going to war against Spain a century before the Rough Riders, since Cuba could be "seized without difficulty."
11. Tom Chaffin, *Fatal Glory* (Louisiana State University Press, 2003), p. 44.
12. Ibid., p. 214.
13. Quoted in Thomas, *Cuba*, p. 325.
14. Ibid., p. 361.
15. Ibid., p. 364.
16. O'Toole, *The Spanish War*, p. 96.
17. Gott, *Cuba*, p. 102. The Teller Amendment was the result of a lobbying effort by Tomás Estrada Palma, later Cuba's first president. It helped justify intervention by making it seem "disinterested" and soothed the fears of Cubans opposed to annexation. But it pointedly did not apply to other Spanish possessions, such as Puerto Rico or the Philippines.
18. Thomas, *Cuba*, p. 390.
19. Ibid., pp. 393–394.
20. José M. Hernández, *Cuba and the United States* (University of Texas Press, 1993), p. 53.
21. Louis A. Pérez, Jr., *On Becoming Cuban* (University of North Carolina Press, 1999), p. 101. Pérez writes: "Vast stretches of rural Cuba were reduced to wasteland." According to a later report by the U.S. Tariff Commission, the war destroyed two-thirds of Cuba's wealth.
22. Thomas, *Cuba*, 422.

23. Pérez, *On Becoming Cuban*, p. 108.
24. Thomas, *Cuba*, p. 443.
25. Ibid., p. 468, n. 26. Roosevelt's racist "Big Stick" diplomacy would cast a long shadow over Latin America in the century to come.
26. Ibid., p. 497. More Spaniards arrived in Cuba between 1900 and 1925 than between 1511 and 1899. This is vividly brought to life in Miguel Barnet's novel *Gallego* (Alfaguara, 1981).
27. Gott, *Cuba*, p. 115.
28. See Hyman G. Rickover, *How the Battleship Maine Was Destroyed* (Government Printing Office, 1976).

CHAPTER 8

1. Hugh Thomas, *Cuba, or The Pursuit of Freedom* (Da Capo Press, 1998), p. 544.
2. Alejo Carpentier, *El Amor a la Ciudad* (Alfaguara, 1996), p. 137.
3. Joseph L. Scarpaci, Roberto Segre, and Mario Coyula, *Havana: Two Faces of the Antillean Metropolis* (University of North Carolina Press, 2002), p. 68.
4. John Parker, *We Remember Cuba* (Golden Quill, 1983), p. 148. One of many reminiscences about pre-Castro Cuba in this delightful book.
5. Louis A. Perez Jr., *On Becoming Cuban*, (University of North Carolina Press, 1999)p. 167.
6. Ibid., p. 193.
7. Ibid., p. 169.
8. Robin D. Moore, *Nationalizing Blackness* (University of Pittsburgh Press, 1997), p. 98. The most popular was the Havana Sport, located at Galiano and San José streets, in the heart of Centro Habana. It employed one hundred women of various sizes and shapes.
9. "Ode to a Negro Boxer," *Songoro Cosongo*, 1931. See Nicolás Guillén, *Nueva Antologia Mayor* (Ediciones Union, 1979).
10. Parker, *We Remember Cuba*, p. 9. Parker calls *piropos* "a stimulant for female spirits of all ages."
11. Moore, *Nationalizing Blackness*, p. 45. Performers blackened their skin with burnt cork and wore wigs. The closest equivalent would be U.S. minstrel shows. Moore notes that Cuban blacks were "systematically denied employment in the theater as late as the 1950s."
12. Scarpaci et al., *Havana*, p. 56.
13. See Carpentier, *El Amor a la Ciudad*, p. 101.
14. María Luisa Lobo, Havana, (Monacelli Press, 2000),p. 178.
15. Juan A. Martínez, *Cuban Art and National Identity* (University Press of Florida, 1994), p. 2.
16. Ned Sublette, *Cuba and its Music* (Chicago Review Press, 2004), p. 395.
17. Moore, *Nationalizing Blackness*, p. 176.
18. Luis E. Aguilar, *Cuba 1933* (Cornell University Press, 1972), p. 118.
19. Ruby Hart Phillips, *Cuba: Island of Paradox* (McDowell, Obolensky, 1959), p. 8.
20. *Havana Post*, May 8, 1933.
21. H. L. Lewis, *Cuba To-Day* 10, No. 134, August 14, 1933.
22. *Havana Post*, August 13, 1933.

23. Thomas, *Cuba*, p. 636. As a young man, Batista was known as *el mulato lindo* (the pretty mulatto).
24. Ibid.


CHAPTER 9

1. Ernest Hemingway, *Selected Letters*, edited by Carlos Baker (Scribners, 1981), p. 359.
2. Ernest Hemingway, "Marlin off the Morro," *Esquire* (Autumn 1933).
3. Ibid.
4. Hemingway, *Selected Letters*, p. 390.
5. For more about the fascinating Jane Mason, see Jeffrey Meyers, *Hemingway* (Da Capo Press, 1999), p. 242; Michael Reynolds, *Hemingway in the 1930s* (W. W. Norton, 1997), p. 130; and Bernice Kert, *The Hemingway Women* (W. W. Norton, 1983), p. 240. A fictionalized account of her relationship with Hemingway appears in my novel *Welcome to Havana, Señor Hemingway* (Planeta, 2005).
6. Denis Brian, *The True Gen* (Grove Press, 1988), p. 85.
7. James R. Mellows, *Walker Evans* (Basic Books, 1999), p. 179. A selection of Evans's Cuba photographs was published in Gilles Mora, *Walker Evans: Havana 1933* (Pantheon Books, 1989).
8. Ernest Hemingway, *To Have and Have Not* (Arrow Books, 1994), p. 4.
9. Carlos Baker, *Ernest Hemingway* (Collier, 1969), p. 551.
10. Norberto Fuentes, *Hemingway in Cuba* (Lyle Stuart, 1984), p. 127.
11. Hillary Hemingway and Carlene Brennen, *Hemingway in Cuba* (Rugged Land, 2003), p. 123.
12. Ibid., p. 116.


CHAPTER 10

1. See Rosa Lowinger and Ofelia Fox, *Tropicana Nights* (Harcourt, 2005), p. 26.
2. Hugh Thomas, *Cuba, or The Pursuit of Freedom* (Da Capo Press, 1998), p. 737.
3. Ibid., p. 780.
4. Louis A. Pérez Jr., *On Becoming Cuban*, (University of North Carolina Press, 1999),p. 469. This hellish vision of Havana remains politically correct nearly fifty years after the Revolution.
5. Rosalie Schwarz, *Pleasure Island* (University of Nebraska Press, 1999), p. 148.
6. Ibid., p. 152.
7. Ibid., p. 158.
8. Joseph L. Scarpaci, Roberto Segre, and Mario Coyula, *Havana: Two Faces of the Antillean Metropolis* (University of North Carolina Press, 2002), p. 93. See also Richard Gott, *Cuba: A New History* (Yale University Press, 2004), p. 165; Thomas, *Cuba*, p. 1103.
9. Jaime Suchliki, *Cuba: From Columbus to Castro and Beyond* (Brassey's, 1997), p. 135.
10. Ibid., p. 136.
11. See *Bohemia*, January 11, 1959, p. 56. A reprint of this famous issue with a Christ-like Castro on the cover was published in 1996.

12. Lowinger and Fox, *Tropicana Nights*, p. 7.
13. Pablo Medina, *Exiled Memories* (University of Texas Press, 1990), p. 99.
14. Thomas, *Cuba*, p. 791.

CHAPTER 11

1. *Bohemia*, January 11, 1951, p. 130.
2. Ruby Hart Phillips, *Cuba: Island of Paradox* (McDowell, Obolensky, 1959), p. 397.
3. Wayne Smith, *The Closest of Enemies* (W. W. Norton, 1987), p. 41. Smith notes that regular flights resumed the following day and that most Americans who wanted to leave were gone by January 4.
4. Carlos Eire, *Waiting for Snow in Havana* (Free Press, 2003), p. 206. Eire left Cuba as a child through the "Peter Pan" program.
5. Tad Szulc, *Fidel* (William Morrow, 1986), p. 458.
6. Robert E. Quirk, *Fidel Castro* (W. W. Norton, 1993), p. 210.
7. Szulc, *Fidel*, p. 459.
8. Carlos Franqui, *Family Portrait with Fidel* (Vintage Books, 1985), pp. 12–13. Franqui, a former communist who broadcast Radio Rebelde from the Sierra Maestra and became editor of *Revolucion*, later fell out with Castro and went into exile in Italy. As Cabrera Infante notes in the introduction to this book, the cover shows several versions of the same photograph with Castro—each with someone airbrushed out. Finally, Franqui himself disappears.
9. Quirk, *Fidel Castro*, p. 221.
10. Rosalie Schwartz, Pleasure Island, (University of Nebraska Press, 1997), p. 15.
11. Franqui, *Family Portrait with Fidel*, p. 15.
12. Hugh Thomas, *Cuba, or The Pursuit of Freedom* (Da Capo Press, 1998), p. 1273.
13. Jon Lee Anderson, *Che Guevara* (Grove Press, 1997), p. 165.
14. Ibid., p. 386.
15. John Martíno, *I Was Castro's Prisoner* (Devin-Adair, 1963), pp. 66–67.
16. Norman Sherry, *The Life of Graham Greene*, vol.3 (Penguin Books, 2004), pp. 147–148. Greene was in Havana shooting the movie version of *Our Man in Havana*, starring Alec Guinness.
17. Juan Clark, *Cuba: Mito y Realidad* (Saeta, 1992), pp. 144–145. Other accounts of imprisonment in La Cabaña during the early days of the Revolution include Jorge Valls, *Twenty Years and Forty Days* (Americas Watch, 1986); Huber Matos, *Como Llego la Noche* (Tusquets Editores, 2002); and Armando Valladares, *Against All Hope* (Encounter Books, 2001).
18. Anderson, *Che Guevara*, p. 375.
19. Ibid., p. 453.
20. Ibid., p. 468.
21. Ibid., p. 739.

CHAPTER 12

1. *Granma International*, May 14, 2006.
2. Ibid.

3.  *Granma International*, May 21, 2006.
4.  Jon Lee Anderson, "Castro's Last Battle," *New Yorker*, July 31, 2006.
5.  Roberto González Echevarría, *The Pride of Havana* (Oxford University Press, 1999), p. 90.
6.  Pedro Juan Gutierrez, *Dirty Havana Trilogy* (Ecco, 2002). This review appeared in *Publishers Weekly*. The *New York Times* compared the novel to the work of the Marquis de Sade, calling it "an exploration . . . of human nature stripped to its essentials."
7.  See Tom Miller, ed., *Cuba* (Traveler's Tales, 2004). Cubanophile Tom Miller relates his own experiences in *Trading with the Enemy*, (Atheneum, 1992).

# Acknowledgments

This book is for my parents, who inspired a love for the city of my birth. I am especially grateful to my agent, Esmond Harmsworth, for his enthusiasm and insight. Gustavo Godoy was again the best of traveling companions, and Emilio Cueto proved an invaluable resource. It was a pleasure to work with Gabriella Georgiades, my editor at Palgrave Macmillan, and her able team. Many thanks as well to Esperanza de Varona, Argel Calcines, Georgina and Eugenio Balari, Carmen Teresa Roiz, José Morales, Alberto Insua, Rosa Lowinger, Peter Eckstein, Gary Marx, Claudia Pennington, and the helpful staffs of the Historical Museum of South Florida and the Hemingway Collection at the John F. Kennedy Presidential Library. And as always, Mary. *Gracias.*